THE POLITICAL ECONOMY OF INDUSTRIAL POLICY

The Political Economy of Industrial Policy

Ha-Joon Chang
Faculty of Economics and Politics
University of Cambridge

Published in Great Britain by
MACMILLAN PRESS LTD
Houndmills, Basingstoke, Hampshire RG21 6XS
and London
Companies and representatives
throughout the world

First edition 1994
Reprinted (with alterations) 1996

A catalogue record for this book is available
from the British Library.

ISBN 0–333–58862–2 hardcover
ISBN 0–333–67890–7 paperback

 First published in the United States of America 1994 by
ST. MARTIN'S PRESS, INC.,
Scholarly and Reference Division,
175 Fifth Avenue,
New York, N.Y. 10010

ISBN 0–312–10294–1 (cloth)

Library of Congress Cataloging-in-Publication Data
Chang, Ha-Joon.
The political economy of industrial policy / Ha-Joon Chang.
p.   cm.
"First published in Great Britain . . . by the Macmillan Press Ltd"–
–T.p. verso.
Revision of the author's thesis (doctoral—Cambridge)
Includes bibliographical references and index.
ISBN 0–312–10294–1
1. Industrial policy.   2. Industrial policy—Korea (South)
I. Title
HD3611.C42   1994
338.9—dc20   92–14247
                                                          CIP

© Ha-Joon Chang 1994, 1996

All rights reserved. No reproduction, copy or transmission of
this publication may be made without written permission.

No paragraph of this publication may be reproduced, copied or
transmitted save with written permission or in accordance with
the provisions of the Copyright, Designs and Patents Act 1988,
or under the terms of any licence permitting limited copying
issued by the Copyright Licensing Agency, 90 Tottenham Court
Road, London W1P 9HE.

Any person who does any unauthorised act in relation to this
publication may be liable to criminal prosecution and civil
claims for damages.

10 9   8   7   6   5   4   3   2   1
05 04 03 02 01 00 99 98 97 96

Printed in Great Britain by
Ipswich Book Co Ltd, Ipswich, Suffolk

To my parents

Contents

Preface to the 1996 Reprint   xi
Acknowledgements   xvi

Introduction: The Search for New Patterns of Economic Management   1

1 Theories of State Intervention: A Review of the Literature   7

    Introduction   7
    1.1 Efficiency: the market-failure literature   7
       1.1.1 Public goods   8
       1.1.2 Non-competitive markets   9
       1.1.3 Externalities   10
    1.2 Morality: paternalism and contractarianism   12
       1.2.1 Paternalism and contractarianism   12
       1.2.2 What should the state do?   14
       1.2.3 Some reflections   15
    1.3 Intention: the political economy literature   18
       1.3.1 The autonomous-state approach   18
       1.3.2 The interest-group approach   19
       1.3.3 The self-seeking-bureaucrats approach   22
       1.3.4 Summary   24
    1.4 Ability: the government-failure literature   25
       1.4.1 The information problem   26
       1.4.2 Rent-seeking   27
    Conclusion   31

2 A New Institutionalist Theory of State Intervention   33

    Introduction   33
    2.1 Remedying government failures I: the information problem   34
       2.1.1 Substantive rationality vs. procedural rationality   34
       2.1.2 Mitigating the information problem   35
    2.2 Remedying government failures II: the rent-seeking problem   38

Contents

	2.2.1	The vulnerability of the state	38
	2.2.2	The problem of collective action	40
	2.2.3	Competitiveness of the rent-seeking process	41
	2.2.4	Some reflections: competitive markets and competitive politics	44
2.3	A new institutionalist theory of state intervention		45
	2.3.1	The nature of economic costs	46
	2.3.2	Transaction costs and state intervention	48
Conclusion			53

3 The Political Economy of Industrial Policy — 55

Introduction			55
3.1	The industrial policy debates		56
	3.1.1	Does manufacturing matter?	56
	3.1.2	What is industrial policy?	58
3.2	The logic of industrial policy I: the static dimension		61
	3.2.1	The nature of the coordination problem	61
	3.2.2	Industrial policy as a device of coordination	65
	3.2.3	Concluding remarks: credibility, fairness and flexibility	70
3.3	The logic of industrial policy II: the dynamic dimension		71
	3.3.1	Knowledge, change, and evolution	72
	3.3.2	Industrial policy as a device to promote change	74
	3.3.3	Concluding remarks: the socialisation of risk	78
3.4	Possible problems of industrial policy		79
	3.4.1	Problems of information	79
	3.4.2	Problems of rent-seeking and entrepreneurship	82
	3.4.3	Political problems: legitimacy and democratic control	85
	3.4.4	The problem of supporting institutions	87
Conclusion			89

4 Industrial Policy in Action – The Case of Korea — 91

Introduction	91

4.1	A brief overview of the Korean economic performance	92
4.2	Explaining the Korean experience	97
	4.2.1 A free market?	97
	4.2.2 Market-preserving state intervention?	101
4.3	Major themes of Korean state intervention	108
4.4	The economics of industrial policy in Korea	113
	4.4.1 The evolution of Korean industrial policy	113
	4.4.2 State-created rents and industrial development	117
4.5	The politics of industrial policy in Korea	123
Conclusion		128

Conclusion: The Market, the State and Institutions   131

Notes and References   137

Bibliography   157

Index   173

Preface to the 1996 Reprint

While one writes a book because one thinks that one has something to say that will interest more than just a handful of people, for an unknown first-time author, it was still a wonderful surprise to find out that *The Political Economy of Industrial Policy* has been doing sufficiently well to justify a paperback edition. Since the book was published, I have received a surprising number of responses from many people through various channels. There were some predictable reactions, be they positive or negative, but there were also some which I did not expect when I wrote the book. And for some of these reactions I felt the need to respond in order to clear up the misunderstandings. Moreover, as some of the issues I discussed in the book have seen a flurry of debate in recent years, I felt that I should add a word or two on the more recent developments.

First of all, my use of the concept of transaction costs in analysing the relative costs of different forms of coordination invited a lot of justified and unjustified criticism. One criticism was that transaction costs are perhaps not as important as the costs of coordination failure themselves, and therefore that my emphasis on transaction costs was diverting attention from a more important issue. This was a response that I anticipated at various places in the book, but perhaps I did not do enough to prevent such misunderstandings. I was by no means suggesting that the costs from coordination failures were less important than the transaction costs involved in correcting them, but simply that correcting coordination failures is not without cost, as it is assumed in many economic theories.

The other criticism that I faced due to my adoption of the term 'transaction costs' was that I was advocating the purely 'self-seeking' view of individuals, as many who use the concept tend to be, and that partly as a consequence of this I failed to see other forms of coordination such as 'networks' which are at least partly based on non-selfish, cooperative behaviours. This was, again, an unfortunate misunderstanding. While I certainly did not explore the network as an alternative coordination mechanism to the market or state intervention, this was not because I believed that human beings are so selfish they are incapable of spontaneous cooperation. As I keep emphasising at various places throughout the book, especially in the first two chapters,

I do not subscribe to the pure, 'self-seeking' view of individuals. The reason why I did not deal with mechanisms of coordination based on horizontal cooperation was partly because I did not have enough expertise in the area, and partly because the book was on 'policy' by the state. Indeed, whether the state can make its policy implementation more effective through promoting cooperation among the relevant agents is one interesting issue that we should look at in future.

In choosing to use the term 'transaction costs', and also the term 'New Institutional Economics', I had some misgivings myself. My own definition of transaction is somewhat broader than that used by many other authors writing in the tradition of the New Institutional Economics, and refers to the costs of running the economy or, as I also call in the book, the 'costs of coordination' (see Chapter 2, Section 3.1). And when the term also carried certain ideological baggages to which I do not fully subscribe, such as its emphasis on opportunistic individual self-seeking, I was not sure whether I should use the term. On the other hand, I did not want to create another term in our jargon-infested profession when there is an already accepted term which could convey the meaning sufficiently, if not perfectly, well. Hence my decision to use the term. Unfortunately, although somewhat predictably, this brought about unnecessary misunderstandings amongst many readers, but I still feel that my decision to use the term 'transaction costs' was, on balance, justified.

When one writes on arguably one of the most contentious issues in modern economic debate, namely, industrial policy, one is bound to face the problem that by the time the book gets known to people, the debate has moved on. The book was finalised, except for minor editorial changes, at the end of 1992, and there has been a good deal of controversy in the area since then.

The most prominent of the recent debates was due to the World Bank's *East Asian Miracle Report*, which was published in late 1993. The so-called 'Miracle Report' stirred up a good deal of controversy on industrial policy by arguing that such policy attempted in the East Asian countries was largely ineffective, perhaps except in Japan, and that it is not something that other developing countries can try anyway because they do not have the administrative and other institutional capabilities to carry out such a demanding policy. While there is no need to repeat the detailed criticisms by many authors, including myself, of the methodologies and empirical validities of the Miracle Report's view on industrial policy, I feel that I should present a few salient points in summary form (for details, see the articles published in the special symposium in *World Development*, 1994, no. 4; essays in Fishlow *et al.*, 1994; and Chang, 1995).

First of all, the World Bank claims that the industrial structural transformation that happened in these countries was 'market-conforming' in the sense that their industries became capital-intensive more or less in line with the rise in their income and thereby capital stock. It then argues that this means these changes would have happened even without industrial policy. One problem with this argument is that with the rise in income, which the Bank takes as something that drove the transformation in industrial structure, was actually also the result of the industrial structural formation of the economy, which was shaped by industrial policy. Also, the structural transformation of the East Asian economies may be 'market-conforming' in the very abstract sense that they started from labour-intensive industries and only later moved to capital-intensive industries. Yet there was little 'market conformity' in the process, as the particular industries that developed over time were often selected and nurtured by the state, rather than by spontaneous market forces. Moreover, even if one makes the biggest concession and accepts that the transformation of the East Asian industrial structure was market-conforming, this still does not mean that industrial policy in East Asia had no impact because the *speed* of such a transformation was certainly accelerated by industrial policy. Anyhow, in the absence of actual examples of market-based progress towards an advanced industrial economy during this century (barring the very exceptional case of the colonial city-state, Hong Kong), the burden of proof is really on those who believe that such a progress is feasible.

Secondly, the World Bank rejects the effectiveness of industrial policy in East Asia, especially in Korea, on the grounds that total factor productivity in the 'promoted' industries such as machinery did not grow as fast as that in the 'neglected' industries such as textiles. Even ignoring the fact that the textile industry was in fact one of the most heavily promoted in Korea (as its ability to earn foreign exchange was highly prized by the policy-makers; see Chapter 4, Section 4.1), the total factor productivity growth figures provided by the Miracle Report should be taken with more than a pinch of salt. There are enough contradicting evidences presented elsewhere, as one would expect given the well-known problems of measuring total factor productivity growth. It should also be added that the Miracle Report ignores other important indicators of industrial policy performance such as balance of payments contributions or spill-over effects beyond the two-digit industry level.

The Miracle Report's last line of defence is that industrial policy requires a high institutional capability – such as a capable bureaucracy and a well-developed forum for government-business dialogue – and therefore is not applicable to countries without such capabilities. At one level, I could not agree with this statement more. It is certainly important to take into account one's administrative and institutional capabilities when one is designing a policy. Moreover, I regard this as a welcome improvement over the standard mainstream practice of recommending an essentially same economic model – namely, an idealised version of the Anglo-Saxon economic system – to a bewilderingly wide range of countries regardless of their political and institutional conditions, which naturally often produces very disappointing results. Although one gets somewhat suspicious when the same people who used to ignore political and institutional conditions when applying the Anglo-Saxon model suddenly become concerned about them when it comes to applying the East Asian model, I take this as a very positive sign that our profession is finally realising the institutional diversity of capitalism emphasised in this book.

However, what is missing in the World Bank's new position regarding the question of institutional capability is a discussion of how a country that does not have an adequate institutional capability to administer 'complex' policies can construct such capability. As I point out at various places in the book, the East Asian countries did not start their industrialisation efforts with a competent bureaucracy and good institutions but consciously built them over time. Moreover, one should not forget that, as in production, there is also learning-by-doing in administration, and therefore that a bureaucracy which is intent on eventually administering a complex set of policies should try to build up its capabilities over time by engaging in some degree of complex policies from the beginning. So if a country starts from the assumption that it does not have an adequate ability to implement an intelligent industrial policy and therefore gives up any attempt, it will never learn to do it.

As I repeatedly argue in *The Political Economy of Industrial Policy*, learning from other countries does not mean exactly copying their institutions and policies – which is not going to be successful anyway – but requires first an understanding of the principles that lie behind these successful policies and institutions, and then constructing their 'functional equivalents' (which may or may not serve the given function better) with due attention to local conditions. There is an old Korean proverb that 'he who does not have teeth chews with his gums', which nicely sums up the spirit of my argument. To develop this insight further in the modern context, one could say that if one hasn't got teeth, one should think about buying a set of false teeth or even a food processor. To drive this point closer to home, I can do no better than refer the readers to the quote in the third chapter of the present book from the eminent scholar of Japan, Ronald Dore, on the replicability of some Japanese institutions on British soil.

References

Chang, H-J. (1995) 'Explaining "Flexible Rigidities" in East Asia' in T. Killick (ed.), *The Flexible Economy* (London: Routledge).

Fishlow, A., Gwin, C., Haggard, S., Rodrik, D. and Wade, R. (1994) *Miracle or Design? – Lessons from the East Asian Experience* (Washington, D.C.: Overseas Development Council).

World Development (1994) no. 4.

Acknowledgements

This book is a revised version of my PhD dissertation at the Faculty of Economics and Politics, University of Cambridge. In writing the dissertation, and subsequently the book, I owe my biggest debt to my supervisor Bob Rowthorn. He has taught me how to analyse economic problems with logical rigour without losing sight of history, politics and institutions. He was always willing to listen to my half-baked ideas and discuss them until I could clarify them. Most of all, he has provided me with much more moral support than I deserve. No amount of words can express my gratitude to him.

Ajit Singh, Peter Nolan and Gabriel Palma have always been willing to discuss any problem I had in writing the book and have provided me with continued encouragement. I also want to thank John Sender for teaching me the importance of balancing theory and evidence when carrying out research and Ugo Pagano for introducing me to many of the ideas that form the theoretical foundation of the book.

Mushtaq Khan deserves a special mention for his continued intellectual and personal friendship. Without him the book would never have looked like it does now. I also want to thank Jong-il You, interaction with whom in the last phase of the dissertation was extremely important in clarifying the arguments. I also benefited a lot from intellectual interaction with Richard Wright, whose wideranging knowledge of economic history helped me to put my arguments into perspective. Terence Moll read the whole of the first draft and provided valuable theoretical comments and superb editorial advice. Jon Di John helped me to clarify my ideas in the final stage of the dissertation and provided editorial advice.

Nathan Rosenberg, while he was visiting Cambridge for a year, read about a half of what became the base material for the book and made some important suggestions to strengthen my arguments, with which he did not always agree. Alice Amsden, through her book on Korea and personal contact, provided me with some very important theoretical insights. Robin Matthews read parts of the manuscript and provided some enlightening comments.

Acknowledgements

Ashish Arora, Anuradha Basu, Pranab Bardhan, William Baumol, Jagdish Bhagwati, David Canning, Hendrik du Toit, Geoff Harcourt, Trina Haque, Ho-In Kang, Sandeep Kapur, Paul Kattuman, Zeljka Kozul, Michael Landesmann, Jay-Min Lee, David Lehmann, Sudipto Mundle, Ramaswamy Ramana, Raja Rasiah and Helen Shapiro read parts of the earlier versions of the manuscript and made helpful comments.

In turning the dissertation into a book, I have benefited a lot from discussions with Christopher Freeman, Alan Hughes and John Toye. Although I have not been able to incorporate all the important points they raised, their suggestions and criticisms will prove important in developing my ideas in the future. I also want to thank Wendy Carlin, Chris Edwards, Andrew Glyn, Kyun Kim and Adrian Wood, who read the dissertation and provided advice which proved valuable in the final conversion process. I also wish to thank Ali Cheema, Anjali Mody and Rathin Roy for their help with proof-reading and indexing.

My cousin, Hawon Jang, and cousin-in-law, Chaewha Lim, who is not with us any more, have provided me with a lot of love as well as intellectual stimulation during my PhD years. Terry Fry and Amy Klatzkin, who were my 'adopted family' during my first year abroad, provided me with immense emotional and intellectual support, which continues till these days. Byong Kon Kim not only provided me with another adopted family but also taught me about the world of philosophy and political science.

My brother Hasok has been a long-time intellectual and emotional companion. Without him, my PhD would have been an extremely lonely trip. My sister Yon Hee, brother-in-law Soo Bin Im, and their son Jay Hyuck also provided me with a lot of love. Without them it would have been impossible to survive some of those difficult days. Hee Jeong Kim, my fiancée, walked into my life at the final stage of preparing the book and made the job much more bearable. Finally, I want to thank my parents, whose great love and intellectual support made me what I am now. I dedicate the book to them.

Cambridge, England   HA-JOON CHANG

Introduction: The Search for New Patterns of Economic Management

The quarter century after the Second World War was truly the 'golden age' of capitalism (see Marglin and Schor (eds), 1990, and Armstrong *et al.*, 1991). All the major industrial countries in this period experienced unprecedented growth with no serious inflation and near-full employment, which resulted in a spectacular rise in general living standards. This achievement was impressive enough to establish Keynesian economic management, which dominated the economic policy-making of the major industrial powers in this period, as the ultimate way to run a viable capitalist system, or the 'mixed economy'.[1]

However the collapse of rapid growth and full employment in the mid-1970s in most of the leading industrial economies was a rude awakening to the fact that certain fundamental structural changes in national and world economies occurred during the 'golden age'. The rapid absorption of the agricultural labour force into industries and services eliminated surplus labour and created tight labour markets, often with inflationary consequences. Investments in manufacturing by multinational corporations emerged as an important form of international capital flow, and this, together with the lowering of barriers to other forms of capital movements, made national economic management much less effective. Japan became one of the world's leading industrial countries and the East Asian newly industrialising countries (henceforth NICs), that is, Hong Kong, Singapore, Taiwan, and South Korea (henceforth Korea), became major actors in some world markets, such as textiles, electronics, shipbuilding and steel. Together these changes meant massive dislocations in the old heartlands of world industrial production, that is, the 'rust belt' of the USA and the old industrial centres of Western Europe, resulting in a fundamental transformation in the map of world industries.

The rise of new-right ideas and the election of the Reagan and Thatcher governments in the last years of the 1970s and the early

1980s, partly prompted by the failure of the US and British economies to adjust rapidly to these fundamental structural changes, seemed to herald a 'brave new world' of monetarism and supply-side economics.[2] The apparent failure of the French socialist experiment of unilateral Keynesianism in the early 1980s seemed to strengthen the new right's belief in its new project of 'liberalising' economic systems from the fetters of state intervention and other rigidities created by the advance of collectivism in the guise of the welfare state.

However, by the early 1990s, new-right experiments in the USA and the UK were rapidly retreating, although they will have long-lasting influences in some, if not all, areas of the economy and society.[3] The declining competitiveness of the UK economy (manifested in its massive trade deficits) and the threatened position of the US economy as the world's greatest economic power (manifested in its massive budget and trade deficits) were probably enough to produce various new attempts to examine alternative ways to run the capitalist economy, or alternative patterns of economic management, especially in the latter half of the 1980s.

One important common theme for these new attempts is the recognition that different capitalist countries have in fact long had distinctive patterns of capital accumulation and economic policy-making. The differential performances of different systems of economic management, it may be argued, were not manifest in the golden age when all the industrialised countries were in good shape, but the need for massive economic restructuring since the late 1970s has caused so much strain that the differential abilities of different systems of economic management to adapt to changes seem to have resulted in differential economic performances.

One of the attempts to search for alternative patterns of economic management is the literature on social corporatism.[4] This literature starts with the observation that some, notably Scandinavian, advanced capitalist countries have not experienced the massive unemployment that has characterised many advanced capitalist economies since the late 1970s. These countries combined near-full employment with relatively low inflation and constantly rising levels of income and consumption for most members of society. Still more impressive, and at the same time contrary to the conventional wisdom, was the fact that these countries have restructured their economies successfully in a relatively painless and less divisive manner *despite* strong trade unions (often accused of creating rigidities in the labour market which obstruct structural change) and high taxation (often accused of being a disincentive to hard work and entrepreneurial activity).

The basic explanation for this impressive performance is found in the tripartite bargaining between the centralised employers' organisation, the centralised trade unions and the state, through which the levels of investment, wage and employment in the economy are coordinated to ensure an effective structural change without causing high inflation or mass unemployment.[5] In addition, egalitarian wage policy (especially in Sweden and Denmark) and 'active labour-market policy' (retraining of and migration assistance to the dislocated workers) are identified as the means with which these countries have avoided inhumane and divisive forms of industrial restructuring in which a substantial minority of society bears the whole burden of restructuring, as happened in some other advanced capitalist countries with very high and regionally concentrated long-term unemployment (Rowthorn, 1990).

Another major attempt to find alternative patterns of economic management is represented by the so-called industrial policy debates.[6] Industrial policy, despite its importance in many advanced capitalist countries (notably Japan and France) and some East Asian NICs (notably Korea, Taiwan and Singapore) during the post-war period, was largely ignored until the late 1970s in the English-speaking academic world. The concept of industrial policy does not seem to be recognised as a legitimate topic of academic discussion among economists – for example, *The Palgrave Dictionary of Economics*, despite its wide-ranging interests, does not have 'industrial policy' as an entry. Yet the 1980s saw a rapid rise in interest in this issue following the destruction of old industrial heartlands in the USA and Western Europe, on the one hand, and the spectacular industrial performances of Japan and the East Asian NICs (especially South Korea as the biggest and most diversified among them), on the other.

The supporters of industrial policy argue that the success of East Asian countries is primarily due to the active role of the state in formulating a vigorous economic system that promotes capital accumulation, innovation and productivity growth.[7] They argue that state intervention in these countries is characterised by direct state involvement in the fate (especially investment and technical change) of individual industries. They also argue that the failure of manufacturing in many advanced capitalist economies, especially the USA and the UK, is not just the result of macroeconomic mismanagement but of lagging investment, innovation and productivity growth. They argue that the manufacturing sector in these countries can only effectively be revived through industrial policy, whose direct and particularistic nature stands out in sharp contrast to the indirect and general nature of macroeconomic policy, which was the main pillar of the Keynesian pattern of economic management.

The industrial policy literature, in contrast with the social corporatism literature where a lot of theoretical advance has recently been made, has suffered from the lack of a sound theoretical foundation. This is partly because its proponents have been concerned largely with practical policy issues, but mainly because there was very little in conventional economic theory that could justify such policy. In the absence of theoretical tools to explain why industrial policy works, even its most ardent supporters could do no more than either describe in detail how it works, say, in Japan, without explaining why, or conclude that it works because of the idiosyncratic cultures of the countries in which it is practiced. Fortunately there have been some recent developments in economic theory that can improve this undesirable situation.

The recent rise of 'new institutional economics' has reminded us that the market is not the only, or even predominant, way in which our economic life is organised.[8] It has shown that non-market institutions are integral parts of socio-economic life, and not necessarily unfortunate rigidities that are best eliminated. Another important development in economic theory has been the growing interest in technical change, which has not been properly dealt with in conventional economic theory.[9] The recent literature on technological change has fundamentally changed our view of the capitalist economy. Now we are increasingly inclined to see the capitalist economy as in constant flux where learning plays an important role. The conventional image of the capitalist economy as a system fundamentally in equilibrium and subject only to external shocks (which are responded to by instant and painless adjustments) is becoming less and less appealing. The rise of 'government failure' literature has played an important role in dispelling the 'welfare economics' image of the state as the selfless social guardian.[10] The literature has made us think of how and why the state may fail to do what it is supposed to in textbook welfare economics, and many other interventionist theories.

These theoretical developments, are of course, not totally new in their ideas. Adam Smith, Karl Marx and Alfred Marshall were all, in their own ways, concerned about the development of the division of labour in the capitalist economy and its implication for the organisation of economic and political life. Adam Smith, Karl Marx, Joseph Schumpeter and Friedrich Hayek are only a few of the many great economists who grappled with the idea that the capitalist economy is in a permanent flux of technological development and institutional change. From Karl Marx on the left to George Stigler on the right, generations of economists have been concerned with the role of the state and the logic of interest-group politics in the capitalist economy.

What is new is that these hitherto scattered ideas are now coming together to produce an alternative to the conventional economic theory whose elegant but overly formalistic models have all but eliminated our ability to deal with issues of economic change and the concomitant conflicts among different groups in society. The application of the recent theoretical developments in economics mentioned above to the issue of industrial policy is the new and ambitious aim of the present book.

STRUCTURE OF THE BOOK

The book is organised into four parts. The first chapter reviews the literature on state intervention. Without claiming to be exhaustive or to be doing justice to all individual theories, four groups of literature are reviewed, namely market-failure literature, contractarian literature, political-economy literature and government-failure literature. It is argued that, even ignoring the moral and political reasons put forward, respectively, by the contractarian literature and the political-economy literature, we cannot fully accept the conventional case for state intervention based on the existence of market failures because the very process of correcting such failures may incur costs greater than the efficiency gains from it, as the government-failure literature has correctly pointed out.

In the second chapter we develop a new institutionalist theory of state intervention. New institutional economics has largely concentrated on the theory of firm and contracts, but, as we wish to demonstrate in this chapter, it can provide some interesting insights into the question of state intervention. In this chapter we interpret the costs of state intervention as transaction costs incurred (1) in policy decision and implementation, and (2) as a result of the increase in the incentives for the private sector to spend resources to change the property-rights system by influencing the state. The standard recommendation from the government-failure school in the face of such costs is to get rid of state intervention altogether, but we argue that it is often better that these costs are reduced through institutional and organisational innovations. We then go a step further and argue that, while state intervention incurs certain transaction costs, it can bring about benefits over and above the efficiency gains from the correction of market failures by reducing the transaction costs in the private sector.

The third chapter, which is the central chapter of the book, applies the theory of state intervention developed in the previous chapter to the issue of industrial policy. After briefly reviewing the industrial policy debates, two dimensions of industrial policy are discussed, drawing on Austrian, Schumpeterian and new-institutional economics. On the static dimension, we discuss how industrial policy can overcome the limitation of the market as a coordination mechanism. We discuss how issues like credibility, fairness and flexibility have to be taken seriously for the design of a successful industrial policy. On the dynamic dimension, the role of industrial policy in promoting industrial change is examined. It is argued that changes often require coordination between agents and therefore a certain degree of socialisation of risk may be beneficial in promoting industrial development. The chapter closes with a discussion of the possible problems of industrial policy and remedies to them. Problems of information, entrepreneurship, politics and supporting institutions are discussed.

The last chapter looks at industrial policy in Korea as an example of successful state intervention. We argue that, contrary to popular belief, the rapid development of Korea owes a great deal to the efficiency of state intervention, and especially of industrial policy. A detailed account of Korean industrial policy is given, and an explanation is provided as to how Korea was able to maximise the benefits and minimise the costs of industrial policy. Finally we examine the political and institutional foundations of Korea's successful industrial policy. While recognising the importance of historical and cultural factors, we emphasise the role of conscious political innovation and institution building in the construction of such foundations.

1 Theories of State Intervention: A Review of the Literature

INTRODUCTION

The role of the state in the capitalist economy has been one of the most controversial issues in economics since the birth of the discipline (Deane, 1989). Almost everyone agrees that the state has a role to play, but there is little agreement as to when and how it should act. Perhaps the reason why there is such little agreement is that state intervention is a complex phenomenon involving many contentious issues such as efficiency, morality, power, liberty and legitimacy, to name just a few.

In this chapter we organise our discussion into four parts to make this complex issue more tractable. In the first section we examine analyses of market failure which are mainly concerned with the possible failure of the market mechanism to achieve Pareto efficiency and with the state's role in overcoming such failure. Then we turn to the politico–philosophical debate on whether the state as a political entity should or should not intervene to correct the market outcome, be such correction efficient or not in some sense. Thirdly we consider the political economy – both right-wing and left-wing – literature, which asks whether it is correct to assume that the state serves some 'public' or 'social' purpose rather than individual or group interests. Lastly we examine the government-failure literature, which asks whether the state has the ability to intervene effectively, whatever its intention is.

1.1 EFFICIENCY: THE MARKET-FAILURE LITERATURE

The most developed literature on state intervention is that of market failure or welfare economics. The literature is primarily concerned with the failure of the market mechanism in equating private and social costs and benefits and with the possible correctives to such failures through state intervention.[1] We will examine three groups of arguments in this tradition, that is, public goods, non-competitive markets and externalities.

1.1.1 Public Goods

In the economics literature, goods are usually classified into two categories, that is, private and public. A private good is something that can only be consumed by those who have paid for it, whereas a public good is something that can be consumed by those who did not pay for it as well as those who have paid for it. In other words, supplying a public good to somebody means supplying it to others, not simply because it has to be 'jointly-supplied' or it has 'non-rivalness in consumption', but more importantly because it is not economically feasible to exclude the non-payers. That is, the defining characteristic of a public good is its 'non-excludability' (Olson, 1965, pp. 14–15, 38–40).[2]

Since it is possible for one to consume the good without paying for it once somebody else has paid for it, there is always an incentive to understate one's preference for a public good (Schotter, 1985, pp. 57–63). The possibility of such strategic behaviour means that public goods are likely to be underprovided due to the free-rider problem or the problem of collective action (see Olson, 1965; Hardin, 1982; Elster, 1989). In such a situation, individual rationality leads to collective irrationality, because, through individuals' attempts to maximise their own net benefits (paying as little as possible, given the benefit), everybody ends up suffering from the underprovision. Therefore, in order to provide the optimal amount of a public good, it is argued, the state needs to intervene by taxing people and providing public goods with the revenue (see, for example, Cullis and Jones, 1987, p. 19).[3]

One of the criticisms of the public-good argument is that non-excludability, the fundamental condition for a good to be a public good, cannot be regarded as permanent. According to Peacock (1979a), technological innovation can eliminate the 'publicness' of some goods by solving the problem of non-excludability. He argues that 'even in the most famous "polar case" of a public good, ways and means can be found ... by which the problem of non-excludability can be solved' (p. 133). Although this is a valid point, it should not be taken as implying that technical progress will eventually solve all public-good problems (for example substitution of lighthouses with radio signals), because excludability is more a property-rights problem than a technological problem (see Note 2).

Another important criticism of the argument for state intervention based on the public-good consideration is that it does not necessarily justify state intervention.[4] That is, even if there is a public (collective) good, it is not clear whether the 'collectivity' to provide it should be the state. As Olson (1965) argues, in a small group, optimal public-good provision may be achieved without state intervention because in a small group it is likely that there are individual members who gain so much benefit from the public good concerned that they are better off providing the good unilaterally (pp. 43–52). And even in a large group where this condition does not obtain, state intervention is not always necessary. Public goods may be optimally provided even in a large number setting, if some 'selective incentives' (Olson, 1965) in the form of private goods provided by 'political entrepreneurs' (Popkin, 1979) can overcome the free-rider problem by bringing individual cost/benefit structures in line with the social (or group) cost/benefit structure. Of course these arguments do not allow us to conclude that the public-good problem can always be solved by private initiatives. In many cases, the use of coercion by the state (for example taxation) may be the only possible way to resolve the problem.[5]

1.1.2 Non-Competitive Markets

The existence of scale economies and/or collusive behaviour can result in non-competitive market structures, where individual producers' decisions can affect the quantity and price in the market. When monopoly or oligopoly prevails in a market, the quantity of goods supplied is smaller than in the competitive context, as firms face negatively sloped demand curves.[6] Thus, in a non-competitive market, some consumer surplus will be transferred to firms in the form of 'monopoly profit', and such a transfer will impose a 'deadweight loss' to society (the Marshallian triangle). In this case, it is argued, it is justifiable for the state to intervene to guarantee the optimal output, that is, the output which would have been provided in a competitive setting.[7] Anti-trust legislation, which may involve the regulation of pricing and the breaking up of existing monopolies, is the most frequently used interventionist measure in this regard, but public ownership is another commonly practised and probably more powerful measure.[8]

A powerful argument against state intervention to 'correct' non-competitive markets is that based on the theory of 'second best' (Lipsey and Lancaster, 1956), which points out that rectifying monopolistic situations (or any other price distortion) in some, but not all, markets may not necessarily improve the efficiency of the economy. On the basis of this theory, anti-interventionists argue that no gain is guaranteed by anti-trust intervention which does not eliminate 'distortions' from all markets (Peacock and Rowley, 1979a). However this argument does not discredit fully the interventionist argument because the theory of second best does *not* imply that there can be no gain from such intervention, only that it is not guaranteed. Actually the theory of second best may be used as an excuse for wholesale state intervention, because no global optimality is attainable without letting all the other markets depart from their local optimal conditions.

Another anti-interventionist argument related to non-competitive markets is that state intervention is one major source of such outcomes. For example, Friedman (1962) argues that, '[m]onopoly frequently, if not generally, arises from government support of collusive agreements among individuals' (p. 28). The implication, then, is that the state should stop meddling with the market if it is serious about correcting distortions in non-competitive markets. In the words of Mises (1979), '[i]t is absurd to see the government ... point its finger at business, saying: "There are cartels, therefore government interference with business is necessary". It would be much simpler to avoid cartels by ending the government's interference with the market – an interference which makes these cartels possible [such as protectionism]' (p. 52). Although there can be no doubt that state-administered entry barriers are often sources of monopoly, it should be pointed out that many, if not all, initially competitive markets – through business cycles, structural changes or even sheer luck – have been transformed into non-competitive ones without collusion or state intervention.[9] Indeed, if the assumption of self-perpetuating competitive markets is unrealistic, it may be pointless from the public-policy point of view to argue for or against state intervention in monopolistic markets, since there is no criterion according to which they are to be corrected other than the fictitious perfectly competitive market (Demsetz, 1964).

1.1.3 Externalities

One of the assumptions in textbook economics is that each individual has only to consider his/her own means and ends. Technically speaking, individual preference systems (or utility functions) and production functions are independent from those of others. Externalities exist where there are some spill-over effects from an individual's activities to those of others, leading to a discrepancy between the private cost/benefit structure and the social cost/benefit structure. Of course, interdependence among individual activities cannot be a problem *in itself*, but where its effects are not properly compensated for there arises an 'untraded interdependence' (Nath, 1973, p. 43), namely externality.

At least in principle, it may be possible to overcome this problem by defining property rights more precisely and having negotiations between the parties affecting and affected (for example the owner of the smoke-spewing factory compensating housewives living nearby who have to spend extra time and money on laundry). However, in many cases, it is economically impossible to do so, because of the transaction costs involved in information acquisition, negotiation and contract enforcement (Coase, 1960; Stigler, 1975, pp. 106–7; Dahlman, 1979). In the absence of such a 'property-rights' solution, the state is justified in ensuring the provision of goods with externalities in socially optimal amounts through other means. State provision of goods with positive externalities at subsidised prices (for example education, health, social infrastructure), subsidisation of those who create positive externalities (for example, subsidies to R&D), and taxation of those who create negative externalities (for example pollution tax), are examples of state intervention on externality grounds.

Some anti-interventionists try to dismiss the externality argument for state intervention by assuming that the magnitudes involved are negligible. However, as Baumol (1965) and others have pointed out, the list of externalities can be extended almost infinitely. Most goods create some negative externalities in their production processes in the form of pollution, except in those few cases where proper compensation is made. When considering linkage effects (Hirschman, 1958, ch. 6) or pecuniary externalities (Scitovsky, 1954), many goods may additionally be classified as having positive externalities. Some economists even argue that some goods that have conventionally been treated as lacking externalities, say basic foodstuff, can be seen as creating externalities when they are not consumed in the proper amount and therefore induce crime (Schotter, 1985, pp. 68–80). Moreover, there exists interdependence between individual preferences. For example, people have what Elster (1983, ch. 2) calls counteradaptive preferences – 'the grass is always greener on the other side of the fence'. The psychology of luxury-good consumption – part of one's pleasure derives from the fact that one consumes what others do not – is another example of interdependent consumer preference. Indeed once we begin to accept the pervasiveness of externalities, it seems questionable whether we are justified in having market transactions at all. The important issue here is not whether externalities exist or not, but to explore under what conditions market transactions will be (or should be) adopted and under what conditions non-market institutions, including state intervention, will be (or should be) adopted, as new institutional economics has recently tried.

Some other anti-interventionists argue that correcting one set of externalities leads to another. Friedman (1962), for example, has grave reservations about state intervention based on the externalities argument – the 'neighbourhood-effects' argument as he calls it – pointing out that: (a) it will in part introduce an additional set of neighbourhood effects by failing to charge or to compensate individuals properly; and (b) it creates externalities in the form of 'threatening freedom' (p. 32). This is unconvincing since: (a) whether the gains from eliminating existing externalities are smaller than the losses from the newly-created externalities cannot be determined *a priori;* and (b) unsolved externalities also mean the limiting of someone's freedom – the *affecting* in the case of positive externalities, the *affected* in the case of negative externalities – because one party has the desire to trade but cannot (recall that externalities are untraded interdependences).[10]

1.2 MORALITY: PATERNALISM AND CONTRACTARIANISM

In the previous section we discussed the market-failure argument, the most important element in the traditional argument for state intervention. Another important element in the traditional interventionist argument is the moralistic argument that the state, as a representative of the members of society, may intervene in the market, if necessary, at the cost of efficiency. Can this argument be justified?

1.2.1 Paternalism and Contractarianism

The moralistic argument for state intervention usually takes two forms. Firstly, it is argued that the state may intervene in the provision of 'merit goods', which are 'goods the provision of which society (as distinct from the preferences of the individual consumer) wishes to encourage or, in the case of demerit goods, to deter' (Musgrave and Musgrave, 1984, p. 78). Secondly, state intervention may also be justified if society believes that market-type transactions are not morally acceptable in some areas, for example blood donations or police services. In this case, the argument goes, the state, as the social guardian, should remove such activities from the domain of the market and conduct them itself.

The above argument is often branded as paternalism by those who believe in methodological individualism and its politico–philosophic counterpart, contractarianism (for an exposition of contractarianism, see Nozick, 1974). From the methodologically individualistic point of view, the above argument is flawed in that it attaches an independent will to society, which is no more than a collection of individuals. From this politico–philosophic point of view, the belief that the state should decide on what individuals should produce and consume and in what ways is a first step on 'the road to serfdom' (Hayek, 1972).

Those who believe in individualism–contractarianism argue that 'the individual and not the group should be the basic repository of rights and obligations' (Schotter, 1985, p. 18). Thus it is believed that 'individuals should be allowed, within defined limits, to follow their own values and preferences rather than somebody else's. ... It is this recognition of the individual as the ultimate judge of his ends, the belief that as far as possible his own views ought to govern his action, that forms the essence of the individualist position' (Hayek, 1972, p. 59). Of course, this position 'does not assume, as is often asserted, that man is egoistic or selfish or ought to be' (Hayek, 1972, p. 59). However, no other person or authority can impose his/her or its own ethical judgement on the individual, since the individual knows best what his situation is and what his best option in that situation is. Any interference with the making of individual decisions is seen as violating the innate right to freedom of the individual (Hayek, 1972, 1988; Mises, 1929, 1979; Friedman, 1962).

If we do not, or rather should not, introduce any exogenous ethical code other than that of the individual being the judge of his/her own destiny, contractarianism, whether of the Hobbesian or the Rawlsian variety, becomes the only consistent view of the state, or more generally, of politics. As Buchanan says, 'if politics is to be interpreted in any justificatory or legitimatising sense *without the introduction of supra-individual value norms* [emphasis added], it must be modelled as a process within which individuals, with separate and potentially differing interests and values, interact for the purpose of securing individually valued benefits of cooperative effort. If this presupposition about the nature of politics is accepted, the ultimate model of politics is *Contractarian* [emphasis original]' (Buchanan, 1986, p. 240). The ideal state is then the product of voluntary contracts between free individuals who found some potential gains in restricting the unfettered exercise of the individual free will of other individuals and of their own. Contractarianism in its most consistent form should be based on the unanimity rule. Otherwise, however fair the outcome of a politico–economic system may appear from some other point of view, it cannot be justified from the contractarian viewpoint. Imposing a decision on individuals (which is bound to happen except under the unanimity rule) violates the fundamental principle that individuals should be free to make contracts and not be coerced into any transaction, however beneficial it may appear to an outsider.

1.2.2 What should the State do?

On the basis of individualism–contractarianism, it is argued that any state intervention other than some (rather ill-defined) minimal functions is illegitimate because it violates individual freedom as the ultimate value in human society. Indeed, according to Peacock and Rowley (1979b), what they term 'liberalism' is to be 'prepared to trade off economic efficiency for individual freedom where such a policy conflict becomes apparent' (p. 26).[11]

Mises (1979) categorically states that 'the government's only legitimate function is ... to produce security' (p. 40). To him, any interventionist attempt is doomed to invite in more and more intervention, if the state is serious about achieving its original purpose, leading inevitably to socialism. There is no such thing as 'the third way' (Mises, 1929, 1979).

Hayek (1972) argues that state intervention, except in areas that can be justified on contractarian grounds *plus* some 'even-handed' interventions in non-exchange economic activities (for example production activities), is bound to erode individual freedom. Competition (and its prerequisite, freedom of entry) is seen as the best means of coordinating the economy 'not only because it is in most circumstances the most efficient method known but even more because it is the only method by which our activities can be adjusted to each other without coercive or arbitrary intervention of authority' (Hayek, 1972, p. 36). That is, state intervention is objectionable not only because it is inefficient but mainly because it violates the fundamental values of individualism and hence of contractarianism.[12]

Buchanan (1986) gives a typology of the state functions that can be justified on contractarian grounds. According to him there are three levels of collective action. At the first level are activities involving enforcement of the law. The role of the state here is that of an umpire of a game. The second level involves collective action within the limits of existing laws. Here the role of the state is the financing and provision of public goods and services. The third level involves changes in the law itself, namely changes in the rules of the game. Unless there is a unanimous case for changes in the basic rules of the game of society, the role of the state should be either the enforcement of the rules of the game – namely the protection of property (and human?) rights and the enforcement of voluntary contracts – and the provision of special goods and services whose private provision will be suboptimal from the social point of view – namely the provision of public goods.

Friedman, usually known as *the* anti-interventionist economist, states that '[t]he role of government ... is to do something that the market cannot do for itself, namely, to determine, arbitrate, and enforce the rules of the game' (Friedman, 1962, p. 27). This view is similar to that of Buchanan, but in fact Friedman is much more generous, if more vague, about state intervention than the strict contractarians cited above. His list of legitimate functions of the state is as follows: maintenance of law and order, definition of property rights, service as a means whereby people modify property rights and other rules of the economic game, adjudication of disputes about the interpretation of the rules, enforcement of contracts, promotion of competition, provision of a monetary framework, engagement in activities to counter technical monopolies and to overcome neighbourhood effects widely regarded as sufficiently important to justify government intervention, supplementation of private charity and the private family in protecting the irresponsible, whether madman or child (Friedman, 1962, p. 34).

1.2.3 Some Reflections

Denouncing any moral judgment other than those based on narrowly defined individualism, as contractarian economists tend to do, is as meaningless as citing moral reasons for state intervention without discussing the role of morality in our social and economic life (McPherson, 1984). Individualism is not a 'scientific' point of view which can do without morality, as is frequently contended (for example Friedman, 1962), it is no more than a particular form of morality.

Methodological individualists assume that each individual knows best his/her interest and the constraints he/she faces. This view is not without its problems. First of all there are individuals who even contractarians do not regard as wholly responsible (for example, madmen and children), but the borderline between 'normal' and 'abnormal' is ambiguous, as even Friedman admits (Friedman, 1962, pp. 33–4). And, more importantly, who has the right to decide who is responsible and who is not, if there should be no supraindividual value? Secondly, there is 'no intrinsic reason why individuals should always pursue their own good or why they will always do so better than others can do it for them' (Freeden, 1991, p. 89). As Goodin (1986) notes, people make decisions on incomplete information, ignorance of their future preferences, ignorance of the full consequences of their own actions, deceptive decision frameworks, the desire to avoid responsibility for risks. The existence of implicit preferences for preferences (for example reckless drivers and drug addicts are not to be seen as acting in their best interests) is another case in point. In such situations it is not clear whether we should regard individual decisions as the manifestation of their preferences, and therefore argue against all intervention.

In contractarian philosophy it is argued that the state cannot be regarded as being 'above' individuals, since it is a product of free contracts between independent individuals. Contractarians hypothesise a 'state of nature' where all individuals are free to make contracts but are involved in a state of war against everybody else, which leads to the need for the imposition of an extra-individual authority, through voluntary contracts, in the form of the state.

This 'state-of-nature' scenario is of course a fiction. During the history of mankind, the choice has been the one between one form of authority and another, and not the one between anarchy and authority, as the contractarians put it (for example Nozick, 1974). Even a cursory look at the history of the last few centuries reveals that the building of the modern state was largely initiated by rulers, and not by freely-contracting individuals (Poggi, 1990). Moreover it is in contradiction to historical truth to argue that market-type transactions brought about the state – the opposite view is more correct. The market in its present form is a newer form of social institution compared with other forms, including the state. As Polanyi (1957) persuasively puts it, historical experience shows us that:

> [t]he road to the free market was opened and kept open by *an enormous increase in continuous, centrally organised and controlled interventionism* [emphasis added]. To make Adam Smith's 'simple and natural liberty' compatible with the needs of a human society was a most complicated affair. Witness the complexity of the provisions in the innumerable enclosure laws; the amount of bureaucratic control involved in the administration of the New Poor Laws which for the

first time since Queen Elizabeth's reign were effectively supervised by central authority; or the increase in governmental administration entailed in the meritorious task of municipal reform .... Administrators had to be constantly on the watch to ensure the free working of the system. Thus even those who wished most ardently to free the state from all unnecessary duties, and whose whole philosophy demanded the restriction of state activities, could not but entrust the self-same state with the new powers, organs, and instruments required for the establishment of *laissez-faire* (p. 140).

Of course most contractarians are not so silly as to believe in the 'state of nature' as a historical reality. Buchanan argues that the contractarian argument is an *ex post* conceptualisation or legitimisation of the political process as a complex exchange relationship and not an *ex ante* moral justification of the existing political order (Buchanan, 1986, p. 247). He thus admits that the contractarian argument is not based on actual history but on some arbitrary belief.[13] Nozick (1974) tries to defend the state-of-nature type explanation by saying that '[w]e learn much by seeing how the state could have arisen, even if it did not arise that way. If it did not arise that way, we also would learn much by determining why it did not; by trying to explain why the particular bit of the real world that diverges from the state-of-nature model is as it is' (Nozick, 1974, p. 9). This is peculiar logic. Since it is definitionally impossible that two or more different end-states arise through the same process, it is hardly justifiable to introduce one of them as a 'potential explanation' (as Nozick calls it) of the other. Of course there may be some heuristic value in the exercise, but this advocacy based on heuristic value can only be fully justified when the 'as if' explanation is complemented by the 'as it was' one, unless it can be shown precisely why the 'as if' explanation is superior to the 'as it was' one.

More importantly, contractarianism does not necessarily guarantee a minimal state. For example, if there is a unanimous belief among the members of society that market-type transactions are not morally acceptable in some areas (for example blood donation, defence), taking such activities out of the market may be justified even from the contractarian point of view. That is, what if the individuals in the society gather together to write a new social contract that endorses an interventionist state?[14] It is not satisfactory to argue for a minimal state on the assumption that individuals will opt for a minimal state if they are given a chance, unless we can show that individuals are wealth-maximisers (a common assumption in economics, but nothing more than an assumption) and that the free market will ensure them the maximisation of their wealth (a proposition that has been proven problematic by welfare economics).

1.3 INTENTION: THE POLITICAL ECONOMY LITERATURE

The political-economy viewpoints, both on the left (for example the Marxists) and the right (for example the Chicago school) of the political spectrum, have for long criticised the market-failure approach for too readily assuming that the state will act like Plato's Philosopher King. That is, is it the intention, or the objective, of the state to serve the public? Below, we will examine three arguments questioning such assumptions, namely the autonomous-state approach, the interest-group approach and the self-seeking-bureaucrats approach.

1.3.1 The Autonomous-State Approach

The view that the state should be regarded as 'a dynamic independent force' (Findlay, 1990, p. 195) with its own objective function that is distinct from that of the society as a whole is not new. A stream within the Marxist tradition, originating from Marx's *Eighteenth Brumaire of Louis Bonaparte* (Marx, 1934), has recognised that a certain state may acquire an 'autonomy' from society, if no class is powerful enough to impose its will on the state (for example, Alavi, 1972).[15] One strand in the recently popular 'neoclassical political economy' goes a step further and characterises the state as a 'predator', which, acting as a discriminating monopolist, develops a property-rights structure and a tax system which maximise its 'profit' or net revenue (tax minus expenditure), if necessary at the expense of social productivity.[16] Of course neoclassical political economy recognises that revenue-maximisation by the state is an exercise in constrained maximisation, since the threat of takeover by an alternative ruler from within or without the country imposes a competitive constraint (see North, 1981, ch. 3; Findlay, 1988; Eggertsson, 1990, ch. 10).

The view that the state may act as an entity with its own will (and greed) is a useful antidote to the naive assumption of welfare economics that it will correct market failures as soon as it finds them. Moreover, when the traditional interest-group approach has treated the state as a black box in which interest groups feed their policy inputs, resulting in some disappointingly simplistic policy implications, there seems to be some value in seeing the state as an autonomous entity (Skocpol, 1985; also see 1.3.2 below). However the approach is not without its problems.

First of all, the approach treats the 'autonomous' or 'predatory' state as a unified entity. As recognised even by one of the earlier proponents of the predatory-state approach, the richer institutional context of the modern polity with a bureaucracy and (frequently) a working legislature makes it difficult to apply this simplistic model to an analysis of real-life examples (North, 1990a). In fact the most distinctive characteristic of the modern state is the development of institutional bounds on *arbitrium* (Poggi, 1990, pp. 74–6). In particular, the 'necessity of developing agents (a bureaucracy) to monitor, meter, and collect revenue' (North, 1990a, p. 190) introduces a complication in the form of a conflict of interests between the ruler, who wants to maximise net revenue, and the bureaucrats, who want to maximise the budgets of their own bureaux (see 1.3.3 below for further discussion).

Secondly, talking of state autonomy in the abstract is not very helpful for the understanding of real life problems. Whether we call a state autonomous or not should depend on what issues we are interested in. First, one may wish to investigate the effect of their different degree of autonomy on the actions of different states (for example the Taiwanese state is more autonomous than the Indian state) or the same state at different points of time (for example, the Japanese state in the late nineteenth century was more autonomous than it is now; the Singaporean state may become less autonomous in the future than it has been under Li Kwan Yew). Second, different states may have different degrees of autonomy in different areas. For example the Swedish state may be less autonomous than the Korean state in influencing investment decisions of capitalists, but may be more autonomous in taxing them. Whether or not one should assume autonomy of the state depends on the country one wants to look at, the time period one wants to study and the areas of policy one is interested in.

1.3.2 The Interest-Group Approach

Another group of arguments which question the intention of the state is what we call the interest-group approach. This approach sees the state as 'an arena within which economic interest groups or normative social movements contended or allied with one another to shape the making of public policy decisions' about 'the *allocations* of benefits among demanding groups' (Skocpol, 1985, p. 4).[17] And, the argument goes, since the most powerful groups will be most able to affect the decisions of the state, state economic policies will be inevitably biased towards them.

The most representative of these theories is the 'regulatory-capture' theory of the Chicago school. According to Stigler (1975), the pioneer of this theory, 'regulation is acquired by the industry and is designed and operated primarily for its benefit' (p. 114) through subsidies, entry restrictions, restrictions on substitutes and subsidies to complements, and price-fixing. Political control over this process is limited by the infrequency of voting and the high cost of acquiring information on the side of the voters (Laffont and Tirole, 1988). Introducing the problem of collective action (due to Olson, 1965) in a more explicit manner, Peltzman (1976) argues that the reason why producers – rather than consumers – capture the regulatory agency is that their smaller number makes collective action easier. This version of the interest-group approach then prescribes that the best way to avoid the possibility of regulatory capture is to deprive the state of the power to regulate.

Some Marxists have argued along similar lines, although with different political connotations. They argue that the state, whose existence depends on the reproduction of the dominant mode of production in society, has to serve the interests of the economically dominant class in that society – that is, the capitalist class in the capitalist society (Miliband, 1969; O'Connor, 1973; Gough, 1979). In the simpler version of the theory, the state is seen as defending the capitalist *class* interest, if necessary at the cost of individual capitalists' interests. In this view the solution to the problem of divergence between the 'public interest' and the objectives of the state is to overthrow capitalism and therefore get rid of class divisions and relations of domination, because the public whose interest the state serves will then become the whole of society.

The interest-group approach is useful as a broad framework to understand politics, since it enables us to see how the public is not an homogeneous entity but is made up of diverse groups which struggle with each other to affect the decisions of the state. However, apart from some sophisticated Marxist versions, this approach has the following shortcomings.

First of all, many versions of the approach do not adequately discuss the problem of collective action. As was pointed out by Olson (1965), Hardin (1982) and Hindess (1987), the traditional theories of interest-group politics (both the pluralist and the Marxist varieties) have too readily assumed that all existing interests will be represented. However, even if people have identical preferences they are not necessarily able to act them out due to the difficulty of collective action. As many studies in the tradition of the theory of collective action have shown, which groups can assert their interests depends on how large the group is and whether it is feasible to devise some selective incentive/sanction scheme. In addition, the frequency and duration of the interaction among the members of the group (Axelrod, 1984; Taylor, 1987) and ideology (North, 1981) also matter for the possibility of successful collective action.

Moreover there is the problem of 'agenda formation'. It is not true that all interests can be organised once the configuration of the group is such that the free-rider problem can be overcome. How interests are represented also depends on which issues are more easily put on the public agenda. In a country at any point of time, there exist social norms (or ideologies) according to which some issues simply cannot be put on the agenda for public action, and therefore it is almost impossible to organise an interest group around such issues.[18] 'Certain kinds of argument, powerful though they may be in private deliberations, simply cannot be put in a public forum' (Goodin, 1986, p. 87), or 'although both individual material interests and the interest of particular groups and classes are still the essential forces at play in the politics ... the form in which those interests are publicly expressed and argued over allows for a real "distance" to open up between political and public debate and those interests' (Kitching, 1983, p. 61). The motivation and the capacity of the state also become important variables in determining what kinds of policy alternatives can be discussed, adopted, and implemented, because government leaders and bureaucrats often take initiatives well beyond the demands of social groups (Skocpol, 1985). In other words, the existing forms of politics, the structure of the state apparatus, the prevailing ideologies (or social norms) and so on affect what kinds of interest groups can and would be formed (see Skocpol, 1985, for a detailed discussion).

Thirdly, most versions of the interest-group approach do not adequately deal with the *process* of interest-group politics. Rather, their analysis is 'structuralist' in the sense that the outcome of interest-group politics is seen as predetermined by systemic parameters. Given such a static view of politics, it is more than natural that the proponents of the approach think that the problem of 'biased representation' could never be resolved without destroying the existing social structure (for example a return to the minimal state, the socialist revolution). However, what matters in reality is not only whether a particular social structure allows some or other group to dominate, but also the nature of the *process* of gaining such dominance – in other words, how surplus is appropriated is as, if not more, important as who gets the surplus (Khan, 1989). For example, in some South Asian countries, mobilisation of clientelist groups has become the major channel for surplus appropriation, with some detrimental consequences for capital accumulation (Bardhan, 1984, for India; Khan, 1989, for Bangladesh). Another example is Latin America, where the fractured nature of society produces a volatile pattern of capital accumulation where a growth cycle starts only to be quickly disrupted by hyperinflation and then needs a major social upheaval (for example military dictatorship, austerity programmes) to resume itself (Fishlow, 1990; Amadeo and Banuri, 1991). Interest-group politics may be properly understood only when the particular process of contest for political and economic rights in the society concerned are analysed in detail (for a seminal work in this vein, see Khan, 1989).

1.3.3 The Self-Seeking-Bureaucrats Approach

Another important critique of the 'benevolence' assumption in welfare economics is what we call the theory of self-seeking bureaucrats. The theory is based on the postulate that bureaucrats are in no sense different from other individuals in pursuing their own interests. It is absurd, the argument goes, to believe that one and the same individual will behave altruistically in the office and egoistically after office hours. It is assumed that the bureaucrats are budget-maximisers, following Niskanen's argument that '[a]mong the several variables that may enter the bureaucrats' motives are: salary, perquisites of the office, public reputation, power, patronage, output of the bureau, ease of making changes, and ease of managing the bureau. All except the last two are a positive function of the total *budget* of the bureau during the bureaucrat's tenure' (Niskanen, 1973, p. 22). Since bureaucrats derive utility from higher salaries and greater power of their bureaus, it is rational for them to maximise the budget of their bureaus rather than to optimise the social output.

Although the vote-maximising behaviour of politicians may impose some constraints on the size of the budget (because the politicians, who have to be re-elected, do not want too high taxes), the outcome is likely to be in favour of the bureaucracy. This is due to the fact that the politicians are at an informational disadvantage concerning the cost functions of the bureaux, not only because they lack the expertise to estimate such functions but also because the state bureaux are in monopolistic positions and therefore there is no criterion to gauge their efficiency (Mueller, 1979, p. 157). The politicians, even when they are public-minded, have no more power than to monitor the bureaucracy according to the crude criterion that the total costs of state expenditure should not exceed total benefits (Cullis and Jones, 1987, p. 127). It is thus argued that the bureaucrats, acting as rational and selfish agents, will produce the goods and services under state provision in more than a socially optimal quantity.[19]

The self-seeking-bureaucrats approach can be criticised on the following grounds. First of all, the scope for the realisation of bureaucratic self-interest through overprovision of public goods and services differs according to the institutional setting and the political process around the bureaucracy. For example, if bureaucrats are recruited through written sitting tests (as in Japan or Korea), it is more difficult to expand bureaux (a good way of maximising the budget) than when a higher official can easily recruit anybody he/she wants (as in some developing countries). Also, if the state acts as a 'predator' (see above), it has an incentive to under- rather than over-provide public goods and services (Eggertsson, 1990, pp. 235–6), thus mitigating the tendency of overprovision due to bureaucratic self-seeking. Even in societies where the 'principal' is the diffused public, bureaucrats are not totally free to do whatever they want. Given its claim to be a 'public' agency, the bureaucracy is more vulnerable to 'voice-type' checks – say, media criticism – than private firms are (on the concept of 'voice', see Hirschman, 1970).[20] Indeed, historically there have been institutional developments within modern states that keep bureaucrats from wielding arbitrary powers, such as: competitive exams for appointments; the auditing of expenditure; the development of the principle of equality of citizens before the law; the development of the expectation that office-holders will operate on the basis of the law, their superiors' directives and their own 'science' and 'conscience'; and the subordination of the bureaucracy to ultimate political decisions (Poggi, 1990, pp. 75–6).

More importantly, bureaucrats *can and do* act in a fashion that is not solely self-interested. Often bureaucrats think of themselves, rightly or wrongly, as the guardians of the public (or national) interest, however defined, and act to promote it. One such reason is that 'public-spiritedness', altruism, and so on are often held as a genuine principle, and not as a thin veil to disguise self-interest. As McPherson (1984) puts it, '[i]f whatever moral concerns people have are simply redescribed as peculiar forms of self-interest – she tells the truth because she'll feel guilty if she lies; she voted against the farm bill because it made her feel good to defy the "interests" – then the self-interest hypothesis becomes empty' (p. 77). The second reason is that bureaucrats (like the members of any other organisation) are constantly asked to conform to the organisational objectives of the state, which is always under some degree of pressure to promote the national or public interest.[21] Moreover, as demonstrated by the psychology literature (for example Tversky and Kahneman, 1986), decision frameworks do influence people's decisions. Bureaucrats usually face questions put in terms of public interest, which will invoke a preference-ordering that is different from that used in private decision-making situations (Goodin, 1986). And through the process of endogenous preference formation, they will develop organisational loyalty and other attitudes that differ from what is supposed in the theory of self-seeking bureaucrats (Schott, 1984, pp. 111–17; Simon, 1991).

1.3.4 Summary

As the interest-group approach emphasises, groups in society engage in struggles to ensure property rights over productive assets, to claim more resources from the state budget, and to restrict property rights and the distributive claims of other groups, and in this process, they try, and sometimes succeed, to influence the state to their advantage. Of course it would be problematic to interpret every policy as an outcome of interest-group politics because the state not only responds to interest-group demands but often takes initiatives, for good or bad reasons. In this respect the autonomous- (or predatory-) state approach, which treats the state as an entity with its own objectives, is a useful antidote. However, as was emphasised by the theory of self-seeking-bureaucrats, the state apparatus itself is made up of bureaucrats who act as agents of the ruler (the sovereign in earlier periods and the public in modern democracies). The principal-agent problem here makes it impossible to assume that the state is a unified entity without looking at individual cases in terms of the strength of the hierarchy within the bureaucracy, the independence of high-ranking bureaucrats, the prevalent ideology within the bureaucracy, the recruiting method, and so on.

There can be no presumption that the state will act in the public interest, as is usually assumed in standard welfare economics. However it is equally inadequate to employ another sweeping assumption as to the objective of the state, such as net-revenue-maximisation or budget-maximisation. What kind of objective function the state operates with will depend on: what kinds of interests can be formed and acted out as a pressure on the state; how resistant the state can be to these demands (or how 'hard', in the Myrdalian sense, it can be); what the objectives of the top politicians are; how strongly they control the bureaucracy; how strong hierarchies within the bureaucracy are; how bureaucrats are recruited; what the prevalent ideology within the bureaucracy is and how it is formed; and so on.

1.4 ABILITY: THE GOVERNMENT-FAILURE LITERATURE

In many theories of state intervention it is (implicitly) assumed that the state knows everything and can do everything. Welfare economics is an extreme case of this tendency. In welfare economics it is assumed that the state has all the relevant information for social-welfare-maximising intervention and is able to achieve what it sets out to do. The political-economy literature suffers from the same problem, albeit to a lesser degree. For example, in the predatory-state approach, although the competitive constraint put on the state is recognised, there is a strong presumption that the outcome will be in favour of the state as a 'predator'. The interest-group approach concentrates on whose objectives are imposed on the state but does not properly discuss whether the state can achieve such objectives. The same applies to the theory of self-seeking bureaucrats, where it is assumed that the bureaucrats can assert their own objectives without too many difficulties.

However, recently, the assumption of the 'omnipotent' state has been questioned by arguments which hold that, even if it is 'benevolent' and genuinely tries to improve the efficiency of the economy (although the opposite tends to be assumed among those who hold this view), the state may fail to achieve its objectives. These arguments, which we would call the government-failure literature, have two major strands. One is the informational argument, which points out that the state may be able to collect and process all the information relevant for the correction of market failures only at costs that are greater than the benefits from such correction. The other is the theory of rent-seeking, which argues that state intervention creates additional 'wastes' that may more than offset the benefits it produces. In the following we examine these two arguments, which question the ability of the state.

1.4.1 The Information Problem

When the state contemplates a policy, it needs to spend resources to collect and process information in order to formulate the possible alternatives and make a decision. Even after the policy is decided on it needs to collect and process the information necessary to monitor the compliance of lower-level bureaucrats, on the one hand, and the groups and individuals at whom the policy is targeted, on the other hand.

Part of the information problem is that of insufficient information. According to this argument, the state simply 'does not know better' about the future course of events and such informational deficiency can only be corrected at a prohibitive cost. This is a point which was already made by the Austrian school in the central-planning debate in the 1930s (see Lavoie, 1985, for a discussion of the debate).[22] According to the Austrians, even if it is theoretically possible for the planning authority to 'simulate' textbook welfare-economics prescriptions (as Oskar Lange and others have argued), the amount of information required to do so is so vast that we cannot possibly expect it to collect and process all the relevant information. Indeed the practice of central planning in socialist countries shows that the amount of information that could be processed in time for the writing of the plan is too meagre to allow a plan of even a reasonable sophistication (see Brus, 1972; Dobb, 1974; Brus and Laski, 1989).

A more important dimension of the information problem is the existence of informational asymmetry, or, in the language of modern economics, the principal-agent problem (see Stiglitz, 1987). There exist two types of informational asymmetry in relation to state intervention. Firstly, there exists informational asymmetry between the top decision-makers and the lower-level bureaucrats within the state apparatus.[23] The classic example is the prevalence of shortages in socialist economies due to the attempts of managers of state-owned enterprises to secure sufficient inputs by understating their capabilities (see Dobb, 1970, 1974; Ellman, 1989, chs 2–3). Secondly, there exists informational asymmetry between the state and the policy 'target' entities (for example firms, income groups, individuals). A good example is the existence of firms under infant-industry protection which persistently fail to grow out of their 'infancy' in many developing countries (see Bell *et al.*, 1984). Whatever its source, informational asymmetry means that the state may not be able to implement effectively its policies unless it spends enormous resources to overcome the asymmetry.

Although the information problem is a serious handicap on any attempt for the state to intervene effectively, we think that the problem can be exaggerated.

Problems of information collection and processing exist for state intervention because the rationality of individuals who make up the state apparatus is 'bounded' (Simon, 1983; also see Chapter 2.2.1). Indeed, overcoming the limitations of individual rationality is the very *raison d'être* of human organisations, including the state apparatus (Stinchcombe, 1990). If this is the case, it is unreasonable to criticise the state for having insufficient information while assuming that decision-makers in private organisations (for example firms) know everything they need to know (see Chapter 3.4.1).

Concerning the problem of asymmetric information within the state apparatus, note that the problem exists in any organisation of reasonable size, and not just within the state apparatus. The fact that large organisations, including the state, develop and function reasonably well shows that there are ways and means to mitigate the principal-agent problem, for example by designing an appropriate organisational structure and promoting organisational loyalty (see Chapter 2.1.2). Moreover, asymmetric information may exist between the state and the policy target groups, but it also exists between the parties in private contracts. And, again, the fact that private transactions that involve high informational asymmetry are conducted routinely shows that there are ways to control this problem through organisational innovations.

1.4.2 Rent-Seeking

The theory of rent-seeking argues that state intervention incurs not only traditional deadweight losses but also costs when resources are diverted into unproductive activities by private agents in order to capture rents generated by state intervention (for a survey, see Tollison, 1982; also see essays in Buchanan *et al.* (eds), 1980, and Colander (ed.), 1984).

Rent is defined as 'that part of the payment to an owner of resources over and above that which those resources could command in any alternative use' (Buchanan, 1980a, p. 3), that is, the receipt in excess of the opportunity costs of the resources. An attempt to capture rents, the argument goes, is perfectly rational at the individual level *and* socially productive in a certain context. For example, entrepreneurs innovate to capture the monopoly rent. This entrepreneurial activity is socially productive in a competitive setting where there is free entry, since once rents are created in an industry people will move into the industry and thus drive prices down to competitive levels.[24] However, when the state intervenes to create *artificial* rents, the resources spent to capture them, the theory of rent-seeking insists, may be worth expending from the individual point of view but are wasted from the social point of view, since they are spent in *resource reallocation rather than resource creation*. Buchanan (1980a) states:

> Rent seeking on the part of potential entrants in a setting where entry is either blocked or can at best reflect one-for-one substitution must generate social waste. Resources devoted to efforts to curry [the authority's] favour might be used to produce valued goods and services elsewhere in the economy, whereas nothing of net value is produced by rent seeking. In the competitive market, by comparison, resources of potential entrants are shifted directly into the *production* of the previously monopolised commodity or service, or close substitutes; in this usage, these resources are more productive than they would have been in alternative employments. The unintended results of competitive attempts to capture monopoly rents are 'good' because entry is possible; comparable results of attempts to capture artificially contrived advantageous positions under governmentally enforced monopoly are 'bad' because entry is not possible (p. 8).

Once government restrictions on entry are introduced, rent-seeking activities (and the resulting 'waste' from them) cannot easily be eliminated and some apparently plausible means of eliminating them may merely shift rent-seeking to another level (Krueger, 1974; Posner, 1975). For example the auctioning of monopoly rights (franchise bidding), while eliminating monopoly profit, will transfer the rents to the state, which in turn is likely to lead to higher salaries for bureaucrats. Consequently people will devote 'excessive' time and resources to becoming bureaucrats (say, by investing 'excessively' in acquiring educational qualifications), whose compensation exceeds the real opportunity cost (the compensation for private-sector jobs requiring comparable ability). Even when there is no rent component in bureaucratic compensation, it is likely that people will strive to capture the rent extracted by the state in the forms of tax cuts or subsidies

(Buchanan, 1980a, pp. 12–13). Moreover, according to the proponents of the theory, the existence of rent-seeking activities affects people's perceptions of the legitimacy of the economic system, inviting further state intervention. 'If the market mechanism is suspect, the inevitable temptation is to resort to greater and greater intervention, thereby increasing the amount of economic activity devoted to rent seeking' (Krueger, 1974, p. 302).

On these grounds, the theory of rent-seeking contends that state intervention, be it good-willed or ill-willed, is doomed to generate forms of inefficiency that have not been generally recognised in the standard welfare-economics literature – that is, the 'cost of creating monopoly' (Posner, 1975, p. 823). The policy prescription is that the state should not intervene in a manner which restricts entry. And on a more fundamental level, there is the need for a 'constitutional revolution' (Buchanan, 1980b) to establish a new set of efficient institutions.[25]

The rent-seeking argument provides some interesting insights concerning the interaction between individual behaviours and the institutional setting. It raises the important point that the combined results of individual maximisations can differ sharply according to the institutional settings. However the theory has a lot of problems that may not be obvious at first sight.

First of all, the nature of rent-seeking costs is not clearly defined in the literature, resulting in conceptual confusions (also see Samuels and Mercuro, 1984). In the standard rent-seeking literature, it is customary to regard all resources expended in rent-seeking as wasteful. However rent-seeking may not involve real expenditure of resources but only a transfer of wealth (for example bribery), which does not constitute a social cost.[26] The real costs involved in rent-seeking are costs involved in transferring property rights, that is, transaction costs, and not the transfer elements (Littlechild, 1981; Varian, 1989).[27] Of course, as noted above, the proponents of the theory argue that the transferred rent (for example bribes or the proceeds from franchise bidding) will, at some level, be competed for, for example through excessive investment in education or lobbying for tax cuts. However, such an argument is based on the assumption that within the social system there is *at least one* area into which entry is unrestricted, be it education or the political market of lobbying, which we argue may not be the case (see Chapter 2.2.3 for a more detailed discussion). In addition it should also be noted that, when we relax the assumption of full employment implicit in the theory of rent-seeking, even an apparently unproductive activity can be useful for society (recall the famous Keynesian example of the 'hole-digging' exercise).[28]

Moreover, the wastes from rent-seeking may not even be the major costs from state-created rents. Rent-seeking cost is often of a *once-and-for-all nature,* because once a rent is granted an entry barrier into the rent market is likely to be erected, which will discourage potential entrants from spending resources to dislodge the incumbent. A more serious danger is that state intervention may protect or even encourage inefficient producers or production methods, with a long-lasting efficiency consequence (see also Littlechild, 1981). This problem is not explicitly discussed in the rent-seeking literature, which normally assumes that all rent-seeking agents are identical and use optimal production methods. However, in the real world, there is no guarantee that someone who is competent (or even lucky) at seeking rents is equally competent as a producer, although this may well be the case if rent-seeking takes the form of franchise bidding.

Thirdly, in the rent-seeking literature it is usually assumed that restrictions on entry will only be created by state intervention. This is a strongly biased view. Firms are always anxious to deter potential entrants. Anything from the secrecy of production technologies, to excess capacity, to the brand loyalty of consumers can be used as an entry barrier. The implicit belief behind the theory of rent-seeking – that competitive markets are self-reproducing – is unwarranted (see 1.1.2 above). Krueger's (1974) assertion that the existence of state intervention, and hence rent-seeking, will erode people's faith in the market mechanism, leading to calls for more and more intervention, is also based on this dubious belief in self-perpetuating competitive markets.

Most importantly, rent-seeking may be directly unproductive, but 'indirectly productive'. Rent-seeking is only unambiguously harmful for society when it can be assumed that 'the initial institutional creation of an opportunity for rent seeking [creation of entry barriers] ensures a net destruction of economic value' (Buchanan, 1980b, p. 359). However the costs of rent-seeking may well be more than offset by the dynamic gains of productivity growth which the rent allows, say, by enabling firms to increase R&D expenditure (Littlechild, 1981) – this is precisely the reason why we have, for example, patent systems (given the public-good nature of technological knowledge) and infant-industry protection (given the possibility of learning by doing). Of course, the theory of rent-seeking is correct in arguing that free entry is necessary to guarantee the beneficial effects of rent, but the theory is far too reluctant to acknowledge that the creation of a monopoly by the state may be beneficial for productivity growth if the state can withdraw the rent when necessary (see Chapter 4.4.2).

The reform proposal for a rent-seeking society is also unconvincing. If we can achieve a 'constitutional revolution' and start afresh, then we may talk of non-intervention on a rent-seeking ground.[29] However any realistic person will recognise that the possibility of a successful constitutional revolution is almost nil. In the first place this proposal assumes that, once created, competitive markets will perpetuate themselves. We have repeatedly pointed out that this is not the case. Secondly, the proposal underestimates the power of vested interests, which may not agree to reform. Even Buchanan admits that the majority of individuals are usually losers in rent-seeking games, and therefore the winners will have strong incentives to defend their positions (Buchanan, 1980b). When there is no feasible political platform to achieve such a change, providing such a reform proposal amounts at best to an evasion of responsibility and at worst to an apparently populist rhetoric that amounts to a refusal to reform.

CONCLUSION

Welfare economics elegantly and convincingly spells out why markets may fail and what kinds of interventionist measures the state can employ to correct them.[30] However, as many economists from across the political spectrum argue, the theory is based on a naive set of assumptions about the nature and ability of the state. Even if we do not accept the contractarian argument that the state, being the product of a social contract among free individuals, has no right to intervene in the market, we still have two thorny questions: does the state really serve the public interest?; and can it achieve what it sets out to do?

In relation to the first question we examined three approaches – the autonomous-state approach, the interest-group approach and the self-seeking-bureaucrats approach – and concluded that none of them on its own can provide generalisable assumptions about the objectives of all states, regardless of the time and space where they exist. The question is more of an empirical than a theoretical one. It was suggested that, in order to establish a reasonable set of hypotheses concerning the objectives of a particular state, we should look more carefully at the process of interest group formation and collective action as well as the operation of the bureaucracy in the particular system of political economy in which the state is operating. In doing so, the insights from all the three approaches reviewed can fruitfully be used.

In relation to the second question, we examined two approaches – the informational argument and the rent-seeking argument – which we grouped together as the government-failure literature. It was argued that the importance of the information problem can be exaggerated and that there are ways to mitigate the problem. In relation to the rent-seeking argument, it was pointed out that despite some important contributions, the argument suffers from a few major theoretical deficiencies. Common to these two approaches is their inability (or unwillingness?) to suggest how government failures may be remedied other than by non-intervention. Does this mean that we are condemned to accept failing markets in favour of failing governments as the lesser of the two evils? We will attempt to answer this question in the next chapter.

2 A New Institutionalist Theory of State Intervention

INTRODUCTION

The early debate on the role of the state was conducted in the terms set by welfare economics. The degree of market failure may have been questioned, along with the moral legitimacy and the political intention of state intervention, but no question was asked as to whether well-informed (with welfare economics) and well-intentioned state intervention can actually improve the efficiency of the economy by correcting market failures. With the advent of the government-failure school the terms of debate have considerably changed. Although the possibility of improvement in efficiency through state intervention is still accepted (except by some staunch free-marketeers who deny the existence of market failures), now it is being asked whether the net outcome of such intervention is efficiency-improving when state intervention itself carries certain costs.

We think that the government-failure literature has provided a valuable corrective to the naive belief about the state held by some welfare economists that, once we can somehow have a 'benevolent' state, it will solve all problems. However, as we pointed out in Chapter 1, we are still left with one important question: Is there any way to correct government failures, as there are ways to correct market failures? The first two sections of this chapter look at the information and the rent-seeking arguments examined earlier and suggest how government failures may be remedied, if not completely eliminated. The last section moves a step further and develops what we call a 'new institutionalist theory of state intervention', which incorporates both the market-failure and the government-failure perspectives and suggests some roles of the state that have hitherto been neglected in existing literature.

2.1 REMEDYING GOVERNMENT FAILURES I: THE INFORMATION PROBLEM

2.1.1 Substantive Rationality vs Procedural Rationality

In the standard model of decision-making, the decision-making agent has a well-defined objective function and is aware of an exhaustive set of alternatives (and their respective likelihoods). In this model of what Simon (1983) calls 'Olympian rationality', there may be inefficiency as a result of individual decisions which lead to collective irrationality (for example see Sen, 1982), but there is no inefficiency due to the costs of *making* decisions because everyone knows everything.[1] When we adopt this model of decision-making, the question boils down to securing 'correct' decisions, or in Simon's terminology, substantively rational decisions (on different notions of rationality, see Hargreaves Heap, 1989, and Langlois, 1986b).

However, given the limited cognitive ability – or 'bounded rationality' in Simon's terminology – of individual agents, devising a rational decision-making procedure becomes a more important question than ensuring that each decision is as substantively rational as possible (Simon, 1975). After all, 'the elaborate organisations that human beings have constructed in the modern world to carry out the work of production and government can only be understood as *machinery for coping with the limits of man's abilities to comprehend and compute* in the face of complexity and uncertainty' [emphasis added] (Simon, 1979, p. 501).

Of course this does not mean that substantive rationality does not matter. Especially when we are dealing with complex phenomena, expertise plays an important role, not least because such knowledge is not easily transferable.[2] However the point should not be over-emphasised. As Schelling (1984) argues, '[t]o expect an organisation to reflect the qualities of the individuals who work for it or to impute to the individuals the qualities one sees in the organisation is to commit what logicians call the "fallacy of composition"' (p. 32). In other words, what matters more in a complex and uncertain situation is the rationality of the decision procedure (determined largely by the organisational structure) rather than the substantive rationality of individual decisions (determined largely by the quality of individual members of the organisation) (Simon, 1975, and 1983).

That procedural rationality may matter more than substantive rationality is also suggested by the fact that those East Asian states that have successfully intervened in the economy do *not* in general have well-trained economists as their economic bureaucrats. In his superb study of the famous Japanese Ministry of International Trade and Industry (henceforth MITI), Johnson (1982) points out that the bureaucrats who have been orchestrating successful economic development have usually been lawyers by training (also see Hadley, 1989, p. 300). The same is true for Korea (see Chapter 4.5). More interestingly, Wade (1990) points out that the economic bureaucracy in Taiwan has traditionally been manned by engineers, and not economists.

2.1.2 Mitigating the Information Problem

2.1.2.1 *Improving the decision-making capacity of the state*

As the government-failure literature points out, the limited ability of the state to collect and process information means that successful state intervention can only be achieved at an informational cost. In this regard the resource capability of the state may matter, because an organisation with a larger resource capability will, *ceteris paribus*, be able to collect more information. And indeed in many developing countries the lack of government resources to collect information (for example understaffed statistical agencies) often poses a serious problem. However, as our argument above indicates, the mere fact that we have more information does not mean much when there is a bottleneck in our ability to process it – that is, when there exists bounded rationality.

As the now-extensive literature on organisation and decision-making (for a survey, see Stinchcombe, 1990) demonstrates, the ability of the state (or any organisation) to process information is, more than anything, determined by its decision-making structure, the most important dimension of which is the degree of centralisation (Simon, 1975; March and Simon, 1958). *Ceteris paribus* more layers of autonomous decision-makers result in more time and resources spent on decision-making (for example communication and negotiation costs), and therefore centralisation of decision-making can save costs by promoting quick decision-making.

Of course a centralised decision-making structure runs the danger of resulting in substantively less rational decisions, because centralised decisions can be overly influenced by the information possessed by the top decision-makers, which is likely to be less complete when compared with that possessed by the operative units. Again, however, this does not mean that the most decentralised decision-making structure will be able to secure the best decision. Whether this is the case depends upon the nature of the decision.

People's perceptions of the world, which are bound to be incomplete, tend to become biased according to their personal experiences. In more practical terms, people tend to develop 'sub-goal identification' (Simon, 1991). For example Simon (1979) found that '[t]he businessmen's perceptions of the principal problems facing the company ... were mostly determined by their own business experiences – sales and accounting executives identified a sales problem, manufacturing executives, a problem of internal organisation' (p. 501). And when there exists subgoal identification, it is not necessarily true that leaving the decision to those at the locality will enhance global efficiency. When the problem concerned is of a global nature, the top decision-maker, be he/she the central executive of a firm or a minister of the government, may identify the problem (and hence its solution) more correctly, not because he is a superior being but simply because he does not have the subgoal-identification problem. If the decision is about the global efficiency of the economy (which is likely to be the case when a state is contemplating an intervention), a centralised decision-making structure may be a blessing rather than a curse.

One more point to be made is that the top-decision makers in the state decision-making hierarchy should be assigned only strategic tasks – that is, tasks which relate to the long-term direction of the economy as a whole – and be allowed to delegate more routinised day-to-day tasks to the lower-level decision-makers.[3] In the organisational literature it is found that, when day-to-day tasks and more analytical tasks were vested in the same decision-making unit, '[t]he pressure of regular deadlines and the tasks of supervising clerical personnel usually [gives] the day-to-day activities priority over equally important, but postponable, analytic tasks' (Simon, 1982, p. 81). Given that any individual's ability to process information is limited, freeing the top-decision makers from routinised decisions will enhance the overall ability of the state to process information.

2.1.2.2 Reducing informational asymmetry

If designing a decision-making structure that can secure rational decisions at the lowest costs can alleviate the information problem that results from the limited ability of the state to collect and process information, how can the information problem due to asymmetric information be reduced? As we discussed earlier, there are two kinds of informational asymmetry involved in state intervention. One is that which exists within the state apparatus, between the top decision-makers and the lower level bureaucrats, and the other is that which exists between the state and other agents.

Concerning informational asymmetry within the state, it should be noted that when the person in charge of a subordinate unit (and hence accountable to the top decision-maker) does not have a substantial measure of control over variables influencing the performance of the unit, he/she can always blame others for bad decisions (Simon *et al.*, 1955, p. 78). In this case, the top decision-makers have to spend time and resources on measuring the performance of their subordinates to verify such arguments. To reduce such costs, the degree of discretion available to an organisational participant should be linked to the characteristics of activities performed by him/her. For example, if it is easy to observe job activities and job outputs and to relate activities to output, less discretion should be allowed, and vice versa (March and Simon, 1958, p. 147).

Improving organisational design is not the only way to reduce the informational asymmetry and the resulting 'agency costs' in the state apparatus. As we discussed in relation to the self-seeking-bureaucrats approach, organisational loyalty plays an important role in reducing selfish behaviour among the organisational participants (see Hirschman, 1970, and Simon, 1991, on the role of organisational loyalty). Promoting organisational loyalty among the bureaucrats, therefore, would reduce the agency costs within the state apparatus to a great extent.

Informational asymmetry between the state and other agents also can be reduced through institutional design. For example, the willingness of Japanese firms to reveal the necessary information to the state, which reduces informational asymmetry, is often attributed to the tradition of a close government–business relationship (Okimoto, 1989, p. 156). Nevertheless it should be remembered that this tradition can only be fully exploited because of the role of state-promoted industry associations as information-clearing houses (Magaziner and Hout, 1980, p. 37). The 'plan contracts' between the ministries and the public (and some private) enterprises in France and the establishment of laws for regular reporting from targeted industries in Korea are other examples of reducing informational asymmetry through conscious institutional design (on France, see Hall, 1987, chs 6–8, and Hayward, 1986; on Korea, see Chapter 4.4.1).[4]

2.2 REMEDYING GOVERNMENT FAILURES II: THE RENT-SEEKING PROBLEM

In the standard model of rent-seeking, wherever the state restricts entry economic agents (individuals and groups) will try to capture the rent arising from such restrictions and, in that process, will spend an amount of resources equivalent to the amount of the rent. In order for this result to obtain, a few rather stringent conditions need to be satisfied.[5] First of all, it should be possible for private agents to influence the state. If the state is not open to influence there is no point in spending resources to affect its decisions. The second condition is that there are agents who will engage in rent-seeking activities. This condition may not be met when the rents are granted to an interest group (for example industry) but the individual agents of the potential interest group fail to organise themselves due to the collective action problem. Thirdly, competition should exist in the rent-seeking process, because if there is no need to compete for the rents it is not necessary to spend resources to acquire them. Let us examine these conditions one by one and explore their implications for the reduction of rent-seeking costs.

2.2.1 The Vulnerability of the State

As Congleton (1980) argues, 'artificial scarcity' alone does not create rent-seeking. There should be some means for rent-seekers to influence the outcome of the contest. And since rent-seeking involves state-created rents, the vulnerability of the state becomes a crucial issue, since if the state is invulnerable to outside influence, there will be no rent-seeking however big the rent may be.[6]

One reason why a state may be invulnerable is that its key decision-makers are not dependent on electoral support. A good example is provided by the 'bureaucratic' régimes of Gaullian France, Japan and Korea (for a more detailed discussion of these countries, see Chapters 3 and 4). In these régimes most of the decision-making power concerning economic policies is entrusted to the bureaucrats, who are less vulnerable to influence because of their job security, and not to the politicians whose need for re-election makes them vulnerable to outside influence. Invulnerability of the bureaucracy may be intensified if the state bureaucrats think of themselves as guardians of social interests and refuse to be affected by outside influence (see Chapter 1.3.3).

A state may also be invulnerable because it has voluntarily abdicated its power to make decisions (for this reasoning, see Schelling, 1960, ch. 1, and Elster, 1984, pp. 411–22). If the state legislates that picking the winner will be by methods such as a genuine lottery, equal sharing, rotation, or will be totally arbitrary (although none of these methods is likely to be used to any extensive degree), people will not seek rent for they have no chance of affecting the outcome of the contest. Other policy tools may also reduce, if not eliminate, the vulnerability of the state. Some, though not all, forms of queuing will be among such methods. Unless queuing requires physically waiting in line (for example, the queue can be formed by submitting written applications), forcing people to forego opportunities for other productive activities, the costs incurred in the process of queuing will not be large.[7] Another case of 'abdication' will be the 'indicative-planning' exercise in Japan and France, which can be understood as an attempt by the state to bind itself to a policy and thus make it difficult for individual ministries and bureaucrats to significantly deviate from the announced priorities (see Johnson, 1982, on Japan, and Cohen, 1977, on France). This is a good contrast to the US industrial policy, where the employment of *ad hoc* measures meant that there was plenty of scope to bend the rules (Johnson, 1984).

More interestingly, the state might be vulnerable to pressure but decides on the method of picking the winner so as to generate some beneficial by-products. Picking the winner by observing each contestant's past contribution to social productivity or his/her future prospect for such contribution will have, to borrow from Congleton (1980), a beneficial 'by-stander effect'. For example, contestants in the rent-seeking process may be required to use the wealth effectively to generate more wealth through innovations – in products, production processes and organisations – or to demonstrate benevolence or altruism (Congleton, 1980, pp. 172–3). Thus if the state makes itself vulnerable to the influence of someone who demonstrates his/her productive capabilities, some cost will be incurred to secure the rents (for example R&D costs), but they may be more than offset by the benefits from what the rent-seekers have created in that process (for example better products).

It should of course be remembered that an invulnerable state is not necessarily a good state. For example, when a state is pursuing objectives that are objectionable from the social point of view, as in the predatory-state approach (see Chapter 1.3.1) or as in regulatory-capture theory (see Chapter 1.3.2), we may want it to be vulnerable to pressure to change its objectives. Moreover, as will be clear from our discussion, different forms of invulnerability will have different efficiency implications, although they may be equally effective in reducing rent-seeking costs. For example, in choosing the recipient of the rent, if the state makes itself invulnerable to influences other than someone's productive contribution, the outcome is likely to be much more positive than when it simply abdicates its power and chooses the recipient at random.

2.2.2 The Problem of Collective Action

Rents are often granted to a group of agents (for example industry, firms in a region) rather than to individuals. This is partly because 'influencing activities' (the phrase owes to Milgrom and Roberts, 1990) requires a large set-up cost (for example one may need an industry association in order to lobby) but also because the principle of 'fairness' often demands that agents with identical attributes receive equal treatment. If a particular contest for rent, for whatever reason, requires organising an interest group, such a contest may not happen due to the collective-action problem. That rent-seeking might suffer from the collective-action problem (since it usually involves organising an interest group) has already been pointed out by Tullock (1984). Tullock, however, does not clearly specify that the problem of collective action exists only for *some* kinds of rent, that is, the ones generated from a public source of rent (named after a public good) – or from property rights that allow open access to those within the relevant group.[8]

There are some rents which simply *cannot* be shared with others. Rents from industrial licensing and patents are cases in point. The sources of these rents are private goods in the sense that the sharing of them with others reduces one's benefit. In this case the problem of collective action simply does not exist, and therefore Tullock's argument does not hold. The problem of collective action *does* exist when the rent is generated from a public good. Tariff protection is a case in point, since the fact that others are getting tariff protection does not reduce one's benefit from the protection. When the source of the rent is a public good (although the rent itself is a private good – an analogy is that a fishery might be a public good but the fish caught from the fishery are private goods) and when the potential rent-seekers fail to organise themselves, rent-seeking may not arise and therefore there may be no waste from rent-seeking, as Tullock argues.

If this is the case, the magnitude of rent-seeking costs is affected by the types of policy tools used. Certain types of policy tools (for example tariff) are less prone to rent-seeking than others (for example industrial licensing) because they have the collective-action problem, although both types of tools may create comparable amounts of rent. This means that, *ceteris paribus*, by using more public tools of intervention (and thus deliberately creating the collective-action problem among potential rent-seekers), the state may reduce rent-seeking costs.

2.2.3 Competitiveness of the Rent-Seeking Process

One basic assumption of the theory of rent-seeking is 'that getting a monopoly whether by influencing the government or by getting it privately is essentially a competitive industry' (Tullock, 1984, p. 228). The assumption of competitiveness is important because if there is no competition, there is no need to spend resources to influence the state's decision to one's favour and hence there is no waste from rent-seeking. Contrary to what is usually assumed in the standard literature, however, rent-seeking does not always, and not even predominantly, involve a large number of equally positioned competitors. Especially in many developing countries, the oligarchy, which has an exclusive access to state-created rents, is so deeply entrenched that the rent-seeking industry can hardly be described as competitive.

The limiting case of non-competitive rent-seeking will be monopolistic rent-seeking where there is only one contender for the rent. For example an incumbent firm in, say, the petrochemical industry may become the sole contender for the rent from tariff protection because it happens to have a monopoly position due to the state's industrial licensing policy or due to scale-economy reasons (natural monopoly). Or Mr Brown may be the sole contender for the rent from the license for the new automobile plant because every other potential seeker of this rent knows that he is a brother-in-law of the prime minister and is certain to get the license. In such situations the sole contender for the rent does not have to spend anything to get the rent, and therefore no rent-seeking cost is incurred, both from the individual and from the social point of view.

The more general case of non-competititive rent-seeking is that of oligopolistic rent-seeking. Small numbers, of course, do not necessarily guarantee less rent-seeking. There can be cut-throat competition even in a rent market with a small number of participants. However a small-number setting is inherently different from a large-number one. In the former case an individual's best response is affected by the response of all others (and the common knowledge about this fact), whereas in the latter case one can act as if one's action does not affect, and is not affected by, those of other individuals. In a small-number situation, therefore, one cannot take the environment as given, since one is a part of the environment. This means that there exists strategic uncertainty resulting from interdependence between individual decisions.[9]

More interestingly, when communication is possible players in the small-number setting may be able to overcome strategic uncertainty by devising a binding contract between themselves. Here there arises the possibility of collusion. The competitors for a particular rent might agree, and make a binding contract between themselves, that only one will bid for the rent at a price that is far lower than the rent, and that they will split the spoils (the rent minus the price), rather than compete the rent away. Let us elaborate on this point with an example.

If two firms are contending for a monopoly position that will yield a rent of 100, and if they have an even chance of getting the position, we can suppose a payoff matrix as shown in Figure 2.1. In this example, if both *A* and *B* bid for the rent, each has an expected payoff of 0, because each runs the risk of spending the sum equal to the expected value of the rent (that is 50) but not getting the rent, one out of two cases (0.5 × [100

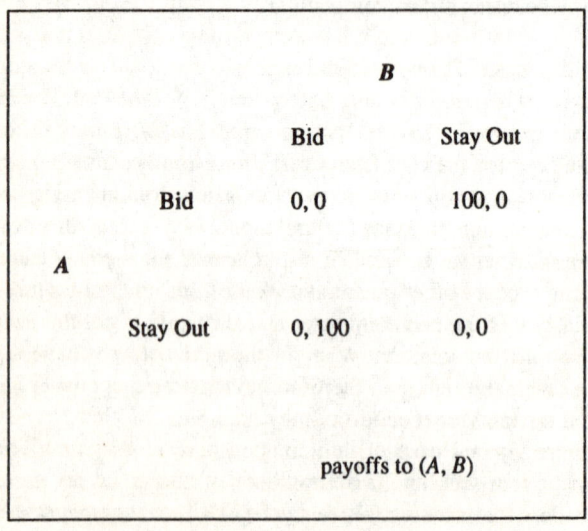

		B Bid	Stay Out
A	Bid	0, 0	100, 0
	Stay Out	0, 100	0, 0

payoffs to (*A*, *B*)

Figure 2.1 An example of duopolistic rent-seeking

− 50] + 0.5 × [0 − 50] = 0). However, if the two firms can write a binding contract such that one of them will stay out of the contest, they can acquire the rent without spending any resource. In this case the social cost involved may be nil. Of course this simple example ignores the fact that the possibility of such collusion will depend on the feasibility of making credible commitments, the possibility of side payments, and other conditions related to bargaining (for a more detailed discussion of these conditions, see Schelling, 1960), but it shows that non-competitive rent-seeking is likely to incur less rent-seeking costs than a competitive one due to the inherent likelihood of collusion.

The above discussion shows that when the rent-seeking process is less competitive, it is more likely that the total costs arising from the process are lower. This happens basically because there exist entry barriers into the rent market. Of course, one may argue that resources will still be wasted even in the case of non-competitive rent-seeking because people will spend resources to build up entry barriers to the rent market. We agree that this is sometimes the case – for example I may spend resources in building personal ties with the industry minister in order to build barriers against future rent-seeking contests. However, in a world with imperfect foresight, the scope for such action may be seriously limited – I cannot be sure how helpful the minister will be in a later, and unforeseen occasion when I want to bid for a rent.[10]

Even if the entry barriers to the rent market are sufficiently high that there are few rent-seeking costs, there may be costs from 'second-tier' rent-seeking if the state distributes the rent extorted through franchise bidding or bribery (see Chapter 1.4.2). For example, if the rent extorted by the state is distributed to bureaucrats in the form of higher salaries, and if anyone can become a bureaucrat with a certain educational qualification, people may invest an excessive amount of resources in education.[11] Likewise, if the state extorts some part of the rent in the form of, say, bribery and distributes it in the form of tax cuts, which are up for grabs by any interest group, interest groups will spend resources to secure such rents. These examples of second-tier rent-seeking, however, still assume that there is unlimited entry at *at least one* level of the political economy. However, if entry is contained at some level and if, as a result, competition does not overflow into other levels, the rent extorted by the state may not be totally dissipated. And although this outcome may have undesirable political and distributional consequences, it may be a less wasteful outcome. For example, if entry into the bureaucracy is open only to a tiny minority, or if only the most powerful group is able to secure a new tax cut, there may be no second-tier rent-seeking and hence no rent-seeking cost to society, although income distribution may become skewed as a result.

2.2.4 Some Reflections: Competitive Markets and Competitive Politics

Fundamentally, what causes rent-seeking is the existence of political competition, and *not* the absence of economic competition (which causes rent but not rent-seeking). If this is the case, restricting political competition seems to be a solution to the problem of rent-seeking. Above we suggested some ways in which this can be done. However the proponents of the theory of rent-seeking would ask: why not attack the root cause of the problem, that is, why not eliminate all the rents simply by freeing the markets from state interference? Why bother about politics when separating economics from politics will solve the problem?

This view, however, is based on the assumption that there is no reason to restrict competition (and thus create rents) in markets. As Schumpeter (1987) and Richardson (1960) have persuasively shown, however, there is a need for restrictive practices (which create rents), in order to achieve innovation and long-term investment, which are the causes of dynamic growth of the economy. Even if the state does not intervene, the market in a dynamic economy is bound to create a lot of rents, and people are bound to spend resources to capture those rents. Then why are the market-generated rents not subject to wasteful rent-seeking whereas the state-created ones are?

The point is *not* that people do not seek rents in markets. As our quote from Buchanan (1980a) in the previous chapter indicates, innovation is rent-seeking *par excellence*. However, rent-seeking in markets is regarded as productive because we *assume* that it creates more resources than it uses up in the process, and not because it does not use up any resource. For example, firms do spend resources on R&D to win the competition, but produce more resources (for example better products) or reduce costs (for example better processes) as a result – although, contrary to the conventional presumption, there is a possibility that such competition will result in waste (see Chapter 3.2.1). Political competition is wasteful only because it is implicitly *assumed* that it does not create any value. However political competition *does* create (if intangible) values. First of all, political activities may involve organisational innovations, which may ultimately reduce the costs of political competition in the future – for example it will be cheaper to have a political party than to let millions of people bargain with each other. Moreover political activities are often ends in themselves and people may derive value from the activities *per se* as well as from the products of such activities (see Hirschman, 1982, pp. 85–6).[12]

Then, whether competition, be it economic or political, is wasteful or not – that is, whether it creates more resources than it spends – is a moot point. Especially in the case of political competition, there is no unambiguous way to measure the value of its output. Even if we follow the proponents of the theory of rent-seeking in assuming that political competition creates no value whatsoever, there are ways and means to reduce the costs from rent-seeking, essentially by restricting competition at one level or another. The real question, then, is at what level of the overall system of political economy – for example education, bureaucratic recruitment, interest-group activities, market competition – should competition be restricted and at what level should it be encouraged? The answer to this question can only be determined with reference to the concrete political economy of the society concerned, and not on the basis of the simplistic model of political economy envisaged by the proponents of rent-seeking in which there exists no entry barrier other than the ones created by the state.[13]

2.3 A NEW INSTITUTIONALIST THEORY OF STATE INTERVENTION

Up to now we have discussed how the costs of state intervention may be reduced, or in other words, how government failures may be corrected. We argued that there are ways and means to devise institutional schemes to reduce the costs of state intervention while not foregoing the possible benefits from such intervention – for example by improving efficiency through correction of market failures or by encouraging productivity growth by granting infant-industry protection. In this section we generalise our discussion and suggest a 'new institutionalist' theory of state intervention, which allows us to look at the problem of state intervention in a more balanced manner and reveal some important roles of the state that have hitherto been neglected.

2.3.1 The Nature of Economic Costs

In neoclassical economics, of which welfare economics is a branch, the only 'economic' problem is that of achieving allocative efficiency between the production units. As the famous definition of economics by Robbins goes: '[e]conomics is the science which studies human behaviour as a relationship between ends and scarce means which have alternative uses' (Robbins, 1932, p. 16). What is curious here is that solving this economic problem does *not* require any cost and the only cost in our economic life is the cost involved in the material production, which is seen as an engineering problem, and *not* as an economic problem.

In this framework market failures are inefficient in the sense that the economy does not achieve the degree of social welfare that is theoretically attainable, or what Demsetz (1964) calls the 'nirvana' state, but they still do not impose any real cost to society. And better still, such inefficiency in resource allocation (market failure) can be remedied by the state and the remedy costs nothing to society, because what the state does, so to speak, is announce new prices at no real cost.

Recently, however, there have been arguments criticising this framework on the ground that the *achievement* of efficiency may be a costly activity – independent of the hypothetical costs arising from *the state of not achieving efficiency*.

In relation to production, two groups of argument have been put forward against neoclassical orthodoxy. Firstly, the literature on technical change points out that technology is not a blueprint but that it contains a lot of tacit knowledge which cannot be put to work without a costly process of learning (for example training costs).[14] Secondly, the Marxian labour-process literature, the efficiency-wage argument, and the theory of team production all argue that production is not merely an engineering process but is also a labour process in which workers have control over their effort, and therefore it may be costly to organise production (for example monitoring costs).[15]

In relation to resource allocation also, two kinds of arguments have been raised. Firstly, the transaction-cost branch of new institutional economics argues that market exchange (or market transaction), through which resource allocation is achieved in the market economy, is not costless as assumed in neoclassical economics because bounded rationality requires us to spend resources to set up safeguards against the opportunistic behaviour of the trading partner (for example the cost of writing and enforcing the contract).[16] Secondly, the government-failure literature argues that the process of resource allocation by the state is not costless as assumed in welfare economics, if only because the state is not an omniscient and omnipotent being (for example costs of information processing).[17]

Thus seen, the recent theoretical developments emphasise that *achieving* efficiency – or coordinating the behaviour of interdependent but independent agents – is costly, independent of the hypothetical costs arising from actually falling short of what Demsetz calls the 'nirvana' state. From this point of view, the costs of actually producing goods (which are inevitable due to the law of physics, so to speak) are not the only costs of our economic life, and a significant portion of economic costs are made up of the costs of actually allocating resources between production units and managing the production process within the production units. These costs of coordination between and within economic units, which are to be differentiated from pure engineering costs, have recently come to be called transaction costs.[18]

Transaction costs exist because economic activities (be it the production process or the allocation process) involve not only interaction between people and things but also interaction between people.[19]

For economic interaction between people to start at all, the rights of individuals need to be defined. Property rights have to be assigned and their boundaries defined – I may own my knife but I may not be allowed to kill people with it. Rights over other entitlements (for example social security, working conditions, and product safety) also have to be negotiated and defined. These are all costly processes that require information-collection and processing, bargaining, and contract writing. After the rights structure is defined, it is necessary to maintain the given rights structure, and this will also require resources for policing and enforcement. Moreover resources will continually be spent by those who want to redefine the rights structure – for example, through enclosing open fields, spending on R&D to acquire patents and lobbying to secure tariff protection – and by those who want to defend the existing rights structure.

Even *within* the existing rights structure it will be costly to acquire and process the information necessary to arrange the contract – say, concerning the contracting partner and the likelihood of each possible future event – and bargain over it. It will often be necessary to incur costs to actually write the contract. Once a contract is made, the adherence of the contracting partners to the contract needs to be monitored. This involves measurement costs (Milgrom and Roberts, 1990) and policing costs. When a breach of contract is suspected it may be necessary to incur costs to settle the disputes (for example the cost of lawsuits). Once the breach of contract is ascertained, enforcement of the contract will become necessary and this will also incur costs.

2.3.2 Transaction Costs and State Intervention

If transaction costs are the costs incurred for the purpose of defining and redefining the property (and other) rights of economic agents, on the one hand, and of writing, monitoring and enforcing contracts within the existing rights structure, on the other hand, the costs of state intervention may also be reinterpreted as transaction costs. Informational costs, which are costs necessary for the state to decide on a policy and effectively implement it, are obviously of this kind (analogous to such costs for private contracts). Costs of rent-seeking, as costs involved in the process of redefining the property rights structure, can also be classified as transaction costs (see Chapter 1.4.2; see also Varian, 1989; Milgrom and Roberts, 1990).[20] Reinterpreting the costs of state intervention as transaction costs allows us to make some important observations in relation to the theory of state intervention.

In neoclassical economics the allocation of resources is a costless process whether it is achieved through the market (that is, market transactions) or through the state (that is, state intervention). What counts is only the difference between the allocation actually achieved and the ideal allocation in the 'nirvana' state. Given such a scheme, it is no wonder that the government-failure literature could criticise welfare economics on the rather obvious grounds that state intervention incurs certain (transaction) costs. However many in the government-failure school are misleading the argument by implicitly comparing the ideal market, which is costlessly run, with the real state, whose activities are costly.

In the real world, *both state intervention and market transaction are costly*. Therefore the comparison must be between the costs of allocating resources through market transactions (or the transaction costs of market allocation) and the costs of allocating resources through state intervention (or the transaction costs of state allocation). Thus seen, the real question is whether the state can achieve the same allocative efficiency at a lower cost than the market can do, and not whether state intervention is costly *per se*. Introducing transaction costs into our scheme allows us to introduce a role of the state which has hitherto been neglected in conventional economic theory, that is, the role of lowering transaction costs in the economy. Let us discuss exactly what the state can do in this regard.

Various authors in the tradition of new institutional economics have suggested that one important role of the state is to institute a well-defined property-rights system and effectively enforce it (Coase, 1960; Matthews, 1986; North, 1981). A clear and effectively enforced set of property rights is seen as saving transaction costs, because otherwise people whose decisions are interdependent may have to spend an inordinate amount of resources in order to resolve the externalities problem. Of course instituting a well-defined property rights structure and enforcing it, in theory, need not be done by the state, but the monopoly on the legitimate use of violence by the state means that it is often, if not necessarily, the most cost-effective agent in doing so (Matthews, 1986, p. 910). Historically, too, transaction costs in market exchanges have been substantially reduced only with the involvement of the state in establishing and enforcing property and other rights (Polanyi, 1957; Coase, 1988; North, 1990b).

The role of the state in reducing transaction costs does not stop at instituting and enforcing a property-rights (and other rights) system. Another important role is to reduce the macroeconomic instability of the economy through aggregate demand management. Given the necessity of stability in the environment for agents with bounded rationality to make any calculation (Simon, 1983, pp. 19–20), increased macroeconomic instability will lead people to divert resources into activities that are intended to create microenvironments that will make rational calculation possible. Spending resources on writing, monitoring and enforcing long-term supply and subcontracting contracts – instead of going into spot-market transactions, which do not require high transaction costs – is the most obvious example of such activities (Richardson, 1972). Financial hedging and inventory holding are equally important examples. The costs involved in these activities are all transaction costs in the sense that they are not necessary from a purely engineering point of view. With reduced instability of the system, there will be less of these activities and consequently less transaction costs in the economy.

There are also areas other than macroeconomic stabilisation to which our insights about the role of the state in economising transaction costs apply. Macroeconomic instability is essentially a case of coordination failure between the activities of disparate individuals (Leijonhufvud,

1981). According to Koopmans (1957), coordination failure may occur due to secondary uncertainty, which exists due to the 'lack of communication, that is from one decision maker having no way of finding out the concurrent decisions and plans made by others (or merely of knowing suitable aggregate measures of such decisions or plans)' (p. 163). If this is the case, we can extend our argument to the coordination problem in general.

A special case of the coordination problem is that of 'pure' coordination, which exists when there are multiple equilibria that are equally preferred by every party involved (see Figure 2.2). In this case, although the agents are indifferent between different outcomes (that is, there is no clash of interests), there is no guarantee that all of them will go for one particular equilibrium. Deciding which side of the road people should drive on is an obvious example of the pure-coordination problem. No one would *ex ante* mind driving on the left or on the right as long as everybody else does likewise, but it is still necessary to decide on which side of the road people will drive. Although a spontaneous norm may emerge to resolve the coordination problem (Schotter, 1981), reaching a coordinated outcome may involve high transaction costs (for example the cost of bargaining), especially when many agents are involved. And in this case, the state may intervene to provide the norm for coordination, consequently reducing the transaction costs involved in the process.

		B	
		Left	Right
A	Left	(1, 1)	(0, 0)
	Right	(0, 0)	(1, 1)

Payoffs to (*A*, *B*)

Figure 2.2   An example of the 'pure' coordination problem

A more generalised problem of coordination exists 'if the payoff space of the game it defines is such that at any equilibrium point, not only does no player have any incentive to change his behaviour, given the behaviour of the other players, but no player wishes that any other player would change either' (Schotter, 1981, p. 22). In this case, everyone would prefer a coordinated outcome to an uncoordinated outcome, but it may be that each may prefer a particular coordinated outcome.[21] A schematic example of such a case is given in Figure 2.3, where two VCR producers, A and B, are using two different types of technology, say, VHS and Beta technologies, but want to introduce a national product standard, which will bring about network externalities or what David (1985) calls 'system scale economies'. In Figure 2.3, A (B), being a VHS (Beta) producer will prefer the standard to be VHS (Beta) technology, but both will prefer either of the coordinated outcomes to the uncoordinated ones.

		B	
		VHS	Beta
A	VHS	(2, 1)	(0, 0)
	Beta	(0, 0)	(1, 2)

Payoffs to (A, B)

Figure 2.3 An example of the generalised coordination problem

The transaction costs involved in resolving this generalised coordination problem through private negotiations are likely to be higher than in the case of the pure coordination problem, because more intense bargaining may be necessary due to different people's preferences for different outcomes (that is, there is a partial clash of interests). Such costs will be particularly high when many agents are involved, which means a multitude of bargaining over, writing, monitoring and enforcing the contract.[22] And indeed some in the tradition of new institutional economics (for example North, 1990b) have suggested that superseding private attempts at coordination with state intervention may greatly reduce transaction costs in the economy (although they do not put it in this particular way).[23] State imposition of a system of weights and measures (North, 1990b) and of technological standards (see Porter, 1990, ch. 12, for examples) are good examples of this.

In order to achieve the coordinated outcome, the state need not completely supersede market transactions, as in our examples above. Indeed such an exercise may be prohibitively costly, as the examples of central-planning practice in the socialist countries show (Coase, 1988; for further references, see Chapter 1.4.1). There exist ways in which the state can reduce the transaction costs in the economy without necessarily superseding all market transactions.

First of all, the state can reduce the transaction costs within the economy by changing the institutional configuration of society. The state can provide legal backing to organise agents into large groups and thus reduce the number of necessary bargainings (and consequently the transaction costs involved). Social corporatism in Scandinavia or Austria, whereby the workers and capitalists are respectively organised into encompassing organisations and conduct nationwide bargaining, is a good example of this – although the transaction-cost aspect of social corporatism has been little discussed (see the Introduction to this book for references).[24]

Secondly, the state can intervene, through its influence on the education system and the mass media, to promote a national 'ideology' or value system, which will help to reduce the costs involved in the exchange of information and bargaining.[25] As Arrow (1974) observed, it is 'easier to communicate with other individuals with whom one has a common approach or a common language' (p. 42), and therefore contracts between agents sharing the same ideology will reduce the bargaining, monitoring and enforcement and other transaction costs required (North, 1981, ch. 3).[26] This is obviously what people have in mind when they say that a homogeneous society like Japan or Korea is easier to manage than a heterogeneous one like the USA or India. Although this role of the state may be objected to on the ground that it can be used to foster 'false consciousness' and other undesirable qualities among the people, it is undeniable that an ideological campaign can play a tremendously important role, as can be seen in its role in the process of rapid industrialisation in many late-developing countries such as Japan, the Soviet Union, China and Korea (see Chapter 4.5 for the Korean case).

Most interestingly, the state may save transaction costs in the economy by providing a focal point, or consensus, around which decisions can be coordinated (on the concept of 'focal point', see Schelling, 1960). For example, investments in complementary projects may be made only at high transaction costs when they are agreed upon through private bargaining (Richardson, 1971, 1972). If this is the case, the provision of a focal point by the state may save the transaction costs involved in these bargaining processes. A good example of this is the Japanese and the French 'indicative-planning' exercises, where the state provides a 'vision' for the future economy and induces private agents to work toward the same goal (see Johnson, 1982, on Japan; Cohen, 1979, on France).[27] For example, in the Japanese case, 'a sense of overall direction to the overall evolution of the economy has been provided by the annual economic white papers of the Economic Planning Agency with their thematic titles and by the forward looks or 'visions' published every two or three years by the MITI, via the Structure Council ..... In practical terms, these documents provide criteria or orientation against which countless individual decisions by private and public officials can be tested and hence given *order and coherence which could otherwise only be achieved by a much higher degree of centralisation*' [emphasis added] (Renshaw, 1986, p. 144).[28]

CONCLUSION

While recognising that state intervention to correct market failures inevitably incurs certain costs, which may indeed exceed the benefits from improved allocative efficiency, we argued that such a possibility does not warrant the *laissez-faire* policy prescription of the government-failure school. Information costs can be reduced through appropriate changes in the organisational structure of the bureaucracy and in the values held by the members of the bureaucracy and society. Rent-seeking costs may also be reduced through changes in the rules of political competition and the tools of state intervention.

Drawing on the insights of new institutional economics, which emphasises that the market is not the only viable coordination mechanism, we constructed a theory of state intervention that sees the state – along with the market, the firm and other economic institutions – as an important device of coordination. We emphasised that the state may resolve the coordination problem at a lower cost than the market (and other economic institutions) and thus reduce transaction costs, which are the costs of coordination, in the economy. Institution of an effective property-rights system, macroeconomic stabilisation, organising society into large groups, promoting national ideologies, and coordinating complementary investment decisions are examples of such a role. This type of intervention is particularly attractive because it is relatively cheap compared with other types, which may indeed incur large transaction costs (for example central planning).

Our theory of state intervention provides a framework that can incorporate insights from the various theories of state intervention we examined in Chapter 1. Our theory considers both the benefits and the costs of state intervention, in contrast with the market-failure approach and the government-failure approach which deal, respectively, with only the benefits or the costs of state intervention.[29] Although our theory is still far from satisfactory, we think it can serve as a good starting point for the construction of a sophisticated theory of state intervention that allows us to look at the problem in a more balanced and realistic way. In the next chapter we apply our theory of state intervention to the area of industrial policy and demonstrate how it improves on the existing theories of state intervention.

3 The Political Economy of Industrial Policy

INTRODUCTION

Until recently there existed a moderate consensus on the agenda of the debate on the role of the state, although there were intense debates concerning how best to achieve the individual items on the agenda. The items on the agenda included an improvement in income distribution, the achievement of macroeconomic stability, the provision of public goods (for example infrastructure, education and environmental protection) and, more controversially, anti-trust activities. State intervention in industry was, except anti-trust activities, looked at with suspicion as opening the window of opportunity for business interests to loot the state exchequer. This suspicion seemed more than natural when state intervention in industry – or industrial policy – did not make theoretical sense according to the conventional framework. Nevertheless, as we mentioned earlier, the recent rise of East Asian economies where the state has implemented strong industrial policy measures with great success has aroused interest in industrial policy, as manifested in the ongoing debate on the applicability of industrial policy in other, notably Anglo-Saxon, countries.

In this chapter we argue that industrial policy not only makes sense but can sometimes provide a better alternative both to the unregulated market and to other forms of state intervention (for example central planning). After reviewing the industrial policy debates, we introduce some recent theoretical developments in the studies of economic institutions and technical change and spell out the logic of industrial policy, both from the static and the dynamic points of view. Regarding the former, we discuss why the market mechanism may lead to coordination failures and why such failures can be costly. Then we discuss the role of industrial policy in overcoming such failures. Regarding the latter, we discuss the nature of economic change and see what role industrial policy can play to promote it. We then move on to discuss possible problems of industrial policy. Problems of information, rent-seeking, politics and institutions are examined.

3.1 THE INDUSTRIAL POLICY DEBATES

Despite the fact that industrial policy, far from being a novelty of East Asia, has been an integral part of economic policies of many advanced capitalist countries during the post-war period, it has become an important issue only recently. In the English-speaking world the OECD has been the pioneer in this area (see the series of country studies published by OECD in the early 1970s). In the UK industrial policy became a controversial issue with the (not hugely successful) introduction of industrial policy programmes by the Labour government in the late 1970s.[1] The famous UK deindustrialisation debate also, to a degree, discussed industrial policy as a possible way to halt deindustrialisation and revive the economy.[2] During the 1980s, studies of various European countries' policy responses to the industrial crisis of the late 1970s also emerged.[3] The issue of industrial policy, however, has probably been most hotly debated in the USA, especially in the early 1980s, with the *Harvard Business Review* as the major forum.[4] The recent rise in strategic-trade-policy literature has also been heavily influenced by (and has influenced) the industrial-policy debates.[5]

3.1.1 Does Manufacturing Matter?

One of the central points made by the proponents of industrial policy is that manufacturing does matter, although a pro-manufacturing attitude does not necessarily imply an endorsement of industrial policy.[6] The proponents of industrial policy argue that the UK and the US economies are deindustrialising (the shrinking share of industrial output and employment in the national economy) due to neglect of the manufacturing industries, and that, given the vital importance of the manufacturing sector for a prosperous economy, this is a dangerous sign (Cohen and Zysman, 1987). They think that macroeconomic measures, albeit important, are not sufficient for a vigorous development of manufacturing since allocation of capital is more important than aggregate capital formation for productivity growth (Reich, 1982, p. 75). The conclusion, then, is that the state should intervene to promote industrial development, if necessary using industrial targeting (Reich, 1982; Johnson (ed.), 1984).

Many opponents of industrial policy argue that the advanced capitalist economies are moving towards becoming post-industrial economies, where service activities become the centre of economic life (for example Bhagwati, 1988, pp. 110–14). Given that the tendency to move towards service activities is dictated by market forces (that is, demand for services increases as income rises), the argument goes, favouring manufacturing is not only unnecessary but also harmful. That is, favouring manufacturing would block the natural-selection mechanism of the market by hampering the necessary reallocation of resources towards service activities, and therefore damage the long-term viability of the economy (for example Burton, 1983). Therefore, it is argued that we need not, and indeed should not, have policies that favour manufacturing, not to mention industrial policies geared to the needs of specific sectors (for the most sophisticated version of this argument, see Bhagwati, 1989).

Confusion about the very concept of deindustrialisation and lack of understanding of the logic of long-term structural change (away from manufacturing towards services) seem to have produced many ill-informed discussions on the deindustrialisation issue. Fortunately some recent studies have spotted the source of confusion and clarified some of the major theoretical issues (Rowthorn and Wells, 1987; Baumol et al., 1989). The conclusions emerging out of the 'manufacturing-matters' debate are the following.

First of all, the long-term structural shift towards a service economy does not happen solely because people want more services as they grow richer, as was believed by some proponents of the theory of post-industrial economy. The major reason for such a structural shift in employment towards services seems to be the (relative) cost-inflation of services due to their lagging productivity growth (compared with that of manufacturing), rather than a real shift in demand towards services as incomes rise.[7]

Secondly, deindustrialisation, defined as the decrease in the share of manufacturing employment in total employment (and the decrease in the share of manufacturing output in total output *in current prices*), is an inevitable long-term result of differential productivity growth rates between manufacturing and services, and is not necessarily related to the declining competitiveness of the economy's manufacturing sector. Even successful exporters of manufactures, such as Japan and West Germany, have experienced deindustrialisation in this sense, which implies that, contrary to what was believed by those who condemned deindustrialisation as a sign of industrial decline, deindustrialisation and industrial decline are not one and the same thing, although industrial decline can affect the timing and scale of deindustrialisation (see Rowthorn and Wells, 1987, ch. 1). Therefore it is wrong to argue that an economy's manufacturing sector is in trouble solely on the ground that it is deindustrialising in terms of the above definition.

Thirdly, the fact that deindustrialisation is an inevitable long-term trend does not necessarily mean that a country can ignore manufacturing completely and rely fully on services. This is largely because many services are either basically non-tradable (for example governmental services, legal services, child care, elementary and secondary education) or have a large non-tradable component (for example transportation, distribution), although there are other services that have become, or are rapidly becoming, tradable (for example financial services, management consultancy, higher education). With a growing share of services in national income, compensating productivity growth in manufacturing is needed – on the reasonable assumption that no dramatic increases in productivity in agriculture and services are likely in the foreseeable future – if a country wants to maintain its income level without running into balance-of-payments problems.

3.1.2 What is Industrial Policy?

A major problem with industrial policy issues is that the very concept of industrial policy is not clearly defined, resulting in heated but often fruitless debates. A good example of this is the discussion on the postwar Japanese experience, which inspired many of the industrial-policy debates. Opponents of industrial policy point out that subsidies and governmental loans to industries in Japan are small (in relative terms), even smaller than in many European countries, and on this ground claim, as the title of one article goes (Trezise, 1983), that 'industrial policy is not the major reason for Japan's success'. Proponents of industrial policy argue that the non-quantifiability of the famous Japanese 'administrative-guidance' system makes people underestimate the success of Japanese industrial policy (Boltho, 1985). Unless we define what we mean by industrial policy, we cannot judge who is correct and who is not.

Reich (1982), the most prominent proponent of industrial policy in the USA, includes the following policy measures in his definition of industrial policy: favouring promising industries; creating skilled workforces; developing infrastructure; regional policy (p. 75). Pinder (1982), a British proponent of industrial policy, goes a step further and regards all of the following as components of industrial policy: general industrial support policies such as manpower policy; fiscal and financial incentives for investment; public investment programmes; public procurement policies; fiscal incentives for R&D; firm-level policies such as specific R&D support; antitrust policy; merger policies to create 'national champions'; support for small firms; regional policies such as the development of physical and social infrastructure and the establishment of industrial complexes; generalised trade protection; sectoral policies such as the organisation of recession cartels in depressed industries; product upgrading in labour-intensive industries (pp. 44–52).

The tendency to adopt an encompassing definition exists even among those who oppose industrial policy. Donges (1980), an ardent European critic of industrial policy, categorically states that industrial policy 'embraces all government actions which affect industry' (p. 189). Corden (1980) also implicitly adopts this definition when he states that 'the best industrial policy may be to provide an adequate infrastructure, some limits on the powers of monopolies and cartels, an education system that helps to generate the human capital for industrial success, indicative guidance about industrial prospects (without compulsion or subsidies), stability and simplicity in the system of taxation, a free and flexible capital market and a steady movement towards zero sectional protection, whether direct and indirect' (pp. 182–3).

Despite the fact that all the above policies would have implications for industrial development, we do not think that classifying every policy that affects industrial development as industrial policy is a useful way to proceed. In the above examples, industrial policy is used as a catch-all term for policies affecting industrial performance, that is, effectively, every economic policy. Such a practice *overloads* the concept of industrial policy, rendering the concept meaningless.

Johnson (1984) provides a more focused definition of industrial policy by defining it as 'a summary term for the activities of governments that are intended to develop or retrench various industries in a national economy in order to maintain global competitiveness' (p. 7), but falls into the same trap of overloading the concept when he includes not only what he calls 'micro' policy of 'industrial targeting' but also such policies as 'governmental incentives for private saving, investment, research and development, cost-cutting, quality control, maintenance of competition, and improvements in labour-management relations' (p. 9) into the category of industrial policy.

As Johnson (1984) rightly points out (p. 9), targeting or micro-industrial policy cannot succeed without favourable macroeconomic conditions. However, why should all policies that constitute preconditions for the success of another policy be treated as components of the latter? If one adopts this logic, one can argue that targeting should be a component of macroeconomic policy because, under certain conditions, it is possible for targeting to have an impact on such macroeconomic variables as savings and investments. For example, targeting some big projects and financing them through inflationary means may increase *ex post* savings. However, does this make such industrial targeting a macroeconomic policy? We think not. In our opinion the best way of defending industrial policy is not to include in it everything that is good for industrial development, but to narrow its definition and demonstrate that its benefits are bigger than its costs.

Landesmann (1992) makes an important contribution by emphasising the *particularistic*, or discriminatory, nature of industrial policy. According to him, industrial policy is 'designed to be *specific*, i.e., directed towards particular industries, firms, regions, groups in the labour market, etc., rather than general ... Implicit in industrial policy formulation and execution are therefore always trade-offs between different groups, regions, industries, etc.' (p. 245). According to this definition, we may exclude such general policies as creating skilled workforces or improvements in labour–management relations from the realm of industrial policy, making the concept more focused.

However Landesmann's concept of industrial policy is still somewhat overloaded, because it includes policies designed to affect both particular regions and particular groups in the labour market. True, industrial policy affects different regions and different groups differently, but its effects on particular regions and groups are better viewed as *by-products* than as aims of the policy. Likewise regional and group-oriented policies may affect particular industries (for example setting up an industrial park for the garment industry in a high-unemployment region), but this does not make them industrial policies.[8]

The existing definitions of industrial policy, then, tend to be too overloaded to be useful in practice. We propose to define industrial policy as a policy aimed at *particular industries* (and firms as their components) to achieve the outcomes that are *perceived by the state* to be *efficient* for *the economy as a whole*. This definition is close to what is usually called 'selective industrial policy' (for example, by Lindbeck, 1981).[9]

In our definition, first of all, we emphasise the words *particular industries*, and therefore implicitly exclude policies designed to affect industry in general (for example educational investment, infrastructural development) and policies aimed principally at categories other than industry (for example regional policy, 'group-oriented' policy) from the domain of industrial policy. Secondly, we emphasise the word *efficient* to stress that the guiding principle of industrial policy in its purest form is efficiency, and not other aims (for example equity). Following our discussion in Chapter 2, efficiency is defined more broadly than in conventional economics and includes transaction-cost economising as an important dimension. Thirdly, we emphasise the phrase *the economy as a whole* to stress that, although it is directed at specific industries, industrial policy ultimately aims to improve the efficiency of the economy as a whole and not just that of particular industries. Therefore, in an industrial-policy régime, whenever the efficiency objective of an individual industry and that of the whole economy clash with each other, the latter is permitted to dominate.[10] Lastly, we emphasise the phrase *perceived by the state*, to stress that the perception of the state may not necessarily be correct or justifiable to everyone.[11]

3.2 THE LOGIC OF INDUSTRIAL POLICY I: THE STATIC DIMENSION

We defined industrial policy as a policy intended to affect particular industries to achieve outcomes that are perceived by the state to be efficient for the economy as a whole. More concretely, it means that there is a case for the state 'selectively monitoring entry, establishing mechanisms to make possible more *ex ante* coordination than is possible through market mechanisms alone, and for governmental regulation or overview to constrain or supplement profit incentives' (Nelson, 1981, p. 109). However, what is the logic behind opting for *ex ante* coordination by the state instead of *ex post*, or 'spontaneous' (in Hayek's words), coordination by the market? Broadly we can say that this is because markets fail, but this seems hardly enough. To answer this question we need to look more closely at the nature of the coordination problem the market mechanism is supposed to solve but often fails to do.

3.2.1 The Nature of the Coordination Problem

In the model of perfect competition, upon which mainstream industrial economics is based, there is no need for *ex ante* coordination of the plans of different agents regarding production and pricing decisions (Pagano, 1985, ch. 8). In this 'perfect decentralisation model', as Demsetz (1982) aptly calls it, there is no need for *ex ante* coordination because assumptions are made to ensure that the actions of individual agents are negligible – infinitesimally small in the limiting case -- in the sense that a *unilateral* action of a single agent is unable to change the aggregate outcome (Khan, 1987, pp. 831–4). When individual agents are negligible, there is no interdependence among individual agents and hence no need to coordinate their activities *ex ante*.

One crucial assumption to guarantee the total absence of interdependence supposed in the neoclassical model of perfect competition is that production technology is characterised by decreasing returns to scale (DRS) – at an infinitesimally small output level in the limiting case. Even under the widely-used assumption of constant returns to scale (CRS) – not to mention the disturbing case of increasing returns to scale (IRS) – the perfect-competition model does not guarantee a solution to the coordination problem, as was pointed out long ago by Richardson (1960, pp. 31–2). When CRS technology prevails in a large-number setting, *ex ante*, firms may behave as if the demand curve is horizontal (that is as if they are individually negligible), but *ex post* there is no guarantee that the market will clear, since an individual firm, not being bound by production technology, can produce as much as it wants. In other words there is no way to determine the number of the firms and their respective outputs in an industry characterised by a CRS production technology, as is recognised even by standard neoclassical textbooks (for example Varian, 1984, p. 88). Therefore even with CRS technology there may be so few firms in a market as to give rise to interdependence and consequently to the need for *ex ante* coordination.[12]

Of course the coordination problem will not exist except in the case of IRS technology if all the firms can correctly predict how much the other firms will produce, as implicitly assumed in textbooks. However, as Hayek (1949a) remarks, '[t]he statement that, if people know everything, they are in equilibrium is true simply because that is how we define equilibrium' (p. 46). If everybody knows everybody else's plan, then why do we need a price system or any other coordination mechanism? In other words, equilibrium in the perfect-competition model is attained only because the coordination problem is assumed away from the beginning!

As Hayek (1978) somewhat derogatorily says, 'a *state* of affairs which economic theory curiously calls "perfect competition"', that is, 'a situation in which all the facts are supposed to be known' leaves 'no room whatever for the *activity* called competition' (p. 182).[13] He argues that '[t]he peculiar nature of the assumptions from which the theory of competitive equilibrium starts stands out very clearly if we ask which of the activities that are commonly designated by the verb "to compete" would still be possible if those conditions were all satisfied... Advertising, undercutting, and improving ("differentiation") the goods or services produced are all excluded by definition – "perfect" competition means indeed the absence of all competitive activities' (Hayek, 1949b, p. 96).

Models of oligopoly in the neoclassical tradition recognise the coordination problem arising from the indeterminacy of the market outcome in a small-number setting. However their solutions to the coordination problem are not entirely satisfactory. The usual solution to the problem is to employ the concept of the mixed (or randomised) strategy (for example patent race in Rasmusen, 1989, pp. 295–8). However a mixed strategy does not guarantee an optimal solution except in the probabilistic sense that, if the situation occurred an infinite number of times, randomising one's actions would yield the highest average payoff. When the situation is not recurrent, employing the concept of probability is less than meaningful (for a classic discussion, see Knight, 1921, Part III), and it is therefore dubious to describe the mixed-strategy equilibrium as optimal. For example, how can firm A's strategy regarding its investment in production capacity for a 4Mb memory chip be 'randomised' in any meaningful sense, when, given the speed of technical progress, it is clear that the next round of investment will be in a 16Mb memory-chip capacity?

One way of avoiding the difficulty of employing probabilistic behaviour by individual agents in non-recurrent situations is to interpret the mixed strategy as an 'evolutionarily stable strategy' (ESS), whereby individual agents do not randomise their actions but there are sufficient different types of agents in the population for the aggregate outcome to be the same as when individual agents randomise (for the concept of ESS, see Maynard Smith, 1982). However, even in the biological world where the concept originated, the ESS equilibrium holds only approximately, because '[genetic] heterogeneity and changing conditions must mean that often populations are not perched at adaptive peaks. *Even when the conditions are constant*, selection becomes progressively weaker towards the peak of a continuous fitness function; *infinite time and infinite populations would be needed to achieve the peak itself* [emphasis added] (Parker and Maynard Smith, 1990, p. 31). And the intuitive meaning of ESS becomes even less clear in many industrial markets where the conditions change so rapidly that the selection mechanism does not have time to work to its full extent and where the agents (being humans) learn and change not only their 'genes' (behavioural characteristics) but also the selection mechanism (the environment) and consequently the ESS itself (see 3.3.1 below).

The deficiency of the unregulated market as a coordination device was already recognised by Marx, who saw firms as islands of planned economy in the capitalist sea of anarchy. According to him, '[t]he same bourgeois consciousness which celebrates the division of labour in the workshop, the lifelong annexation of the worker to a partial operation, and his complete subjection to capital, as an organisation of labour that increases its productive power, denounces with equal vigour every conscious attempt to control and regulate the process of production socially, as an inroad upon such sacred things as the rights of property, freedom, and the self-determining "genius" of the individual capitalist.... [I]n the society where the capitalist mode of production prevails, anarchy in the social division of labour and despotism in the manufacturing division of labour mutually condition each other ...' (Marx, 1976, p. 477).[14] Marx saw an enormous waste of resources in the failure of the market as a coordination device (what he called the anarchy of the social division of labour) and hoped to extend the *ex ante* coordination that already existed in the firm to the economy-wide level – what he called the despotism in the manufacturing division of labour or what Williamson (1975) calls the 'hierarchy' – through central planning or at least some form of central coordination of individual activities (Pagano, 1985, ch. 3).[15]

Why *are* coordination failures 'wasteful'? There are coordination failures, the counterargument may run, but are not such failures corrected via the competitive process whereby firms perish unless they correct their mistakes? If so, why should any *ex ante* coordination be necessary? For example, it may be argued that even when an industry is characterised by IRS technology, it would still not require *ex ante* coordination, because if more than the optimal number of firms enter the industry, some will inevitably go bankrupt through competition, thereby finally achieving the optimal outcome.

The above reasoning assumes that resources invested in the bankrupt firms can be instantaneously and costlessly shifted to other activities. Nevertheless it is only in the financiers' world (or the economists' world?), where every asset is 'general' and 'liquid' (as in Keynes' concept of liquidity preference), that any investment, if found unprofitable, can be instantly withdrawn at no, or at most little, cost.[16] However, in modern industrial economies, assets are often specific to investments and therefore cannot be redeployed without a loss in its value (for the concept of 'asset specificity', see Williamson, 1975 and 1985). In a world with asset specificity, *ex post* coordination through the market can be wasteful, as Marx argued, because a coordination failure that involves specific assets means a net reduction in the amount of resources available to the economy.[17]

If the market fails to solve the coordination problem and if such failure can produce waste, there is a case for non-market, or *ex ante*, coordination (Pagano, 1985, ch. 8). As new institutional economics demonstrates, the firm (or the hierarchy, in Williamson's words) is the most representative form of non-market coordination, but other diverse forms of non-market coordination mechanisms exist. As Winter (1988) puts it, '[m]arkets appear and disappear; firms expand in scope and then turn back toward specialisation; quasi-firms and quasi-markets proliferate' (p. 168).[18] Central planning is also an institutional device to solve the coordination problem (Richardson, 1971), and industrial policy is another such device.

3.2.2 Industrial Policy as a Device of Coordination

One characteristic of modern industrial economies is the use of production technologies that require large fixed-investments, mainly in the form of machinery.[19] Large fixed-costs mean a decreasing average cost curve, or scale economies. Moreover, a large part of these fixed assets are specific or 'sunk' in the sense that their costs cannot be fully recovered when sold elsewhere. Scale economies often force firms to produce at a scale that will allow no more than a few firms in an industry, because, by producing at the most efficient scale, a firm can undercut its competitors and force them out of the industry. Out of fear of extinction, other firms have to adopt the same (or more efficient) technology or perish. The outcome is an oligopolistic industry in which strategic interdependence among the decisions of the firms exist.

Under certain likely conditions, strategic interdependence may lead to inefficiency (see below; also Telser, 1987 and Yamamura, 1988), providing a case for state intervention. The intervention needed here is *not necessarily* an antitrust-type policy, because the benefits from breaking up the oligopolistic firms (that is reduction in the deadweight loss) may be more than offset by higher production costs due to suboptimal scales of production. Below, we show the role of industrial policy in this context.

3.2.2.1 Investment coordination

An industry whose cost structure is characterised by significant scale economies is likely to experience a price war – firms selling at long-term losses (or at prices that do not cover fixed costs) to undercut competitors. Under adverse demand conditions, which might occur due to factors like external shocks (for example a rise in energy prices) and a slower demand growth than was expected at the time of the investment decision, firms in the industry might prefer to engage in a price war rather than forego sales, and hence incur heavier losses due to their inability to recover fixed costs. This makes an industry with scale economies subject to the dangers of underinvestment or overinvestment, which may not be easily resolved through the market mechanism.

In a new industry (or an expanding industry) with scale economies, if many of the potential entrants expect that enough others would enter the industry to start a price war, there may be insufficient entry, resulting in a suboptimal level of output – a case of underinvestment. On the other hand, if they expect that not many competitors would enter, too much investment may be undertaken, because then they have an incentive to install as much capacity as possible to reduce their unit costs (which would provide a distinct advantage in future competition) – a case of overinvestment. However, in Richardson's words, 'overinvestment, by causing a collapse of prices, will penalise all suppliers' (Richardson, 1971, p. 441). And if some firms go bankrupt in this process, the resources put into their investments will have been wasted, insofar as they involve specific assets.

Since under- and over-investment are essentially problems of strategic uncertainty (each potential entrant not knowing the intentions of others), the state can intervene in this industry to assure optimal entry by guaranteeing potential entrants that there will not be more than optimal entry. It can do this through arbitrating private bargaining among potential entrants, but also by superseding private dealing and thus reducing the transaction costs involved in such bargaining. Licensing entry and regulating capacity expansion are the most common forms of state-imposed investment coordination. The negotiated industrywide investment plans (the so-called 'investment cartels') in Japan during the 1960s for industries like steel, vinyl chloride, synthetic fibres, pulp, paper, cement, petroleum, petro-chemicals, cars, machine tools and some branches of electronics are classic examples of investment coordination achieved through state-led private negotiation (Dore, 1986; Magaziner and Hout, 1980). An interesting variety of investment coordination is 'conditional entry' whereby the state links the number of entrants (or the scale of new capacity) to changes in demand conditions. An example of conditional entry is the Korean passenger-car industry, where, faced with a lagging demand growth, the state forced one of the three existing firms to exit on the condition that it would be allowed back when demand expanded (see Chapter 4.4.2).

3.2.2.2 Recession cartel

Even industries with optimal capacity may experience price wars if there are unforeseen fluctuations in demand due to, say, downturns in the business cycle, a sudden import penetration, changes in raw-material prices or world recession (in the case of export-oriented industries). If the fall in demand is temporary, it may be desirable to organise a 'recession cartel', whereby individual firms limit their production for a limited period of time, rather than allow a price war.

In the conventional wisdom, cartel arrangements are strongly opposed because they are seen as creating allocative inefficiency (that is deadweight loss) in the process of transferring consumer surplus to producers (that is the process of creating monopoly profit). However the costs of cartels (that is the deadweight loss) should be weighed against their possible benefits. First of all, as we have already discussed, when there are specific assets involved price wars can lead to bankruptcy and therefore social waste. Recession cartels may allow such waste to be avoided. Moreover, even assuming that there is no waste involved in bankruptcy, prohibiting recession cartels may increase allocative inefficiency in the longer run. As Okimoto (1989) points out, without a recession cartel stronger firms will survive at the cost of weaker ones, eventually extracting more monopoly profit after the recovery. Thirdly, and most importantly, letting firms engage in a price war may have disastrous consequences for long-term productivity growth if firms have to reduce their investment levels in order to make up their losses from the price war.

As was common in the interwar period in many advanced capitalist countries, recession cartels may be organised through private initiatives. Nevertheless such cartel arrangements may be costly to organise, for example, when a large number of firms are involved, due to the cost of overcoming the collective-action problem. For another example, if the sellers do not publicly quote prices and make separate deals with separate buyers (say, because the number of the buyers is small), it will be difficult to detect breaches of the cartel agreement (Tirole, 1988, p. 241). In this case the cartel may have to spend a lot of resources on monitoring. Or if the history of the industry is such that firms do not trust each other, working out an arrangement may incur a large bargaining cost. If, for whatever reason, it is costly to make a recession cartel work on private initiatives, the state may intervene and organise a more credible arrangement, thus cutting down the transaction costs involved (for examples of state-led recession cartels in Japan, see Magaziner and Hout, 1980, and Dore, 1986).

3.2.2.3 Negotiated exit/capacity scrapping

If the demand downturn turns out to be of a long-term nature, the cumulative costs of a recession cartel may exceed its benefits. In this case, apparently, there is a need for market forces to weed out the weak. However leaving the adjustment to the new long-term demand situation to market forces can also be costly. A permanent fall in demand requires some firms to exit, but this may cause a war of attrition, whereby no firm wants to exit first because it will benefit by staying if others exit first (Ghemawat and Nalebuff, 1985; Fudenberg and Tirole, 1986).[20] A war of attrition can lead to a protracted price war, leaving everybody worse off than they would have been with timely exits (Tirole, 1988, p. 313).

Of course, if there is no specific asset involved the form of adjustment in this situation may not matter because exit (and the consequent redeployment of physical and human capital) does not cost anyone anything. However when the assets involved are specific there is a case for orderly exit or capacity scrapping. Obviously, if there are no transaction costs, the parties involved may work out a contract with side-payment schemes. However the existence of transaction costs hinder such contracts, and there is a case for state intervention. Orderly exit or capacity-scrapping arrangements organised or assisted by the state can take the following forms.

First of all, some firms can exit altogether in return for some side-payments. Side-payment may take the form of direct compensation by the remaining firms, as seen in the Japanese textile industry in the early 1980s (Dore, 1986).[21] State subsidies may quicken the process, especially when negotiations over side-payments prove difficult. Mergers can also make it easier to devise side-payment schemes, as seen in the reorganisation of the French chemical industry (Hall, 1987, pp. 208–9). Side-payment can also take the form of an increase in a firm's share in other markets in return for exit from one market. This option may be feasible if the firms concerned belong to larger entities simultaneously operating in multiple markets (for example conglomerates) – the 1980 industrial reorganisation programme in Korea is a good example of this (see Chapter 4.4.2).

Secondly, all firms can scrap some of their capacities according to some norm, for example according to each firm's share in total industrial capacity or according to its market share. The best examples are seen in the capacity-scrapping arrangements in the Japanese aluminium, shipbuilding, textile, petrochemical and steel industries in the 1970s and the 1980s (Dore, 1986, p. 142; Okimoto, 1989, p. 110).[22] The advantage of capacity scrapping over an exit arrangement is that it can improve the vintage structure of capital, thus raising overall productivity (on the vintage effect, see Salter, 1960). A capacity-scrapping arrangement may need state intervention more than an exit arrangement does because it is more difficult to monitor the compliance of the parties involved. It is fairly obvious whether a firm is in operation or not, but it is difficult to observe whether a firm really has scrapped its capacity. The presence of government inspectors in capacity-scrapping processes, as in some Japanese capacity-scrapping arrangements, may help to solve this problem (see Dore, 1986).

Thirdly, there is the interesting practice of 'mothballing', defined as stripping equipment down and concreting in the mountings so that it requires a good deal of time and effort to rehabilitate it, as practiced in Japan (Dore, 1986, p. 142). This mitigates the problem of credibility that is inherent in recession cartels by making cheating costly. However it keeps open the option of returning to the former levels of production if necessary (although at a cost) and therefore avoids the risk of scrapping too much capacity due to an unduly pessimistic forecast of future demand. As a hybrid between recession cartels and capacity-scrapping arrangements, mothballing may be appropriate when it is uncertain whether the demand downturn is permanent, while recession cartels (capacity scrappings) are appropriate when the demand downturn is certain to be temporary (permanent).[23]

Fourthly, with state arbitration or even decree, firms can divide a market into segments and exit from some segments in return for the exit of others from the segments where they are given permission to stay. Such a segmentation arrangement may be a good idea when the industry can easily be divided into segments (for example, ships over or under a certain tonnage). One example of such market-segmenting or specialisation arrangement is given by the reorganisation of the Korean electronic telephone-switching-system industry in 1980, when faced with serious overcapacity, each of the four incumbent firms was forced by the state to specialise in a different product (see Chapter 4.4.2). The market-segmentation arrangement in the Japanese industrial machinery industry in the late 1960s is another such example (Dore, 1986, pp. 137–8).

3.2.3 Concluding Remarks: Credibility, Fairness and Flexibility

In the first part of this section we discussed why the market mechanism may fail to solve the coordination problem, and why coordination failures can be costly. In the second part we discussed how state intervention can prevent and/or redress coordination failures. Investment coordination, recession cartels and negotiated exit/capacity scrapping were examined.

Common to all these forms of industrial policy is the problem of strategic uncertainty. Of course the existence of strategic uncertainty does not necessarily mean that state intervention is the optimal solution. After all many non-market institutions enable long-range planning by reducing strategic uncertainty (Schumpeter, 1987, pp. 102–3; Eatwell, 1982, p. 210).[24] Long-term supply contracts, technological cooperation and vertical integration between firms all fall into this category (Richardson, 1972). In a situation of strategic uncertainty, making one's commitment credible is vital in working out a coordinated outcome. And, as we argued, state intervention can help overcome the problem of credibility in such situations. Investment coordination by the state is a way of avoiding overinvestment and underinvestment due to the difficulty of making credible commitments concerning one's investment decision. A state-led recession cartel is a way of overcoming mistrust inherent in a private recession-cartel arrangement. The presence of government inspectors in capacity scrapping or mothballing arrangements can also help to make the commitments credible.

Another problem common in all the arrangements we discussed is that of devising a scheme that is considered fair among the participants. Decisions regarding the quota of each firm in recession cartels, which firms should exit, which firm should cut how much capacity, and so on, all involve the question of fairness. The capacity or the market share of each firm may provide focal points for such fairness, but they need not do so necessarily, especially when the firms involved are heterogeneous. For example, in the case of Japanese shipbuilding industry, '[t]he large companies and efficiency-oriented civil servants wanted to see the big companies cut capacity, and many of the small companies to close down. The small companies wanted the large ones to take all the cuts. Companies which had newly invested in up-to-date berths . . . wanted special exemptions' (Dore, 1986, p. 145).[25] Although the state may not necessarily be better situated to work out a 'fair' norm, it can help this process by representing the national interest, which may serve as a focal point in negotiations.

The third problem is the question of flexibility. The limits of human cognition (or bounded rationality) mean that the demand (and other) forecasts on which investment decisions are based can prove wrong.[26] For example, even if demand has fallen substantially, we do not know whether this situation will last long enough to justify exit or capacity scrapping. And if it is not implausible that demand might improve in the future, it may be wise to bear certain short-term costs, say through a recession cartel, in order to keep open the option of exploiting improved demand in the future.[27] Conditional entry is one device to maintain flexibility in an expanding industry. Mothballing is a device to maintain flexibility in declining industries where demand is unlikely to improve.

3.3 THE LOGIC OF INDUSTRIAL POLICY II: THE DYNAMIC DIMENSION

In the previous section we paid little heed to endogenous technical change, considering mainly changes in demand. However we cannot possibly ignore this issue, as the very strength of the capitalist system is its ability to generate endogenous technical change. By its nature technical change is an unpredictable process, and no one, including the state, can claim superior knowledge of its future course. Moreover, it is often argued, technical change is an evolutionary process, whereby only those who develop better technology survive. Therefore some opponents of industrial policy argue (for example, Burton, 1983) that, however well industrial policy may solve the 'static' problem of coordination, it will do more harm than good in the long run because it hampers the workings of the natural-selection mechanism of the market economy.

After all, does not the failure of central planning prove that the coordination problem (which it solved at least to a degree) may be far less important than the attainment of dynamic efficiency? Indeed the advocacy of central planning is usually based on the proposition that a centrally-planned economy can solve the coordination problem as well as, if not better than, a market economy, and not that it generates more dynamism (see essays by Lange and Taylor in Lippincott (ed.), 1938; see also Lavoie, 1985, ch. 4).[28] As Rosenberg and Birdzell (1986) argue, '[t]he failure of planning can be attributed in part to its conception of an economy system as a lifeless machine, without the internal capacity to change, adapt, grow, renew, reproduce itself and shape its own future. Plans ... do not ordinarily provide for creating extensive classes of people with capacity to engage in independent economic activities not envisioned by the plan. But a growth system is like a living organism with impulses of its own. The result of planning for growth is to produce an economy that is, if not a wholly lifeless statute of the real thing, at best a tame zoo-bred shadow of the natural animal' (p. 331). How then can industrial policy cope with the problem of change? Before we answer this question we need to look more closely at the nature of economic change.

3.3.1 Knowledge, Change and Evolution

According to Hayek and the Austrian school, the essence of our economic problem is that those variables treated as data by orthodox (that is neoclassical) economics keep changing (Hayek, 1949b, pp. 93–4). The market, far from already embodying all the information necessary for coordination, can only gradually reveal them through a competitive process (Kirzner, 1973, ch. 1). Hayek (1949c) argues that '[t]he various ways in which the knowledge on which people base their plans is communicated to them is the crucial problem for any theory explaining the economic process, and the problem of what is the best way of utilising knowledge initially dispersed among all the people is at least one of the main problems of economic policy – or of designing an efficient economic system' (pp. 78–9).

According to Hayek, human knowledge can never be fully codified, and therefore the crucial question in economics becomes: '[h]ow can the combination of fragments of knowledge existing in different minds bring about results which, if they were to be brought about deliberately, would require a knowledge on the part of the directing mind which no single person can possess' (Hayek, 1949a, p. 54).[29] In particular, as Svennilson puts it, when the knowledge involved is technical knowledge, 'only a part, and mainly the broad lines, of [such] knowledge is codified by non-personal means of intellectual communication or communicated by teaching outside the production process itself' (quoted in Rosenberg, 1976, p. 155).[30]

The virtue of the market mechanism, according to this argument, is that it acts as the most economical mechanism through which dispersed agents exchange information without explicit coordination. If this is the case, the market mechanism may need be preserved to promote economic change, because it is 'highly conducive to the achievement of many different individual purposes not known as a whole to any single person, or relatively small group of persons' (Hayek, 1978, p. 183).

If we recognise the importance of competition in generating change, should we not understand the market process as an evolutionary process, whereby natural selection operates to pick the winners? And does this not mean that industrial policy is harmful because it attempts to tinker with the natural-selection mechanism, which is beyond any human comprehension? We think likening economic process to an evolutionary process is a helpful analogy.[31] However an analogy is an analogy, and therefore should not be taken too literally.

First of all, biological evolution is characterised by the *lack* of conscious planning (Gould, 1983; Dawkins, 1986), whereas economic evolution is characterised by the human ability to learn consciously (from one's own and others' experience) and accordingly change one's behaviour. That is, mutation at the genetic level is essentially a random process, whereas economic mutation – or 'industrial mutation' in Schumpeter's language (Schumpeter, 1987, p. 83) – is often subject to *intentional* changes.[32] That this is the case is potently demonstrated by the examples of some late-developing nations which forged ahead by overcoming initial disadvantages *through conscious learning*, despite the existence of 'cumulative causation' – where the initial (dis)advantage leads to further (dis)advantages – in modern industrial economies (Abramovitz, 1986; Nelson, 1991).[33]

Secondly, biological evolution is essentially a Darwinian process in which only hereditary characteristics can be transmitted, whereas economic evolution is essentially a Lamarckian process in which acquired characteristics can also be transmitted (Hodgson, 1988, p. 143). This is because human beings have the ability to codify knowledge (for example, languages and signs), and, more importantly, store it (for example, books, computer memories), however limited such ability may be. And that acquired characteristics, and not just hereditary characteristics, can be transmitted means that learning plays an important role in the process of economic evolution.

Thirdly, natural selection in the biological world, while systematic, is independent of the actions of the units of selection, that is, the individual organisms. However the selection mechanism in economic life is not 'natural' in the sense that it is totally out of reach of the *conscious* attempts by the objects of selection (in this case, firms) to change it to their advantages. The participants in economic life enhance their ability to survive not only by changing themselves (the genes) but also by changing the environment (the selection mechanism). For example, a firm operating in an industry with network externalities (for example typewriters, computers, telecommunications) can change its chance of survival by spreading its own technology -- for example by encouraging other smaller firms to produce clones of its products or by providing loans to its customers. Advertising is another example whereby firms change their possibility of survival by changing the selection mechanism – that is, consumer preference.

3.3.2 Industrial Policy as a Device to Promote Change

In the previous section we examined the nature of change in the capitalist economy. In particular we examined the evolutionary argument, which likens the process of change in the capitalist economy to biological evolution. We argued that the fundamental difference between biological and economic evolution is that, in the latter, the units of selection have the capacity to *intentionally* 'mutate' and change the selection mechanism itself, at least to a degree. This is essentially due to the human ability to learn, especially from others, and to the ability to pass on (at least part of) the knowledge acquired through codification (for example by writing a book on Japanese business management) and institutionalisation (for example by introducing some elements of Japanese business management). How then can industrial policy be used as a means to promote economic change and learning?

3.3.2.1 Economic change, coordination and industrial policy

One important point not addressed by the opponents of industrial policy who employ the (misunderstood) evolutionary argument is that economic changes may require coordination to be successful. In a world of interdependence, the existence of a better alternative does not necessarily mean the advent of a change. For example, there exist more efficient alternatives to the QWERTY typewriter (and computer) keyboard, but an agent (or even a group of agents) who unilaterally shifts to an alternative keyboard will be penalised unless others also opt for it (David, 1985). More generally, when interdependence prevails between economic agents, changes would not automatically be made without the guarantee that complementing changes would also be made (Richardson, 1960, ch. 2).

For example, if a successful computer industry depends on a strong semiconductor industry, people will be reluctant to invest in the computer industry unless there is a credible commitment for adequate investment by the potential investors in the semiconductor industry, and vice versa.[34] As Abramovitz (1986) argues, if 'the capital stock of a country consists of an intricate web of interlocking elements', then 'it is difficult to replace one part of the complex with more modern and efficient elements *without a costly rebuilding of other components*' [emphasis added] (pp. 401–2). Now, '[t]his may be handled efficiently if all the costs and benefits are internal to a firm', but when the capital stock is '*interdependent in use but divided in ownership*', and thus the accompanying costs and benefits of change are divided among different firms and industries, 'the adaptation of old capital structures to new technologies may be a difficult and halting process' [emphasis added] (p. 402).[35]

Although it is possible that potential investors in complementary projects may devise a contract between themselves, such a contract may be costly to draw up, particularly when there is asymmetry in asset specificity of investments between different investors (the failure of the complementary investments to materialise can be more damaging to the investor with greater asset specificity). State intervention in this case may cut sharply the transaction costs involved in such contracts. Such intervention need not involve financial resources such as subsidies. As we discussed earlier, governmental announcements (for example the French and East Asian 'indicative-planning' exercise) may suffice if they can provide obvious focal points for coordination between complementary investments (see Chapter 2.3.2).[36] Financial incentives provided by the state, say, for cooperative research in new industries, although not necessary, may make the state's commitment to its announcement more credible by serving as a signalling device (Porter, 1990, ch. 12). Thus seen, industrial policy that coordinates complementary investment decisions may be essential for economic change in a world of interdependence, rather than be an obstacle to it.[37]

3.3.2.2 Codifiability of knowledge, product cycle and industrial policy

The limited codifiability of technical knowledge requires that we have to incorporate the problem of knowledge generation into our industrial-policy framework. The problem of knowledge generation is captured in more practical terms by the theory of the 'product cycle' (see Vernon, 1987), which is known to be incorporated into Japanese industrial-policy practice (Okimoto, 1989, ch. 1; Magaziner and Hout, 1980, ch. 4).[38]

According to this theory, a young market is characterised by a phase of experimentation in which different ways of doing the same thing vie with each other. As the market matures, most technical knowledge becomes codified and easily transmittable. When a few technologies emerge as the best-practice ones, they are adopted across the industry, as firms learn from the experiences of others. As a market matures and finally becomes senile, the discovery potential in that market gradually diminishes (as knowledge becomes more codified) and the role of 'competition as a discovery procedure' (Hayek, 1978) is accordingly reduced.[39] Let us examine how the idea of the product cycle can be incorporated into the practice of industrial policy.

In the infant stage of an industry, where experimentation is necessary to generate new knowledge, industrial policy should encourage it. More aggressive experimentation and learning can be encouraged by providing firms with a more stable environment (through, say, patent systems, subsidies, tariffs or other types of entry barrier), as the familiar infant-industry argument goes. At this stage it would also be necessary for the state to set up institutional arrangements that can cope with the new externalities generated by this new industry (Nelson and Soete, 1988, pp. 633–4). Moreover industrial policy has a valuable coordinatory role to play at this stage. Introducing national product and, if necessary, process standards, coordinating competing investment decisions to prevent underinvestment and overinvestment, and ensuring that complementary investments are made will all be useful at this stage.

As the industry matures, experimentation becomes less important. According to Hayek, when 'we have a highly organised market of a fully standardised commodity produced by many producers, there is little need or scope for competitive activities because the situation is such that the conditions which these activities might bring about are already satisfied to begin with. The best ways of producing the commodity, its character and uses, are most of the time known to nearly the same degree to all members of the market' (Hayek, 1949b, p. 103). When the technology has been stabilised and codified, on the one hand, and the institutional arrangements necessary to cope with with new configurations of asset specificity and the resulting uncertainty have been set up, on the other hand, the 'static' dimension of industrial policy, which we discussed earlier, becomes more important.[40]

As an industry enters its senile stage, production shrinks, labour is shed and capacity is scrapped. The material and human resources employed in an industry may be highly specific to that industry so their redeployment may be extremely difficult, or even impossible. In the face of a possible loss in value of specific assets, the owners of the assets will resist change, and this may result in a considerable waste of resources if a war of attrition among the firms concerned or protracted labour disputes take place. The role of industrial policy in this phase will be to encourage private negotiations regarding exit and capacity scrapping between the relevant agents, or even to impose a centralised solution when negotiations reach a stalemate. Retraining and relocation programmes organised by the state will also greatly assist the process of negotiation by reducing the would-be displaced workers' resistance to the firm's decision to exit or scrap the capacity.

3.3.2.3 Diversity of innovatory sources and industrial policy

Nelson (1981), in discussing the innovation mechanism of the capitalist economy, argues that the waste that is bound to be generated by competitive innovative attempts (say, due to duplication) may be a price worth paying to avoid the dangers of relying on a single mind for innovation (that is monopoly). Or as Abramovitz (1986) puts it, 'in the uncertainty that obscure early effort to explore new fields, it would be quite unwise to concentrate all effort on a single approach to a still cloudy goal' (p. 41). This is because innovation is basically a chase after a moving target, a job at which nobody can claim absolute superiority. That is, 'were man omniscient and omnipotent, he would not choose to organise his R&D activities through private enterprise [given the wasteful nature of competitive R&D activities]. The case for private enterprise as an engine of progress must be posed in recognition of bounded rationality' (Nelson, 1981, pp. 108–9).

This is a powerful argument. Unless human rationality is unbounded, there will be a pressing need to preserve a diversity of the sources of knowledge in an ever-changing world – although this statement should *not* necessarily be interpreted as an advice against all 'collusive' behaviours amongst firms (Jorde and Teece, 1990, pp. 81–2).[41] However, does the state have any role to play, if this is the case? Should it not just leave things to evolve on their own?

One point against the apparent *laissez-faire* implication of this 'diversity' argument is that imperfections in the capital market put a follower firm in a disadvantaged position if there is a high fixed-investment requirement.[42] In this situation the state can act as a surrogate capital market and subsidise a potential entrant that is deemed to be at least equally capable as the incumbent firm except in its financial ability. State-organised venture-capital schemes conducted in countries such as Korea, France and the United Kingdom are good examples of this.

The state can contribute to increasing the diversity of innovatory sources in a more direct manner. For example it may expand the pool of potential entrants into an industry with high R&D components by subsidising related R&D activities by firms who operate in similar lines. Or, alternatively, it may encourage related basic research in universities or public laboratories, which will publicise the results of their research. This of course carries some possibility of duplication, but it may be a price worth paying to preserve and develop diversity.

3.3.3 Concluding Remarks: The Socialisation of Risk

In the first half of this section we discussed the nature of change in the capitalist economy. We argued that the process of change in the capitalist economy is best characterised as a quasi-biological evolutionary process whereby the agents can and do change both their own 'genes' (behavioural characteristics) and the selection mechanism (or environment). Drawing on this argument, we discussed the dynamic dimension of industrial policy in the second half of the section. It was pointed out that coordinating changes, encouraging experimentation and preserving diversity are the most important roles industrial policy can play.

The crucial theme emerging from our discussion in this section is that of the 'socialisation of risk', whereby risks involved in economic changes are borne by society rather than by individuals. In the models in the orthodox tradition, where individuals make decisions in an atomised fashion, risks involved in changes are necessarily borne by the individuals. To those who subscribe to this view, the socialisation of risk opens doors to the moral hazard of excessive risk-taking by those individuals whose risks are borne by society (see 3.4.1 below). However in the real world many changes involve interdependent decisions. If the risks involved in these situations have to be solely borne by the individuals, necessary changes may not come about. The socialisation of risk through state intervention is a means of promoting changes that involve interdependence.

Contrary to what is implicitly assumed in mainstream economics, the capitalist economy has developed on the basis of the growing socialisation of risk. As Rosenberg and Birdzell (1986) argue, '[t]he West has grown rich, by comparison to other economies, by allowing its economic sector the autonomy to experiment in the development of new and diverse products, methods of manufacture, modes of enterprise organisation, market relations, methods of transportation and communication, and relation between capital and labour' (p. 333). And in such a process, institutional arrangements that, by 'internalising benefits and externalising costs of private investment' (North, 1981, p. 62), allow experimentation and risk-taking *beyond a scale whose risk can personally be borne out by the experimenter* (for example systems of limited liability) have played an important role. The socialisation of risk through state intervention, then, may be seen as but one extension of these already existing institutional arrangements.

3.4 POSSIBLE PROBLEMS OF INDUSTRIAL POLICY

3.4.1 Problems of Information

One common objection to industrial policy is based on problems of information (for example Burton, 1983; Grossman, 1988). There are two major elements in this argument (also see Chapters 1.4.1 and 2.1). First of all, it is argued that the state does not possess enough information to decide correctly on the future industrial structure of the economy. This is, according to our earlier classification, the problem of 'insufficient information'. Secondly, it is argued that the state is at an informational disadvantage vis-à-vis the firms that are subject to industrial policy. The firms, the argument goes, may use their informational advantage to extract more than they deserve on social grounds (a moral hazard problem). This is the problem of 'asymmetric information'.

With the exception of some staunch free-marketeers (for example, Burton, 1983), those who employ informational arguments (for example, Cairncross *et al.*, 1983; Grossman, 1988; OECD, 1989) support a generalised industrial policy targeted at *certain types of activities rather than at particular industries* (for example, investment, R&D), against selective industrial policy – the type of policy we defined as industrial policy proper at the beginning of the chapter. If the state has all the relevant information, the argument goes, particularistic interventions may work, but since this is unlikely to be the case, the state should support productive behaviour in general rather than pick the winners on the basis of incomplete information (Price, 1980; Lindbeck, 1981).

3.4.1.1 Insufficient information

Concerning the insufficient-information argument, note first that insufficient information does not prevent us from planning our future economic life. Actually the uncertainty of the future is exactly the reason why we plan for the future. Overcoming uncertainty is one of the most important functions of business management, especially in large modern corporations (Richardson, 1960; Williamson, 1975; Stinchcombe, 1990). A firm chooses its production technology, capacity, liquidity position, inventory level and so on, to minimise the potential loss in case of abrupt changes in environmental factors such as market demand, macroeconomic conditions and the state of technological development – in other words, to overcome parametric uncertainty. A firm goes into long-term binding contracts concerning its purchases of raw materials, labour power, parts and equipment, on the one hand, and its sales of products, on the other, to minimise a potential loss in the event of opportunistic behaviour by its business partners – in other words, to overcome strategic uncertainty. It is inadequate to argue that the state should not attempt to plan the future of the national economy because of insufficient information, when firms can and do plan their own future despite – or rather, precisely because of – insufficient information.

Secondly, the informational requirement for intelligent state intervention is not always so great as to disallow state intervention altogether. Entrepreneurs themselves often operate on the basis of informed guesses or of 'animal spirits' in making investment decisions. Frequently much of the information used by the firm to make investment decisions – for example estimates of present and future demand, the availability of best-practice technology, the financial situation of the firm, the distribution network of the firm – are readily available to anybody, and not just to the firm itself. Moreover, a large part of the information used by the firm is acquired from external sources such as consultants, research institutes and state agencies (for example a central statistical bureau). Thus seen, it is not necessarily true that the state suffers from insufficient information whereas the firms do not. In fact one of MITI's resources in dealing with the private sector has been its 'superior information' (Okimoto, 1989, p. 145), thanks to the more extensive informational network in the hands of the state (also see the Korean case discussed in Chapter 4).[43]

Thirdly, in the context of late development (on the concept of late development, see Gerschenkron, 1966), the problem of identifying desirable industrial structures is far less serious. This is because late-developers can have the 'second-mover advantage', by which they can watch the countries on the frontier of economic development and learn from their experiences.[44] Even in a country like Japan, which was pretty close to the frontier of industrial development, it is recognised that '[s]etting priorities, picking the next likely winners, has not been difficult throughout the post-war period when the objectives of policy were primarily "catching up" objectives' (Dore, 1986, p. 135). The insufficient-information argument loses most of its force in the case of late-developers (that is almost all countries) where the scope for 'conscious mutation' is great (also see Dore, 1989).

3.4.1.2 Asymmetric information

Concerning the asymmetric-information argument, note first that asymmetric information is not confined to the relationship between the state and firms, but is a ubiquitous problem in economic life, as we have repeatedly pointed out. Informational asymmetries exist between firms and lending institutions and between managers and shareholders. It exists, moreover, *within* the firm itself, that is, between headquarters and subsidiaries (or other component parts of the firm). If the asymmetry of information is always so severe as to disallow state intervention, neither financing somebody else's investment projects nor managerial planning can be justified. After all, large modern corporations came into being despite the dangers of the principal-agent problem, because there are ways of controlling managerial excesses (see Chandler, 1962). And likewise there *are* ways and means to reduce informational asymmetry between the state and firms (see Chapter 2.1.2).

Secondly, the problem of asymmetric information is not unique to industrial policy as defined by us, but it applies to other policies too. Moreover, general industrial policy, which its supporters assume to have no moral-hazard problem due to asymmetric information (for example Corden, 1980, pp. 182–3; Balassa, 1985, p. 319), may suffer even more acutely from such a problem. As contracts become more and more general, the contingencies to be considered become more and more numerous, resulting in prohibitive transaction costs in drawing up effective contracts. This means that general industrial policy can be compromised by unforeseen contingencies. An interesting example is the US 1981 tax-code provisions, which were originally intended to boost industrial R&D but ended up subsidising advertising firms (Lawrence, 1984, p. 140, n. 45). Industrial policy, as defined by us, being particularistic in its nature, tends to involve contracts that are more custom-designed and hence allow fewer unforeseen contingencies and less moral hazard. The use of plan contracts with specified targets between the state and individual firms in France is the best example of preventing moral hazard through the use of custom-designed policy (see Hall, 1987, p. 207).

Thirdly, the asymmetric-information argument assumes that local information is always better than global information because it is more finely-meshed.[45] However, as we pointed out earlier, people with localised information may make a substantively less rational decision due to the subgoal-identification problem (see Chapter 2.1.2). If the aim of industrial policy is to improve the efficiency of the economy as a whole, it may actually be better, under certain circumstances, *not* to be affected by the localised information possessed by the firm. Especially when the decision involves externalities that are not borne out by the firm, the state can make a better decision solely due to the more global nature of its information, and not because it is a superior being.

3.4.2 Problems of Rent-Seeking and Entrepreneurship

The ever-changing nature of the capitalist economy – or Schumpeter's 'gales of creative destruction' (Schumpeter, 1987) – and the consequent pervasiveness of uncertainty gives entrepreneurship a vital role to play in the capitalist development process as the generator and/or finder of new knowledge (Schumpeter, 1987; Dobb, 1925; Kirzner, 1973; Nelson, 1986). However, as Baumol (1990) argues, depending on the incentive structure in the economy, the existing stock of entrepreneurial talents may be diverted away from productive purposes into unproductive or even destructive ones. According to him, entrepreneurial talents can be used for destructive purposes when rents are granted to those who are best at destroying existing assets (for example warmongering in Europe in the Middle Ages). They can be used for unproductive purposes when rents are granted to those who are best at transferring existing assets, as in rent-seeking (also see North, 1990b, ch. 8).

The state has a major role to play in preventing the diversion of entrepreneurial talents into unproductive venues by reducing profitable opportunities in those areas. As argued in Chapter 2, the nature of unproductive activities is that they are transaction-cost-generating activities, and many such activities exist because of strategic uncertainty. As we discussed, the reduction in macroeconomic instability through appropriate macroeconomic management would reduce the need for activities that are specifically designed to deal with it (for example financial hedging), and therefore limit the diversion of entrepreneurial talents into these activities (see Chapter 2.3.2). The same applies to activities intended to deal with more specific coordination problems. Investment coordination through indicative planning and the establishment of national product standards are areas where the state can intervene to reduce strategic uncertainty inherent in the coordination problem and therefore the scope for unproductive entrepreneurship.

Another crucial condition for entrepreneurship to be a productive activity is that the rent accruing to the entrepreneur should be durable but not permanent, as already pointed out by Marx (1981) and Schumpeter (1987). In general people pursue rents primarily because they value the quiet life that follows from the acquisition of a monopoly position, and not because they are devoted to the cause of productivity growth (although this may be the case in certain contexts). Therefore, if the monopoly position (and the accompanying rent) is too quickly eroded, there will be little incentive to innovate (Schumpeter, 1987, pp. 104–5). However, if the monopoly position lasts too long, the cumulative deadweight loss due to its existence will ultimately cancel out the initial productivity gains made in the process through which such a monopoly position was established. Thus the important question is: how can it be ensured that the rent lasts long enough to motivate people to capture it but short enough to force people to keep improving productivity (Richardson, 1960, ch. 3)? In employing industrial policy measures, which are bound to create rents, this question becomes particularly relevant. Then how can the state ensure that the rents are durable but do not become permanent?

One obvious way is to use the patent system. The patent system, by guaranteeing a monopoly position, frees the innovator from the fear of being caught up with, but at the same time, by limiting the length of such a guarantee, ensures that the cumulative deadweight loss will not ultimately cancel out the initial productivity gains. However, when it is not just a particular product or process that enhances social productivity but a whole investment project (say, through spillover effects), the patent system may not be used. And in this case, the necessary incentive, the rent, needs to be created in other ways such as subsidies, import protection and industrial licensing.

If the rents are created by means other than the patent system, the crucial question becomes whether the state is able to withdraw the rent whenever necessary. This means, first of all, that when it is contemplating an industrial policy, the state should set strict performance criteria so that the rents would not go on regardless of the performance of their recipients. For example, in France the provision of state aid to ailing industries dependent on their performance is not unrelated to the relative effectiveness of those aids (Hall, 1987, p. 210). Secondly, the state has to ensure that it has the power to punish the firms if they resist the elimination of the rents. It is not a coincidence that industrial-policy exercises were more successful in France, whose state has control over the banking sector, than in, say, the UK, whose state has had only a limited control over the flow of financial resources in the economy.[46]

In addition, some industrial policy measures that may be used as means to preserve diversity – for example, venture-capital schemes and subsidisation of related commercial R&D and basic research – can also be used as means of keeping rents from becoming permanent. Even when new entry does not add to diversity (that is when the entrants have the same technology and organisational structure), prohibiting the incumbent firm from expanding its capacity beyond what is justified by scale-economy considerations and allowing new entrants can prevent permanency of the rent.

3.4.3 Political Problems: Legitimacy and Democratic Control

As we discussed in the Introduction, an industrial-policy régime is not merely a technical means to achieve efficiency, it is fundamentally a régime of political economy. This means that a discussion of industrial policy cannot be satisfactory without discussion of the political problems associated with it. There are several political problems related to industrial policy, but we shall discuss only the two which are the most relevant in this context – legitimacy and democratic control.

3.4.3.1 Legitimacy

Some may argue that industrial policy should not be used because it undermines the legitimacy of the state. First of all, by opening the door for special interests, industrial-policy practice can erode the image of the state as a social guardian and therefore make people question its intentions.[47] Secondly, industrial policy gives bureaucrats the power to allocate property rights and hence creates scope for bureaucratic corruption. In addition to its efficiency consequences (for example an industrial license may go to an inefficient producer), corruption may have consequences for the legitimacy of the political system (Krueger, 1990, p. 18). If industrial policy may endanger the legitimacy of the political system, should we not refrain from it, whatever its efficiency gains may be?

First of all, it should be pointed out that legitimacy is concerned with the socio-economic system as a whole, of which the political system is only a part. People may be generally disenchanted with the outcome of the socio-economic system – for example, high income-inequality – even if the state is impartial and honest. For example Dobb (1925) argues that monopoly 'may give occasion for a psychological tendency to antagonism and distrust on the part of dependent groups and classes towards those in a position of advantage.... If this happens ... the society may cease to have the "general will" which is supposed to exist in a harmonious democratic community; its sections may not respond to the same idealistic appeals, and their latent antagonism may prevent them from subordinating their own sectional interests to the success of the whole' (pp. 157–8).[48] The problem of legitimacy is much more fundamental than whether or not a particular government, or a specific type of policy, is open to corruption.

Moreover, although the erosion of legitimacy is a serious danger when conducting industrial policy, it is by no means a possibility confined to industrial policy. Other, more general, policies may also suffer from the problem of legitimacy. For example monetary policy may *prima facie* appear to be immune to interest-group activities, but it is well known that industrialists often lobby for expansionary monetary policies whereas financiers usually lobby for tight monetary policies. And there is no guarantee that such lobbying would not involve corruption and therefore endanger the legitimacy of the state.

3.4.3.2 Democratic control

The fact that an industrial-policy régime apparently requires an élite bureaucracy has often raised concerns about democratic control. Especially among those who believe in parliamentary democracy of the Anglo-Saxon variety, the weakness of legislature in 'industrial-policy states' such as Japan and France (not to mention Korea, which has been non-democratic for the major chunk of its modern history) has been a great concern. To them the fact that bureaucrats, who are not subject to popular mandate, are powerful means that the whole political process is rigged to ensure that efficiency dominates democratic values.[49] They believe that industrial policy is less subject to democratic control because it is open to bureaucratic discretion, in contrast with other 'even-handed' or general policies.

Against this view, it should firstly be pointed out that some degree of bureaucratic control is necessary for any society of reasonable sophistication, because 'many decisions have to be taken in response to rapidly changing situations and cannot, except at the cost of total stasis and chaos, be "left" until a highly democratic decision-making process has been completed. Almost immediately then, in any real situation it becomes necessary to delegate powers from larger, more democratic bodies . . . to smaller, more "efficient" bodies. However, once such delegation has occurred, a great deal of the real day-to-day decision-making power is taken out of democratic channels and placed in the hands of small minorities which may then be beyond the effective control of the larger bodies' (Kitching, 1983, p. 39). That is, there may be a certain trade-off between democratic control and efficiency in decision-making. However no *a priori* criterion can tell us which mix of democratic control and efficiency – including the one existing in an industrial-policy régime – is the most desirable.

Secondly, it is not just industrial policy that suffers from the problem of democratic control. For example, those who criticise industrial policy usually support an independent central bank, but it is not clear to us why the democratic credentials of an official in the Japanese MITI or the British DTI should be viewed with suspicion whereas those of a German Bundesbank official should be accepted without question. No policy is free from the personal discretion of the policy-maker. Moreover other policies may be even less subject to democratic control than industrial policy due to their less transparent nature (Dore, 1987, pp. 199–201). Industrial policy usually clearly reveals the beneficiaries of the policy, whereas other policies (for example monetary policy) often do not clearly reveal who is benefiting from them. Such transparency may make it easier to exercise democratic control over industrial policy than in the case of other policies, if there is a will to do so.

3.4.4 The Problem of Supporting Institutions

Opponents of industrial policy often point out that 'industrial-policy states' have a particular set of institutional arrangements, especially an élite bureaucracy with a wide discretionary range and a cooperative government–business relationship.[50] They argue that it is difficult to change institutions and therefore that industrial policy cannot be a realistic option for other countries, that lack such institutional arrangements, no matter what merits it may have.

Although an effective industrial-policy régime does require an appropriate set of supporting institutions, the difficulty of building it should not be exaggerated. Countries learn from their own past experience and from other countries and engage in institutional innovations. For example in Japan many of the institutions that are often said to have arisen because of Japan's unique culture are actually products of conscious institution building. The fact that Japanese labour, product and financial markets were vastly more volatile in the early 1950s than they have been since shows that the renowned 'collectivist' characteristics of the Japanese are not 'just a "hangover" of ancient (feudal) cultural traditions' (Dore, 1986, p. 250) but also products of conscious institutional innovation (see also Magaziner and Hout, 1980, p. 2).

Moreover, institutional innovation does not necessarily take a long time. The famous Japanese lifetime employment is basically a postwar creation (Johnson, 1982, p. 14). The French state, which is renowned for its interventionist and 'modernising' attitude, was famous for its *laissez-faire* and 'anti-modern' attitude before the Second World War (Cohen, 1977; Kuisel, 1981). The well-known Swedish labour–capital consensus emerged in a relatively short period of time out of one of the most contested industrial relations in Europe of the 1920s (Korpi, 1983).

Moreover learning from other countries with different institutions does not necessarily mean that a country has to exactly copy their institutions. It is often possible to create functional equivalents of foreign institutions. For example the Swedish 'active labour-market policy' and Japanese lifetime employment are very different institutional arrangements, but they are functionally equivalent in creating a positive attitude among workers toward technological change by guaranteeing them jobs. In this regard, the following quotation from Dore (1986) is well worth consideration:

> [Learning from the Japanese experience] need not mean that we [the British] have to become Japanese, absorb the Confucian ethic, or raise our sense of national identity to the Japanese levels. What it does mean is that we should ask ourselves whether there are not other ways in which some of the things which Japanese institutions and traditions achieve for the Japanese might be obtained by other methods, other institutional arrangements, more consonant with our own tradition. If close co-operation and consultation between managers and workers seems to be a precondition for rapid innovation in manufacturing firms, and if it is difficult to achieve this, given our adversarial traditions, what forms of industrial democracy or workplace decision-sharing might substitute for the easy acceptance of bureaucratic hierarchy which facilitates co-operation in Japanese firms? If we cannot have, and do not want, lifetime employment to be the norm, if we want to preserve a more mobile system with the greater personal freedom which that provides, can we at the same time devise schemes which would give British employers the same incentive to invest in training their employees as the lifetime employment expectation gives Japanese employers? If the crucial aspect of the Japanese system of financing industry seems to be the way in which it facilitates long-term planning and investment, and reduces preoccupations with next year's bottom line, is there any way in which our own financial institutions could be mended to achieve the same effect, without necessarily modelling our stock exchange on Japan's? If inflation control in Japan crucially depends

on institutionalised wage leadership and a nationally simultaneous pay settlement date, does that not suggest the wisdom of re-examining the many suggestions that have been made for introducing synchro-pay in Britain? (p. 252).

CONCLUSION

The common reaction to the argument for industrial policy has been one of suspicion and incredulity. The opponents of it regard industrial policy either as a bureaucratic meddling that is at best irrelevant – for example, 'Industrial policy is not the major reason for Japan's success' (Trezise, 1983, title) – or as a peculiar form of state intervention that works only in countries with a particular culture – for example, 'Industrial policy: It can't happen here' (Badaracco and Yoffie, 1983, title). Such reactions are more than understandable when thinking that orthodox economic theory hardly recognises any form of coordination other than the idealised perfect market and ignores the role of endogenous technical change and learning.

However, as we have tried to show, industrial policy is a policy practice that can be firmly anchored in economic theory if we incorporate recent developments in economic theory that take seriously the issues of institutional diversity and technical change. As a coordination mechanism, industrial policy can be most efficient in a context where interdependence and asset specificity are important. In this context, coordination through the market would incur high bargaining costs and coordination through central planning high information costs, while industrial policy is likely to incur little of both types of cost. When we take the issue of technical change into account, industrial policy also emerges as a superior way to promote it. Industrial policy does not kill off the profit motive – which is the most important, if not the only, driving force behind technical progress – as central planning would, and, through the socialisation of risk, it can promote changes that are additional to what the market can produce on its own.

Industrial policy, needless to say, is no panacea. Like any other policy, or any other form of economic coordination, it has its own costs and benefits. Its benefits seem to have more than offset its costs in success stories like those of Japan and Korea, but we have plenty of other examples that show that its costs may overwhelm its benefits. The real question is not whether industrial policy can work or not (because it does), but how it can be made to work. In this chapter we have tried to provide some theoretical grounds for identifying the economic, political and institutional conditions under which industrial policy would work and have suggested some ways and means to achieve them. The next chapter, which looks at the Korean experience, demonstrates how they have been achieved in practice.

4 Industrial Policy in Action – The Case of Korea

INTRODUCTION

That industrial policy has played an important role in the postwar economic development of countries such as France and Japan is widely accepted. However the role of industrial policy in another important industrial-policy state, Korea, is less well known, despite the fact that the Korean state has, as we shall see below, much more actively employed industrial-policy measures than its French or even its Japanese counterparts. This rather unsatisfactory state of affairs is partly due to the ideological climate of the Cold War era. For those economists who were on the side of the 'free world', it was unthinkable that a successful non-socialist economy such as Korea may not be a free-market economy. And consequently they turned a blind eye to the active role of the state in Korean development. More important than the ideological climate, however, was the inability of neoclassical economics to accommodate other institutions (or devices of coordination) than the perfect market and the perfect state.

By applying the theories of state intervention and industrial policy developed in the previous chapters, which acknowledged the diversity of economic institutions, the present chapter provides an account of Korean industrial policy that analyses why things work in Korea as they do. After presenting a brief overview of Korea's economic performance, we critically review some of the mainstream interpretations of the Korean experience that deliberately downplay the role of the state, and particularly of industrial policy. The next section explores some major themes behind Korean state intervention in general. The chapter concludes with an extensive discussion of the economics and politics of industrial policy in Korea.

4.1 A BRIEF OVERVIEW OF THE KOREAN ECONOMIC PERFORMANCE

Since the early 1960s Korea has shown a truly remarkable economic performance in terms of growth and structural change. Between 1965 and 1986 Korea's annual per capita real GNP growth was 6.7 per cent compared with that of 2.9 per cent for the developing world as a whole (World Bank, 1988, Table 1). Table 4.1 compares the growth performance of Korea since 1950 with that of other leading developing countries – Taiwan, China, India, Argentina, Brazil, Chile and Mexico – and of three OECD countries that were at relatively low levels of development in the immediate post-war years – Japan, Italy and Austria. Although the Korean growth performance was respectable before 1964, it was not particularly outstanding. However from 1964 its growth accelerated and, especially in the inter-oil-shock period (1973–9), its growth performance exceeded that of all other countries in our sample, including Taiwan, the world's best growth performer in the post-war period.

Table 4.1 Comparative growth performance of Korea, 1950–87 (average annual growth rates)

	1950–64	1964–73	1973–9	1979–1987	1950–87	1964–87
Korea	6.1	9.6	9.0	7.0	7.6	8.5
Taiwan	8.3	11.0	8.4	7.4	8.8	9.1
China	5.2	6.9	5.0	9.3	6.5	7.2
India	4.3	2.7	3.4	4.6	3.8	3.6
Argentina	3.0	4.9	2.3	–0.4	2.6	2.4
Brazil	5.9	8.1	6.5	3.5	6.0	6.1
Chile	4.2	2.8	2.3	1.6	3.0	2.2
Mexico	6.2	6.6	6.1	1.7	5.3	4.7
Austria	5.5	5.1	2.9	1.7	4.2	3.3
Italy	5.7	5.1	2.6	2.2	4.3	3.4
Japan	9.5	8.9	3.6	3.8	7.1	5.7

Source: Calculated from Maddison (1989), tables B-3,B-4,B-5.

Table 4.2 compares the manufacturing growth rates of some selected developing countries. Between 1963 and 1972, the first decade of Korea's rapid development, Korea's manufacturing sector grew at an annual rate of 18.3 per cent. This performance exceeded that of all other major NICs, such as Singapore (17.0 per cent), Brazil (6.7 per cent),

Mexico (8.7 per cent), India (4.5 per cent), Greece (9.7 per cent) and Spain (10.8 per cent). Thanks to the country's ambitious heavy and chemical industrialisation (HCI) programme launched in 1973 (see 4.4.1 below for details), the growth of the Korean manufacturing sector accelerated even further between the two oil shocks (1973–8), a period when most other major NICs experienced a substantial slowdown in their manufacturing growth. In the ten-year period following the second oil shock (1979–88), Korea's manufacturing growth slowed down to 11.7 per cent, due to reasons such as the slowdown in world-demand expansion after the end of the 'golden age', the growing maturity of the economy (reduced catching-up effect), and the substantial restructuring of the economy in the early half of the 1980s. However this was still an

Table 4.2 Manufacturing growth in some selected developing countries (average annual growth rates)

	1963–72	1973–8	1979–88
Korea	18.3	24.7	11.7
Brazil	6.7[1]	n.a.	1.5
China	← 9.5[2] →		12.6[3]
Chile	4.1	-2.9	2.7
Greece	9.7	4.3	0.4
India	4.5	4.3	8.3
Malaysia	n.a.	n.a.	7.3
Mexico	8.7	7.4	0.0
Singapore	17.0[4]	7.1	6.8
South Africa	6.8	1.3	1.6
Spain	10.8	3.3	1.5

1. For 1963–69
2. For 1965–80
3. For 1980–87
4. For 1966–72

Sources: UN, *The Growth of World Industry*, 1973; UN, *Yearbook of Industrial Statistics*, 1979, 1988; World Bank, *World Development Report*, 1988 (for China).

extremely good performance by international standards, and was second only to that of China (12.6 per cent) in our sample during this period.

The rapid expansion of the manufacturing sector transformed the structure of the Korean economy with a speed that was second to that of no other country in the world. Table 4.3 compares Korea's performance in structural change with that of other developing countries and some poorer European economies (Greece and Spain) between 1965 and 1986. The production structure of Korea, which looked more like that of low-income countries such as India and Kenya in the 1960s, began to look more like that of upper-middle-income countries such as Argentina, Brazil and Spain by the mid-1980s. The Korean manufacturing sector increased its share of GDP by two thirds over a period of 20 year (from 18 per cent to 30 per cent), and the agricultural sector's share of GDP contracted to one third of its size over the same period (from 38 per cent to 12 per cent). In our sample, no other country, including Taiwan – the best growth performer in the post-war world – increased its manufacturing share in GDP by more than one third during the 20-year period.

Not only was there a structural shift from agriculture towards manufacturing, but, more importantly, there was a rapid structural change

Table 4.3 Structural change in selected developing countries, 1965–86

	Per capita GNP (dollars) (1986)	Population (millions) (1986)	Production structure (1965) (as percentage of GDP)				Production structure (1986) (as percentage of GDP)			
			A	I	M	S	A	I	M	S
India	290	781.4	47	22	15	31	32	29	19	39
China	300	1054.0	39	38	30	23	31	46	34	23
Kenya	300	21.1	35	18	11	47	30	20	12	50
Colombia	1230	29.0	30	25	18	46	20	25	18	56
Chile	1320	12.2	9	40	24	52	n.a.	n.a.	n.a.	n.a.
Brazil	1810	138.4	19	33	26	48	11	39	28	50
South Africa	1830	32.3	10	42	23	48	6	46	22	49
Mexico	1860	80.2	14	31	21	54	9	39	26	52
Argentina	2350	31.0	17	42	33	42	13	44	31	44
Korea	2370	41.5	38	25	18	37	12	42	30	45
Taiwan	3580	19.4	n.a.	n.a.	22[1]	n.a.	n.a.	n.a.	29[2]	n.a.
Greece	3680	10.0	24	26	16	49	17	29	18	54
Spain	4860	38.7	15	36	n.a.	56	6	37	27	56

Notes: A=Agriculture; I=Industry (Mining, Manufacturing, Construction, Electricity, Water and Gas); M=Manufacturing; S=Services.
1. For 1960
2. For 1985
Sources: World Bank, *World Development Report*, 1988: Wade (1990), tables 2.2, 2.6; Maddison (1989).

Table 4.4 Korean manufacturing performance, 1963–88 (annual growth rates of production)

ISIC	Industry	1963–72	1973–8	1979–88
*Light Industry**		17.9	18.0	7.6
311/2	Food products	14.7	17.0	8.6
313	Beverages	14.6	18.8	6.0
314	Tobacco	12.5	11.0	3.4
321	Textiles	25.3	16.3	7.2
322	Apparel	22.1[1]	26.7[1]	9.0
323	Leather and leather products	17.9	60.4	10.7
324	Footwear	—[1]	—[1]	6.6
331	Wood products	21.0	11.1	–0.4
332	Furniture and fixtures	5.8	29.3	13.9
341	Paper and paper products	13.0	17.3	11.5
342	Printing and publishing	14.2	11.3	6.2
361	Pottery and china	–7.4	14.0	8.9
362	Glass and glass products	17.4	12.6	10.5
369	Non-metal products	19.2	13.0	8.5
390	Other industries	9.3	12.8	9.8
*Chemical Industry**		17.6	18.1	8.1
351	Industrial chemical	25.7	21.5	7.9
352	Other chemicals	19.7	24.3	11.8
353	Petroleum refineries	33.1[2]	9.5	4.2
354	Petroleum and coal products	12.1	10.9	8.1
355	Rubber products	9.2	19.7	11.6
356	Plastic products n.e.c.	50.3[3]	32.3	7.5
*Heavy Industry**		13.9	39.5	17.4
371	Iron and steel	16.9	34.9	10.5
372	Non-ferrous metal	6.2	33.8	17.8
381	Metal products	4.8	48.6	10.3
382	Machinery n.e.c.	9.4	25.4	18.6
383	Electrical machinery	22.4	44.7	21.8
384	Transport equipment	20.6	46.5	17.5
385	Professional goods	18.5	37.9	13.4
3	*Manufacturing**	17.0	22.1	12.1

* Weighted averages: the weights are, respectively, output at producers' prices (including indirect taxes and excluding subsidies) for 1967, 1975 and 1983.
1. Major group 324 is included in 322.
2. Annual growth rates for 1964–72.
3. Annual growth rates for 1965–72.

Source: UN, *The Growth of World Industry*, 1969, 1973; UN, *Industrial Statistics Yearbook*, 1975, 1978, 1979, 1987, 1988.

within the manufacturing sector. As we can see in Table 4.4, the heavy industries – International Standard Industrial Classification (ISIC) numbers 37 and 38 – which grew much more slowly than the manufacturing sector as a whole between 1963 and 1972 (13.9 per cent per annum as opposed to 17.0 per cent per annum), started to grow rapidly with the launch of the HCI programme and showed an incredible growth performance of 39.5 per cent per annum between 1973 and 1978 – as opposed to around 18 per cent per annum for other industries. Even after the slow down caused by the advent of the 1979–80 recession (for details, see Chang, 1987), heavy industry continued to grow at a much faster pace than the chemical and the light industries (17.4 per cent per annum as opposed to 8.1 per cent per annum and 7.6 per cent per annum respectively between 1979 and 1988). As a result the share of heavy industry in total manufacturing output (in current prices) rose from 16.4 per cent in 1963 to 42.0 per cent in 1987 (calculated from UN Yearbook of Industrial Statistics, 1969, and Industrial Statistics Yearbook, 1988). Since the launch of the HCI programme, chemical industry has also shown slightly faster growth rates than that of light industry, increasing its share in total manufacturing output from 17.1 per cent to 20.1 per cent during the same period.

The magnitude of Korea's intramanufacturing structural change can be put into perspective by comparing it with that of Taiwan. Despite the fact that the Korean economy grew more slowly than that of Taiwan (see Table 4.1), Korea experienced an intramanufacturing structural change of a greater magnitude than that of Taiwan. Table 4.5 compares Korea's intramanufacturing structural change with that of Taiwan between 1965 and 1984. In this period, the share of heavy and chemical industry in total manufacturing output rose by 48.7 per cent in Korea (from 38.2 per cent to 56.8 per cent), whereas that in Taiwan rose by only 17.5 per cent (from 49.8 per cent to 58.5 per cent). Even when

Table 4.5 Intramanufacturing structural change in Korea and Taiwan, 1965–84 (percentages)

Industry	Country	1965	1971	1975	1981	1984
Light	Taiwan	51.2	50.7	46.7	43.4	41.5
	Korea	61.8	54.7	51.6	47.2	43.2
Heavy and Chemical	Taiwan	49.8	49.3	53.3	56.6	58.5
	Korea	38.2	45.3	48.4	52.8	56.8

Source: Adapted from Wade (1990), table 2.8.

considering that Korea was in a 'catching-up' position in relation to Taiwan – Taiwan's industrial structure was more advanced than that of Korea in the early 1960s – this is a striking difference in performance.

From our overview of the Korean experience during the last three decades we can see that its most remarkable feature has been the magnitude of structural change. The fact that Korea's structural change has been much faster than that of the fastest-growing country in the world, Taiwan, seems to suggest that there has been something more than just the 'pull' from market-led demands behind the country's remarkable economic transformation. Especially given that Taiwan is by no means a free-market economy (see Amsden, 1985; Wade, 1990), this seems to suggest that the 'push' factor in Korea must have been extremely strong. We argue that this 'push' was achieved by the strong industrial policy of the state. Before we discuss the conduct of industrial policy in Korea, however, let us critically examine some mainstream arguments that deliberately attempt to downplay the role of industrial policy, and more generally of the state, in the Korean developmental experience.

4.2 EXPLAINING THE KOREAN EXPERIENCE

4.2.1 A Free Market?

With the accumulation of studies that reveal the important role of the state in Korea, the formerly common interpretation of the Korean developmental experience as a free-market and free-trade economy is rapidly losing its popularity.[1] However it is useful to discuss briefly the argument because the more recent mainstream interpretations examined below (4.2.2) can be seen as attempts to rescue the conclusions of the early interpretation.

According to the free-market view, the Korean economy stagnated in the late 1950s after it had depleted the possibility of 'easy import-substitution' in non-durable consumer goods. This inward-looking strategy was trammelled with inefficiencies due to distortions generated by excessive state intervention in various markets. Such chaotic import substitution with multiple exchange rates and across-the-board protection, largely by the use of discretionary quantitative restrictions rather than universal tariffs, allowed inefficient firms to survive and discouraged export activities. This in turn added to the foreign-exchange shortage and hence to pressure for more import restrictions.

The phenomenal growth of the economy, the argument goes, started with the transition from an inward-looking, or an import-substitution, industrialisation strategy to an outward-looking, or an export-led growth, strategy. The turning point in this transition was a series of policy reforms around 1965, whose most important ingredients included: (i) the introduction of a unified, realistic exchange rate régime; (ii) trade liberalisation involving cuts in tariffs and the abolition of most quantitative restrictions; (iii) a substantial increase in real interest rates. These policies are regarded as having radically improved the performance of the economy for the following reasons. Firstly, realistic exchange rates, by making export activities as profitable as they 'should be', allowed Korea to follow its comparative advantage in labour-intensive industries, and therefore to reap the gains from foreign trade. Secondly, trade liberalisation improved the efficiency of the economy by exerting competitive pressures on domestic producers. Finally, the rise in interest rates enabled the economy to invest more by mobilising more savings, on the one hand, and to use scarce capital more efficiently by restoring the relative price of capital near to its 'realistic' level.

In the words of Ranis and Fei (1975), '[s]tabilisation plus dismantling of the various existing direct control measures, on trade, interest rate and foreign exchange, thereby created a more market oriented economy most conducive to access for large numbers of domestic entrepreneurs seeking efficient utilisation of the economy's relatively abundant resources via embodiment in labour-intensive industrial exports' (p. 56).[2]

There is abundant empirical evidence, however, that runs counter to this explanation. Concerning trade-related reforms, Luedde-Neurath (1986) meticulously shows that such reforms were not as thorough as is usually presented and were implemented rather half-heartedly.[3] Firstly, tariffs were still quite high after 'liberalisation', and the bureaucracy retained the power to impose emergency tariffs (for items with 'excessively' fast import growth) without changing the relevant laws. In the second place, quantitative restrictions, usually applied under various special laws and import area diversification regulations, were pervasive even after liberalisation. As late as 1982, 93 per cent of total imports (in value terms) were subject to one or more such restrictions (Luedde-Neurath, 1986, p. 156, table 14.4). Thirdly, prohibitive inland taxes were often used virtually to ban the importation of luxury consumer items that were subject only to non-prohibitive tariffs.[4]

Fourthly, there were many state supports for import substitution, for example subsidised credits to import-substitutors and the purchasers of some domestic products (especially machinery), which in effect acted as import restrictions. Lastly, and most importantly, there was widespread foreign-exchange rationing, which often meant that importation of a certain item was impossible not because it was illegal to do so, but because it was impossible to obtain the foreign exchange to pay for it.

Table 4.6 Real interest rates in Korea, 1960–84 (percentages)

Period	Unregulated financial market[1]	Deposits[2]	Export loans
1960–4	31.1	–6.7	n.a.
1965–9	44.4	26.9	n.a.
1970–4	28.2	–0.2	–16.3
1975–9	24.0	–4.5	–12.5
1980–4	19.7	2.4	1.3

1. Nominal interest rates less consumer price inflation.
2. Nominal interest rates less inflation of the GNP deflator.
Source: Calculated from Dornbusch and Park (1987), p. 419, table 14.

The effect of financial reform also has to be reinterpreted (for a detailed discussion, see Harris, 1987, and Dornbusch and Park, 1987). As can be seen in Table 4.6, the post-reform high interest rates did not last for long, and real interest rates had been negative until the 1980s due to rather high inflation. Nevertheless, savings as a proportion of GNP have shown a rising trend, up from less than 10 per cent in the 1950s and the early 1960s to more than 30 per cent in the late 1980s (see Table 4.7). That is, 'Korea's saving responds little to interest rates. Overall, the Korean experience suggests that there is no need for high positive real interest rates to mobilise saving through the financial system; as long as large negative real interest rates are avoided, the real interest rate is relatively insignificant' (Dornbusch and Park, 1987, pp. 418–19).[5]

Even if liberalisation in Korea was as comprehensive as the proponents of the free market insist, it is not necessarily true that a 'more market oriented economy' is more efficient, as the above quote from Ranis and Fei implies. As the theory of second best tells us, the removal of market distortions in some, but not all, markets does not guarantee that the economy will achieve greater allocative efficiency (Lipsey and Lancaster, 1956). Moreover, even if it is true that the move to a more

Table 4.7 Investment and its financing in Korea, 1953–86 (as percentage of GNP at current prices)

Year	Gross investment	National savings	Private savings	Government savings	Foreign savings
1953	15.4	8.8	11.2	−2.4	6.6
1954	11.9	6.6	9.3	−2.7	5.3
1955	12.3	5.2	7.6	−2.4	7.1
1956	8.9	−1.9	1.0	−2.9	10.9
1957	15.3	5.5	8.6	−3.1	9.8
1958	12.9	4.9	8.0	−3.1	8.0
1959	11.1	4.2	6.9	−2.7	6.9
1960	10.9	0.8	2.9	−2.1	8.6
1961	13.2	2.9	4.7	−1.8	8.6
1962	12.8	3.2	4.8	−1.6	10.7
1963	18.1	8.7	9.1	−0.4	10.4
1964	14.0	8.7	8.3	0.4	6.9
1965	15.0	7.4	5.7	1.7	6.4
1966	21.6	11.8	9.1	2.7	8.5
1967	21.9	11.4	7.3	4.1	8.8
1968	25.9	15.1	9.0	6.1	11.2
1969	28.8	18.8	12.9	5.9	10.6
1970	26.8	17.3	10.8	6.5	9.3
1970	24.6	16.2	11.0	5.2	9.1
1971	25.1	14.5	10.0	4.5	10.5
1972	20.9	15.7	13.8	1.9	5.0
1973	24.7	21.4	18.4	3.0	3.7
1974	31.8	19.3	17.3	2.0	11.9
1975	27.5	16.8	14.5	2.4	10.3
1976	25.7	22.2	17.9	4.3	2.6
1977	27.7	25.4	20.9	4.5	1.2
1978	31.9	27.3	21.9	5.3	4.3
1979	36.0	26.5	20.0	6.5	8.9
1980	32.1	20.8	15.4	5.4	11.5
1981	30.3	20.5	14.9	5.6	9.8
1982	28.6	20.9	14.8	6.1	7.0
1983	29.9	25.3	18.1	7.2	4.7
1984	31.9	27.9	20.9	7.1	4.0
1985	31.1	28.6	21.7	6.9	3.1
1986	30.2	32.8	26.2	6.6	−2.8

Note: The series between 1953 and 1970 and the series between 1970 and 1986 are not fully compatible due to changes in the accounting method.
Source: BOK, *National Accounts*, 1987.

market-oriented economy improved the allocative efficiency of the economy by moving it closer to its comparative advantage, it does not explain why Korea *grew faster* after the reform in the mid-1960s than before. There is very little economic theory to support the view that conforming more closely with comparative advantage (or with any other form of static efficiency) leads to higher growth, as even the leading neoclassical trade theorists admit (for example see Krueger, 1980).

4.2.2 Market-Preserving State Intervention?

Evidence shows that state intervention was pervasive in Korea during its rapid industrialisation period. As Bhagwati (1987) correctly argues, '[t]he key question then is not whether there is governmental action in the Far Eastern economies, but rather how have these successful economies managed their intervention and strategic decision making in ways that dominate those of the unsuccessful ones' (p. 285). And, naturally, some neoclassical economists, including Bhagwati himself, have put forward explanations of the Korean experience that try to reconcile the existence of an interventionist state with the rapid growth of the economy.

One such argument is the theory of virtual free trade régime, which suggests that various measures of state intervention in Korea cancelled out each other to produce a neutral incentive structure (Little, 1982; Lal, 1983; World Bank, 1987). Another is the theory of prescriptive state intervention, which argues that state intervention in Korea does not hinder growth because it leaves room for private initiatives (Bhagwati, 1985, 1987, 1988). In effect these theories argue that, whatever state intervention there may have been in Korea, it did not affect the workings of the market mechanism because it was either self-cancelling (virtual free trade) or porous (prescriptive state intervention). Below, we will examine these arguments in turn, and argue that they are neither theoretically convincing nor empirically correct.

4.2.2.1 *Self-cancelling state intervention?*

According to the proponents of the theory of virtual free trade régime, in Korea there existed widespread price distortions due to one set of state interventions (for example import protection), but these were cancelled out by another set of interventions (for example export subsidies), producing a neutral incentive structure between production for export and production for the domestic market. They also emphasise the fact that Korean exporters had free access to imported inputs at world market prices, and consequently bypassed various import restrictions. The economic crisis in the early 1980s following the HCI drive during the 1970s is presented as proof that a departure from incentive neutrality was a disaster (Lal, 1983).[6]

On the theoretical level, it is not clear how meaningful it is to call the import-substitution-cum-export-incentives régime a virtual 'free trade' régime because there is no reason why the structure of relative prices under this trade régime should be the same as the one under genuine free trade (Yusuf and Peters, 1985, p. 18, n. 49). And if the relative price structures under the two régimes are different, we cannot say that the incentive structure under the former is neutral, because what matters in determining the relative attractiveness between export and production for the domestic market is the *relative* price structure, and not the average incentive (for a more detailed discussion, see Wade, 1990, ch. 5).

Moreover, on the empirical level, it is not true that Korean exporters could freely obtain imported inputs (raw materials and machinery) at world-market prices. Luedde-Neurath (1986, ch. 4) shows that only raw materials can be described as relatively, but not absolutely, freely importable in the Korean trade régime. The importation of machines was heavily controlled in order to promote the domestic machinery industry, which was seen as the vital ingredient in building a well-integrated economy (see 4.3 below). Credits were usually refused to those who wanted to import domestically available machines, and instead subsidised credits, which sometimes amounted to 90 per cent of the product value, were provided to the purchasers of domestic machinery (KDB, 1981, pp. 473–4).[7]

Moreover it is quite incorrect to assert that the promotion of heavy and chemical industry in the 1970s through a departure from incentive neutrality was a failure. As we have already seen in the previous section, since the launch of the HCI programme the growth performance of heavy, and to a lesser degree chemical, industry outstripped that of light industry. By international standards the performances of Korean heavy and chemical industries are extremely impressive. Table 4.8 compares the performance of Korean industries between 1979 and 1988 with those of some countries at comparable levels of development and, except for Brazil, of a similar size. While almost all individual Korean industries performed far better than their counterparts abroad,

Table 4.8 Korea's comparative industrial performance, 1979–88 (annual growth rates of production)

ISIC	Industry	Brazil	Chile	Greece	Korea	Mexico	South Africa	Spain
*Light Industry**		1.5	2.6	0.3	7.8	1.8	2.7	1.6
311/2	Food products	2.2	3.8[3]	0.5	8.6		2.9	
313	Beverages	1.8	1.5	4.0	6.0	2.5	6.4	3.0
314	Tobacco	3.0	−1.1	0.2	3.4		4.2	
321	Textiles	0.0	2.1	0.0	7.2	−0.1[6]	1.2	−0.3
322	Apparel	−0.4[1]	2.1	−2.5	9.0	—[6]	0.1	−3.6[1]
323	Leather and leather products	n.a.	−5.4	−3.3	10.7	n.a.	−1.3	0.4
324	Footwear	—[1]	−3.7	−4.7	6.6	n.a.	−0.5	—[1]
331	Wood products	n.a.	−1.4[4]	−5.5	−0.4	1.1	0.4	0.3
332	Furniture and fixtures	n.a.	12.1	−8.4	13.9		−1.0	n.a.
341	Paper and paper products	4.2	2.3	5.6	11.5	2.7	5.1	3.2[9]
342	Printing and publishing	n.a.	8.0	1.1	6.2	n.a.	2.7	—[9]
361	Pottery and china		16.2	−4.0	8.9		−2.8	
362	Glass and glass products	0.4	2.2	−0.4	10.5	0.6	7.2	−0.1
369	Non-metal products		4.7	1.5[5]	8.5		1.3	
390	Other industries	n.a.	−4.8	0.6	9.8	1.7	6.9	n.a.
*Chemical industry**		2.6	0.6	2.2	7.5	3.4[7]	1.3	0.8
351	Industrial chemical	3.6[2]	1.9	1.4	7.9	3.4[7]	0.8	1.1[2]
352	Other chemicals	—[2]	1.0	3.9	11.8	—[7]	2.2	—[2]
353	Petroleum refineries	1.6	0.3	2.0	4.2	—[7]	n.a.	0.3
354	Petroleum and coal products	n.a.	n.a.	−0.2	8.1	—[7]	n.a.	n.a.
355	Rubber products	2.7	1.8	1.6	11.6	—[7]	1.6	1.7
356	Plastic products n.e.c.	n.a.	n.a.	2.3	7.5	—[7]	4.8	
*Heavy industry**		0.6	1.6	−0.8	17.2	2.7	0.4	2.1
371	Iron and steel		3.6	−0.4	10.5	1.2	0.3	0.8
372	Non-ferrous metal	1.4	2.0	−0.6	17.8		3.8	
381	Metal products		2.0	−0.1	10.3	2.6[8]	−1.3	0.9
382	Machinery n.e.c.	0.1	−1.7	−5.1	18.6	—[8]	−1.3	2.0
383	Electrical machinery	2.1	3.9	−0.8	21.8	—[8]	2.8	3.6
384	Transport equipment	−1.5	−5.5	−1.3	17.5	—[8]	−0.8	2.8

Table 4.8 (cont.)

ISIC	Industry	Brazil	Chile	Greece	Korea	Mexico	South Africa	Spain
385	Professional goods	n.a.	n.a.	−0.8	13.4	—[8]	5.3	7.4
3	Manufacturing	1.5	2.7	0.4	11.7	2.1	1.6	1.5
	1986 per capita GNP (dollars)	1810	1320	3680	2370	1860	1830	4860

* Weighted averages: the weights are 1980 (except for South Africa, which is for July 1980–June 1981) output at producers' prices (including indirect taxes and excluding subsidies), except for Greece, South Africa and Spain, which are at factor values (excluding indirect taxes and including subsidies).
1. Major group 324 is included in 322.
2. Major group 352 is included in 351.
3. Excluding slaughtering.
4. Excluding sawmills.
5. Magnesite roasting is included in mining.
6. Major group 322 is included in 321.
7. Major groups 352 to 356 are included in 351.
8. Major groups 383 to 385 are included in 381 and 382.
9. Major group 342 is included in 341.

Source: UN, *Industrial Statistics Yearbook*, 1983, 1984, 1990.

the difference was especially pronounced in heavy industry, where the Korean performance was truly spectacular.

The advance of the heavy and chemical industries has not been confined to the domestic market. As we see in Table 4.9, which shows the trade performance of commodities at 1- and 2-digit levels between 1977 and 1987, almost all the items promoted through HCI – SITC numbers 5, 67, 68 and 7, which roughly correspond to ISIC numbers 35, 37 and 38 – show (often dramatic) improvements in trade balances during this period. The export–import growth differentials (which shows the rate at which the sectoral trade deficit [surplus] decreases [increases]) of these items are mostly higher than that between overall exports and imports, although, again, the performance of chemical products is not particularly outstanding. This suggests that it was these industries which improved the country's balance of payments during the 1980s. A detailed cost-benefit analysis of the HCI programme is beyond the scope of this chapter, but the above evidence suggests that the HCI programme, far from being a failure, produced impressive growth and trade performance, especially in heavy industry.

Industrial Policy in Action – Korea

Table 4.9 Trade performance by commodity group in Korea, 1977–87

SITC	Commodity	Trade balance (1977)	Trade balance (1987)	Export growth	Import growth	Differ- ential
0	Food and live animals	1.1	0.5	8.2	8.5	–0.3
1	Beverages and tobacco	0.4	n.a.	–1.7	n.a.	n.a.
2	Crude materials, excluding fuel	–7.9	–6.2	4.3	11.7	–7.4
3	Mineral fuel (e.g., petroleum, petroleum products)	–9.9	–6.0	20.4	10.7	9.7
4	Animal, vegetable oil and fat	n.a.	n.a.	n.a.	5.0	n.a.
5	Chemicals and related products	–3.7	–3.7	19.6	16.6	3.0
51	Organic chemicals	–1.9	–2.0	16.0	16.0	0.0
52	Inorganic chemicals	n.a.	n.a.	n.a.	16.3	n.a.
53	Dyes, tanning colour products	n.a.	n.a.	n.a.	16.3	n.a.
58	Plastic materials	–0.8	–0.5	40.2	17.0	23.0
59	Chemical materials n.e.c.	n.a.	n.a.	n.a.	20.4	n.a.
6	Basic manufactures	7.2	4.5	12.9	15.2	–2.3
61	Leather, dressed fur, etc.	–0.5	–0.4	23.7	15.4	8.3
62	Rubber manufactures n.e.c.	n.a.	0.6	16.3	n.a.	n.a.
63	Wood and cork manufactures n.e.c. (e.g., plywood)	n.a.	n.a.	–14.1	n.a.	n.a.
64	Paper products	0.2	0.1	16.5	19.8	–3.3
65	Textile yarn, fabric, etc.	3.5	3.0	14.1	15.2	–0.9
66	Nonmetal mineral manufactures n.e.c. (e.g., cement, glass)	1.0	0.2	8.5	22.2	–13.7
67	Iron and steel	–1.1	0.5	19.6	11.7	7.9
68	Non-ferrous metals	–0.8	–0.8	27.3	18.4	8.9
69	Metal manufacture n.e.c. (e.g., tools, cables, cutlery)	2.1	1.2	10.7	15.5	–4.8
7	Machines and transport equipment	–3.6	3.2	24.7	16.9	7.8
71	Power generating equipment	–1.5	–0.7	31.7	12.0	19.7
72	Machinery for special industries (e.g., textile machinery)	–2.0	–2.1	22.6	17.0	5.6
73	Metal working machinery	n.a.	n.a.	n.a.	11.2	n.a.

Table 4.9 (cont.)

SITC	Commodity	Trade balance (1977)	Trade balance (1987)	Export growth	Import growth	Differential
74	General industrial machinery n.e.c. (e.g., furnaces, pumps)	−2.4	−1.9	35.6	15.5	20.1
75	Office machinery (e.g., computers)	−0.0	0.8	39.3	28.5	10.8
76	Telecommunication and sound equipment (e.g., TV, phone)	1.2	4.4	25.4	15.3	10.1
77	Electric machinery, n.e.c. (e.g., transformers, microchips)	−0.2	−0.0	23.6	22.6	1.0
78	Road vehicles	−0.4	3.1	48.2	18.5	29.7
79	Other transport equipment (e.g., ships, aircraft)	1.2	0.4	35.3	10.3	25.0
8	Miscellaneous manufactured goods	14.7	14.9	16.2	19.6	−3.4
84	Clothing and accessories	n.a.	n.a.	13.8	n.a.	n.a.
87	Precision instruments n.e.c. (e.g., measuring equipments)	−0.4	−0.8	18.9	22.6	−3.7
88	Photo equipment	0.1	−0.0	15.6	17.6	−2.0
89	Miscellaneous manufactured goods n.e.c. (toys, arms, wigs)	1.8	2.9	20.5	18.2	2.3
9	Goods not classified by kind	n.a.	n.a.	n.a.	n.a.	n.a.
Total		−3.8	7.0	16.8	14.3	2.5

1. All figures are percentages.
2. Data for each commodity group appears only if the value in each year is greater than or equal to 0.3 per cent of the total trade for that year.
3. Trade balance for commodity i is $(X_i - M_i)/\Sigma(X_j + M_j)$, where X_i (M_i) is exports (imports) of commodity i and X (M) is total exports (imports).
4. Export and import growth rates are average annual growth rates between 1977 and 1987 in current value terms.
5. The differentials are the differential between the export and import growth rates.

Source: UN, *Yearbook of International Trade Statistics*, 1980 and *International Trade Statistics Yearbook*, 1987.

4.2.2.2 Porous state intervention?

The theory of prescriptive state intervention proposed by Bhagwati (1985, 1987, 1988) tries to resolve the (self-imposed neoclassical) dilemma of an interventionist state in a rapidly growing economy by characterising the Korean state as a 'do' (or a prescriptive) state, in contrast with a 'don't' (or a proscriptive) state, such as India. According to this theory, state intervention in Korea does not hinder growth because it is less stifling. According to Bhagwati, 'although a prescriptive government may prescribe as badly as a proscriptive government proscribes, a proscriptive government will tend to stifle initiative, whereas a prescriptive government will tend to leave open areas (outside of the prescriptions) where initiative can be exercised' (pp. 98–9). That is, state intervention works in Korea because it is porous, or allows the private sector to circumvent it.

On a superficial level, it is hardly objectionable that an obstructive state will not be very helpful for business, and, by implication, economic growth. However on closer examination we find the theory of porous state intervention theoretically and empirically unconvincing.

In a world with scarce resources (and therefore with opportunity costs), doing something means not doing something else. In this world, saying *'do A'* is often equivalent to saying *'don't do **not** A'*. And there can be no presumption that saying *'do A'* (= *'don't do **not** A'*) will allow more initiatives than saying *'don't do A'* (= *'do **not** A'*). A prescriptive state can be as stifling as a proscriptive one, since it can force private enterprises to do so many things against their will that they are left with few resources to do what they want, even if these activities are not explicitly forbidden. Likewise a proscriptive state may allow a lot of initiative if it proscribes only a few things. If we adopt the liberal concept of negative freedom ('freedom from'; see also Chapter 1.2), we may say that one has less freedom under a prescriptive state than under a proscriptive one, because private enterprises with a state prescription are coerced to execute the prescription, whereas private enterprises with a state proscription are not coerced into any particular action and therefore can choose the best option from whatever is not forbidden by the state, and thereby exercise initiative.

The Korean state's prescriptions were certainly stifling in many ways. The Korean state prescription for private firms to invest in heavy and chemical industries in the 1970s was a proscription against investing in less risky and often more profitable (partly due to higher protection) consumer-goods industries. The best example in this regard is the shipbuilding industry, which has, since 1973, grown literally from scratch to become the world's second largest in less than a decade.[8] The Korean shipbuilding industry was set up in direct response to a personal command from the then president, Park Chung Hee, against the will of the Hyundai group, the boldest of Korean business groups, who are all, in any case, famous for their boldness (Jones and Sakong, 1980, pp. 119–20, 357–8). Moreover, if private firms could not be made to do something, the Korean state did not hesitate to set up public enterprises, making the share of public enterprises in GDP almost equal to that of India, whose state is regarded by Bhagwati as the classic example of an obtrusive proscriptive state (Jones and Mason, 1982, pp. 22–3). In a country like Korea where private firms depend almost totally on the state-run banking sector for their investment funds (see 4.5 below), the state's channelling of money into public enterprises can have a very visible impact on private initiative.

Moreover, when a knowledgeable magazine observes that 'most business activities are prohibited unless expressly approved' (*FEER*, 30 May 1991, p. 54), we begin to wonder whether the degree of *proscriptive* intervention by the Korean state has been so minimal as to warrant the description *prescriptive* without serious qualification. In addition to restrictions on the prices of foreign exchange and credit (that is exchange rates and interest rates), there was a legally implemented direct price control over all marketed products up to 1973. And even after 1973 the state reserved the right to impose a price ceiling when necessary. No price change is conceivable without formal and/or informal state permission, except in some unimportant markets.[9] In addition to price controls almost all important Korean industries have had restrictions on entry, capacity and technology (see 4.4.1 below). Frequently the Korean state reorganises industries which it thinks have too many firms, through state-led mergers and market-sharing arrangements (see 4.3 and 4.4.2 below). It is not clear to us how anything could be more stifling, if so many firms have so little freedom to decide what and how to produce and at what price.

4.3 MAJOR THEMES OF KOREAN STATE INTERVENTION

If the remarkable growth and structural-change performance in Korea was not the result of free play of market forces but was orchestrated by the state as we have suggested, exactly how has state intervention worked in Korea? Before we look at details of the policy measures employed in Korea, we need to look at the general direction in which the Korean state was driving the economy. In this section we present a stylised account of the major themes of state intervention in Korea. The account draws both from the revealed and, especially, the stated policy objectives, which are to be found in various policy documents but which have hardly been investigated by other researchers.[10]

The basic theme of state intervention in Korea has been the making of an 'independent economy' (Jarip Gyongjé) (see various Five-Year-Plan [FYP] documents and EPB, 1982).[11] Until recently the balance-of-payments constraint has been the main concern of Korean policymakers, and, as Michell (1982) points out, even exports were regarded more as a means to reduce the unfavourable external balance than as the engine of growth (p. 196). Policymakers have regarded the ultimate solution to the problem of dependence on foreign savings for financing of investments (Table 4.7) to be the construction of an economy with the degree of technological capability that would permit a reasonable living standard without a chronic balance-of-payments deficit. It was believed that the cause of the balance-of-payments problem lay in the underdevelopment of the capital and intermediate goods industries, and therefore that 'a shift towards heavy and chemical industries is imperative in order to increase the independence of the Korean economy' (WP, 1970, p. 340) – a principle known in Korea (and Japan) as 'upgrading' the industrial structure (also see, Second FYP, pp. 9–10; Third FYP, p. 1).

To Korean policymakers, industrial upgrading required giving priority to investment, which was essential for growth (WP, 1968, p. 48). Therefore, macroeconomic policy was geared towards the need to create an expansionary environment – if necessary through inflationary measures – which was seen as vital for a sustained high level of investment through its effect on investors' confidence.

Until the late 1980s, of course, there existed a persistent savings gap, which had to be filled by foreign savings (see Table 4.7). Although the filling of the savings gap was believed to depend ultimately on the rise in income level (a Keynesian savings assumption), serious attempts were also made to repress consumption demand through policy measures, expressed in unashamedly paternalistic terms like 'the need to establish a *sound* consumption pattern' [emphasis added] (Fourth FYP, p. 27). The banks, which are mostly owned by the state, were instructed not to make consumer loans. The heavy reliance on indirect taxes was also justified –

against the accusation that they are less equitable than income taxes – in terms of their discouraging effect on consumption (Third FYP, p. 16). The control was even stricter when it came to consumption that involved foreign-exchange expenditure. For example, foreign holidays were banned until the late 1980s when the country finally became a net exporter of capital, and imported luxury goods were either banned or were subject to high tariffs and inland taxes (see 4.2.1 above). One outcome of such anti-consumption policies was low passenger-car ownership, which was discouraged by high taxation and restrictions on consumer loans until very recently. Despite Korea being a major exporter of passenger cars, Koreans have owned far fewer passenger cars than people in other developing countries with a comparable income level. In 1985 there were 73.5 people per passenger car in Korea, whereas the corresponding figures in 1983 were 27.0 in Taiwan, 21.8 in Chile, 16.3 in Malaysia and 15.2 in Brazil (NRI, 1988, p. 190, table 9-8). Given such a clear (stated and revealed) anti-consumption bias, Korean macroeconomic policy may be more appropriately understood as 'investment management' rather than as 'aggregate-demand management'.

Maintaining a high investment level through investment management, however, was seen by Korean policymakers as necessary but not sufficient to upgrade the industrial structure in a short period of time. Macroeconomic policy measures were seen as ineffective in rapidly upgrading the industrial structure due to their uncertain impact on specific sectors, and consequently they took second place to industrial policy. It was explicitly stated that 'the market mechanism cannot be entirely trusted to increase the competitiveness of Korean industries [in the world market]' (WP, 1984, p. 123), and therefore that sectors with high-productivity growth potential had to be identified by the state and designated as 'promising strategic industries' or 'priority sectors', and given custom-designed financial, technical and administrative supports (see 4.4 below for details).

Although macroeconomic constraints often set severe limits on the conduct of industrial policy, industrial policy has been actively used whenever deemed necessary and practical. When the aim of macroeconomic stability clashed with the aim of upgrading the industrial structure, the latter was usually allowed to dominate, as testified to by the fact that preferential (subsidised) loans directed to the priority sectors increased faster than general (non-subsidised) loans during recession periods, when the availability of financing can be a matter of life and death for firms (Ito, 1984; Chang, 1987). That is, even when the increase in the overall money supply was contained, the priority sectors were guaranteed financing at the cost of non-priority sectors. The unfair nature of such policy has been widely criticised inside and outside Korea, but the dominant attitude in policy-making circles has been that being unfair in the short run is justified in the long run by the greater benefits generated by the priority sectors in the form of faster growth.

In moving towards high-productivity sectors, the biggest concern for Korean policy-makers was that these industries are often characterised by large scale economies (for example WP, 1968, p. 174). The strong emphasis on scale economies in Korean economic policymaking is exemplified by EPB (1982), which diagnoses the causes of troubles in the heavy and chemical industries in the early 1980s – an example that is often thought to be the classic case of overly ambitious investments by economists of neoclassical persuasion – as 'the lack of scale economies due to the participation of too many firms in each industry' (p. 222), that is, in our terminology, the failure of investment coordination.

The prevalence of scale economies in many priority sectors posed two challenges to Korean policymakers. One was that individual firms in these sectors needed to be large in order to obtain the minimum efficient scale of production.[12] Firms were often instructed by the state to build plants of efficient production scale, which, given the small size of the domestic markets, had the beneficial side-effect of compelling them to start exporting as soon as possible in order not to incur losses due to low capacity utilisation. And whenever firms were thought to be smaller than the minimum efficient scale, state-initiated or state-subsidised mergers were implemented.[13] The most dramatic example of this was the 1980 reorganisation of six major industries (see 4.4.2 below for details). The merger of two automobile producers in 1965, of five PVC producers in 1969 (see KDB, 1981) and the mergers within the fertiliser, shipping and overseas-construction industries in the 1980s (see Leipziger, 1988) are other examples. The second challenge from the presence of large scale economies was the high possibility of 'excessive competition', a term used by Korean (and Japanese) policymakers to describe the well-known propensity of industries with large sunk costs to engage in price wars. As a result serious attempts were made to restrict entry and regulate capacity expansion in such industries.

The apparent antitrust implication of the above policies (merger, entry restriction and so on) has been regarded as secondary, because the

Korean policymakers thought that excessive competition could result in social waste (for example, WP, 1968, p. 173). In traditional textbook economics where it is believed that large numbers guarantee competition and small numbers hamper it, the notion that there can be excessive competition and that it can result in social waste may not be readily accommodated. However, as we argued earlier, competition is not a costless process in the presence of specific assets (See Chapter 3).

Korean policy-makers have regarded competition as a means to achieve efficiency rather than as an end in itself. This view is exemplified by the 6th FYP document, which states that collusive behaviour should be allowed, and even encouraged, in 'promising industries' that need to 'increase R&D, improve quality, attain efficient production scale' and in 'declining industries' that need to 'scale down their capacities' (p. 79). Likewise, the antitrust law (the Law for the Regulation of Monopoly and for Fair Trade), which came into being in 1981, after four abortive attempts at legislation (in 1964, 1966, 1969 and 1971), claimed to be concerned mainly with restricting anti-competitive *behaviour*, rather than market concentration itself, although the growing criticism of the concentration of economic power into the hands of conglomerates brought about an amendment (in 1986) with stronger restrictions on cross-investments between members of the same conglomerates (Paik *et al.*, 1988, pp. 28–9, 40–2).

Another important theme of Korean state intervention is the policymakers' attitude towards foreign firms. Korean policy-makers have regarded assimilation of advanced technology by domestic firms as a vital condition for effective industrial upgrading.[14] To them, this meant tight state control over foreign direct investment.[15] Of course the persistent savings gap had to be filled, but Korean policy-makers tried to avoid foreign direct investment and contracted (all state-guaranteed) foreign loans to do the job, if they could afford it. As a result the share of foreign direct investment in total foreign capital inflow (except foreign aid) during 1962–83 was a mere 5 per cent (Amsden, 1989, p. 92, table 5).

Although restrictions on foreign direct investment have been weakening recently, even the latest version of the Law for Importation of Foreign Capital (amended in 1988) – which is regarded as a liberal one by Korean policy-makers – specifies that foreign direct investment should be restricted in priority industries, infant industries, industries using large quantities of imported raw material, consumer (especially luxury) goods industries, polluting industries, and agriculture and fishery – which can mean practically all industries, if the state so wishes.[16] Even when foreign direct investment was allowed, foreign majority ownership was practically banned, with some rare exceptions, outside the free trade zones (FTZs). The fact that only 6 per cent of multinationals in Korea (including the ones in the FTZs) are wholly-owned subsidiaries, compared with 50 per cent in Mexico and 60 per cent in Brazil, suggests a substantial degree of state control over foreign direct investment in relation to ownership (Evans, 1987, p. 208). Even technological licensing, which was preferred to foreign direct investment whenever feasible, was subject to heavy restrictions. For example, the latest version of the Law for Importation of Foreign Capital clearly states that technological licensing is banned in industries where local technological capability is deemed to be promising – which, again, can effectively mean any industry.

4.4 THE ECONOMICS OF INDUSTRIAL POLICY IN KOREA

4.4.1 The Evolution of Korean Industrial Policy

Throughout the last three decades the Korean state has chosen several industries at a time as priority sectors and has provided massive support to them. Most of Korea's major industries have been designated as priority sectors at some stage and were developed through a combination of massive support from and heavy control by the state. The designated industries had priority in acquiring rationed (and often subsidised) credits and foreign exchange, state investment funds, preferential tax treatments (for example tax holidays, accelerated depreciation allowances) and other supportive measures, including import protection and entry restrictions.[17] In return for this support, they became subject to state controls on technology (for example production methods, products), entry, capacity expansion and prices.

The practice of giving priority to certain industries identified as important is a common practice in industrial-policy states such as France and Japan. In Korea the practice originated in the very early years of economic development, with the designation of cement, fertiliser, and oil refining in the 1st FYP (1962–6) as 'basic' industries.[18] In the Second FYP (1967–71), chemicals, steel and machinery were designated as priority sectors. And during the Third and Fourth

FYP periods (1972–81), especially through the HCI programme (announced in 1973), non-ferrous metals, shipbuilding and electronics were added to the Second FYP's list of priority sectors. The practice continued in the Fifth and the Sixth FYP periods (1982–91), during which machinery, electronics, automobile, chemical, shipbuilding and various high-tech industries (semiconductor, new materials, biotechnology) were designated priority sectors.

Details of such support and control measures can be seen in Table 4.10, which summarises the measures employed in some selected promotional laws, enacted in the late 1960s and early 1970 (except for textiles) to provide legal backing for support for and controls over priority sectors. Korean policymakers' concern for 'excessive competition' and the resulting 'social waste' is reflected in the laws in the form of entry restrictions and regulations on capacity expansion. Violators of such restrictions could be heavily punished with the revocation of licenses, fines and, in some serious cases, prison sentences. Another interesting feature of these laws is the tight performance-monitoring system. The monthly export-performance monitoring by the Korean state is already famous (see, for example, Jones and Sakong, 1980, p. 97), but all firms in promoted industries were required to report not just on their export performance but also on their performance in other areas. Failure to report regularly and/or false reporting could result in the imposition of fines and prison sentences. Such a system provided the Korean state with up-to-date and detailed information concerning the state of businesses in priority sectors, something which is essential if the asymmetric information problem is not going to weaken the effectiveness of industrial policy.

More recently, various promotional laws were integrated into the Industrial Development Law (enacted in 1986). The novelty of the Industrial Development Law (IDL), compared with the promotional laws, is its emphasis on rationalisation programmes with *limited*, albeit extendable, lifetimes (usually 2–3 years). The rationalisation programmes are custom-designed to the needs of individual industries and aim to provide temporary boosts to industries that need import substitution, capacity upgrading and improvement in international competitiveness, on the one hand, and temporary protection to declining industries that need a smooth phasing-out, on the other hand. Rationalisation programmes based on IDL may be implemented upon application from the industry, but they may also be implemented by the government *without such application*.[19]

Table 4.10 Major content of promotional laws

Major Content (year of enactment)	Machinery (1967)	Shipbuilding (1967)	Electronics (1969)	Petrochemical (1970)	Iron & steel (1970)	Non-ferrous metals (1971)	Textiles (1979)
REGULATIONS							
Entry Restriction	x	x	x	x	x	x	x
Capacity Regulations							
Setting up Facility Standard	x	x					
Capacity Expansion Approval				x	x		x
Incentives to use Domestically Produced Facilities	x		x				
Production Regulation							
Regulation of Material Imports					x	x	
Production Standard and its Inspection	x	x	x		x	x	
Restrictions on Technology Imports	x		x				
Price Control				x	x		
Reporting and Inspection	x	x	x	x	x	x	x
RATIONALISATION							
Rationalisation Programmes	x	x	x	x			x
R&D SUPPORT							
Subsidies to R&D	x		x	x	x		
Joint R&D Projects			x				
FINANCIAL SUPPORT							
Special Purpose Fund	x	x	x		x	x	x
Financial Assistance	x	x	x		x	x	x
Subsidies							
Direct Subsidy	x					x	
Reduced Public Utility Rates	x				x		

Table 4.10 Major content of promotional laws *(cont.)*

Major Content (year of enactment)	Machinery (1967)	Shipbuilding (1967)	Electronics (1969)	Petrochemical (1970)	Iron & Steel (1970)	Non-ferrous metals (1971)	Textiles (1979)
Tax Preferences							
Special Depreciation	x					x	
Tax Reduction/ Exemption	x	x	x	x	x	x	
SPECIAL INDUSTRIAL COMPLEX	x		x	x			x
ADMINISTRATIVE ASSISTANCE							
Facilitating Overseas Activities			x		x		
Purchase of Raw Materials					x	x	
PRODUCERS' ASSOCIATION	x	x	x				x

Sources: Kim (1989), p. 34, table 3.1.; S. H. Lee *et al.* (1989), pp. 52–9.

The measures employed by the IDL can be divided into three groups.[20] First, there are *protective* measures to ease the adjustment process, which include import restrictions on competing products, reductions in tariffs on raw materials, price controls, and outright subsidies. Secondly, there are measures related to the attainment of an *optimal production scale* and the prevention of excessive competition. These include restrictions on entry and capacity expansion, state-initiated mergers, coordinated capacity scrapping and/or exit, market-sharing arrangements (that is subdividing markets into non-overlapping segments). Thirdly, there are measures aimed at raising *productivity*. These include the provision of subsidised credits for such activities as capacity upgrading (or capacity scrapping for declining industries), import substitution of inputs (for example machine parts), subsidies for expenditure on R&D and training programmes, and joint research programmes between the private firms and government-funded research institutes.

As we can see, except for the introduction of limited lifetimes for rationalisation programmes, absent in the promotional laws, the major characteristics of Korean industrial policy changed very little with the introduction of the IDL. The policy measures used are virtually the same, and the discretion of the bureaucracy remains as great as before (because the eligibility criteria are deliberately made vague enough for any industry to qualify). The custom-designed nature of individual programmes also remains strong.

Between 1986 and 1989 automobiles, coal-mining, dyeing, ferro-alloys, fertilisers, heavy construction machinery, heavy electrical equipment, naval diesel engines and textiles underwent rationalisation programmes (for details, see S. H. Lee *et al.*, 1989, pp. 64–72; Kim, 1989). As mentioned before, the rationalisation programmes were custom-designed to meet the different needs of different industries. For industries with a need for technology upgrading and involving large sunk investments – automobiles, ferro-alloys, heavy construction machinery, heavy electrical machinery and naval diesel engines – the emphasis was given to creating more stable environments for major new investments and R&D activities through measures like state-led market-sharing arrangements, entry restrictions and subsidies on investment and R&D. For industries with satisfactory technological capabilities but aging capital stocks – textiles and dyeing – the priority was capacity upgrading, and therefore subsidies were given to producers for scrapping old machines and installing new ones. For the (largely state-owned) fertiliser industry, where the local technological capability was already substantially developed, the programme aimed to introduce more competition in the product market by granting sales licenses to more distributors and by reducing tariffs on fertiliser imports. Coal-mining, which was identified as a declining industry, was under a phasing-out programme, which involved restrictions on entry and capacity expansion, subsidised capacity scrapping, price controls and import restrictions.

4.4.2 State-Created Rents and Industrial Development

If the world operates according to the model of perfect competition, the governments of developing countries should not deliberately seek to develop new industries because this means, *ceteris paribus*, a less efficient use of resources. And this was perhaps what was on their minds when various international lenders, including the World Bank and KISA (Korea International Steel Associates) – a consortium formed by steelmakers from the USA, West Germany, the UK and Italy

– turned down Korea's three applications for loans to build an integrated steel mill in the 1960s (Amsden, 1989, p. 295; Watanabe, 1987, p. 69) or when the Bank of Japan fiercely opposed MITI's effort to develop the automobile industry in the 1960s (Magaziner and Hout, 1980, p. 55). However the fact that an industry is unprofitable in a developing country at present prices does not mean that it should not be promoted, as the spectacular successes of Korea's (state-owned) steel mill and the Japanese automobile industry testify.[21]

In the context of late development, whereby a country develops on the basis of borrowed technologies, if a technology can be put to work, the industry will become much more profitable than in the more developed country where the technology originated. This is partly because the borrower does not necessarily pay the full cost of developing the technology but also because it can combine the technology with cheaper (even when adjusting for its quality) labour. Of course not all producers who borrow technology become more cost-effective than the lenders of the technology. This is so, first, because technology is not a blueprint and it has a certain element that cannot be codified, and therefore requires a (possibly infinitely long) period of learning.[22] Secondly, the firms in late-developing countries do not have access to the social capital (for example skills of the workforce, infrastructure), to which the firms in the developed countries have ready access and for which they do not pay the full costs (Abramovitz, 1986). Due to these reasons firms in late-developing countries will need additional incentives to adopt new technologies. And such additional incentives are exactly what the states in many late-developing countries, from Germany down to currently developing countries, have tried to provide through tariff protection and other forms of state-created rents (for example subsidised credits).

Indeed, as we have shown above, the industrial policy measures used by the Korean state are not radically different in kind from those often associated with economic failure in many other developing countries. This is contrary to the widespread belief that the Korean state's role, 'apart from the promotion of shipbuilding and steel ... has been to create a modern infrastructure, to provide a stable incentive system, and to ensure that government bureaucracy will help rather than hinder exports' (Balassa, 1988, p. S286), while in other developing countries, for example the Latin American countries, 'there are pervasive controls of investment, prices, and imports and decisions are generally made on a case by case basis, thereby creating uncertainty for business decisions'

(Balassa, 1988, p. S287). That is, industrial policy in Korea has been no different in kind from that in other countries in that its essence has been to entice firms into new industries through state-created rents. However, why does industrial policy work so well in Korea and not in many other countries? This is because, as we pointed out earlier, there are dangers associated with industrial promotion through state-created rents, which Korea was able to avoid. The question then becomes: how was Korea able to avoid, or at least minimise, these dangers?

One obvious danger of industrial policy is that it may, by opening up opportunities to acquire wealth through unproductive activities such as influence-peddling, divert entrepreneurial efforts away from productive activities. This is the rent-seeking argument. However, if the waste from rent-seeking activities has been a major obstacle to growth in Turkey and India (for example Krueger, 1974; Mohammad and Whalley, 1984), why has this apparently not been the case in Korea?[23]

As we pointed out earlier, rent-seeking costs are fundamentally transaction costs expended in the process of *seeking* rents (which involve activities like information collection, influence-peddling, and bargaining), and have to be strictly differentiated from the rent itself, which is a pure transfer. Therefore the mere existence of state-created rents – and therefore the *opportunity* of rent-seeking – does not mean that resources will *actually* be spent on rent-seeking. The *realised* magnitude of rent-seeking costs in a society will depend on how state-created rents can be obtained and through which process. For example, as we have shown in earlier chapters, if firms can acquire rents through bribery, and if there is little 'second-tier' rent-seeking, the actual amount of resources spent on rent-seeking may not be large.

In this context it has often been suggested that less resources are spent on influencing the state in Korea, because there is not much point in spending resource to influence a 'hard' state (in the Myrdalian sense) like that of Korea (for example Bardhan, 1984). One difficulty with this view, as is well known to anyone familiar with Korean politics and business, is that the country by no means lacks huge corruption scandals on a regular basis. The head of one of the country's largest companies is reported to have recently complained that '[t]he government has all the power and you have to purchase approval ... [and as a result] we pay as much in extortion – legal, semi-legal and illegal extortion – as we do in legitimate taxes' (*FEER*, 30 May 1991, p. 54). This shows that the Korean state certainly *is* subject to influence, if less than other 'softer' states. The explanation has to be more sophisticated.

A part of the solution to this puzzle lies in the fact that the Korean state is subject to influence, but mainly to influence from a small, exclusive group of agents, the *chaebols* (literally – financial clans). Although the practice has produced some undesirable distributional consequences, limiting the opportunity of rent-seeking to the *chaebols* seems to have reduced rent-seeking costs in Korea in several ways. Firstly, when a small number of people have exclusive access to rents, rent-seeking activities will be less frequent and of smaller magnitude because others may not join in the rent-seeking contests, knowing that they have little chance of success in influencing the state (this is what Bhagwati, 1988, calls the 'brother-in-law theorem'). Secondly, since the *chaebols* as a group have exclusive access to the rent markets, they need to spend few resources to acquire information about the nature of the present opponent, because they are frequently confronted with the same adversaries in different rent-seeking contests. Thirdly, the fact that the *chaebols* are conglomerates, with stakes in multiple markets, also reduces rent-seeking costs by the 'bundling of issues'. A bargaining solution can be more easily devised if there are other related bargains that allow more room for arranging side-payments (Schelling, 1960, pp. 32–3). For example, in the 1980 industrial reorganisation, Daewoo, the third largest *chaebol*, remained in the passenger-car market as one of the duopolists, but was forced to exit from the diesel-engine industry and was forced to specialise in a cheaper variety of product in the electronic-switching-system industry; Hyundai, the second largest *chaebol*, remained in the passenger-car industry in return for forced specialisation in the diesel engine and heavy electrical-machinery industries (more on this later).

Even when the potential waste of rent-seeking is fully realised (and we have repeatedly discussed why this may not be), we think that rent-seeking is *not* the biggest danger of using state-created rents for industrial development. As we mentioned earlier (see Chapter 1.4.2), once a rent is granted it is highly likely that an entry barrier will be set up around the rent market, which will discourage the potential entrants from spending resources to dislodge the incumbent. A more serious danger of state-created rent is that state intervention may protect or even encourage inefficient producers or production methods, with long-lasting efficiency consequences. In Korea access to state-created rents is limited to the *chaebols* which, as conglomerates, are able to operate equally well in almost any line of business. Because of this practice it matters less who gets the rent in Korea than in other developing countries. In other words, state-created rents in Korea may generate a certain amount of once-and-for-all rent-seeking costs, which are likely to be small anyway (due to the reasons given above), but generate few long-lasting production inefficiencies.

In our opinion the most serious problem with industrial policy is that, once implemented, state-created rents may be difficult to withdraw due to political pressure from the recipients of such rents. The existence of infant industries that refuse to 'grow up' in many developing countries is a testimony to such a danger (see Bell *et al.*, 1984). As emphasised by economists such as Marx, Schumpeter and Richardson, the beneficial role of rents as a means to lure (positive rents) and force (negative rents) firms into more productive activities, hinges on the fact that no rent accruing to the innovator is permanent. In a situation where rents are created by the state, these rents may cease to be transitory if the state is unable to withdraw them when necessary.[24]

Korea is no different from other countries in that industrial policy has created many inefficient firms. However what differentiates Korea from other countries is that the Korean state has been willing and able to withdraw support whenever performance (revealed through exporting and fierce competition in the domestic market) lagged (Khan, 1989; Amsden, 1989). Such state discipline, when combined with industrial upgrading (which involves creation of new and often bigger rents in more productive industries), has acted as a powerful incentive for firms to enhance their technological capabilities. The imposition of such discipline, of course, has not been a purely technocratic procedure whereby impartial bureaucrats teach non-performers a lesson, nor has it been a smooth and concensual procedure, as things are usually assumed to be in East Asia. It has, rather, been a process of continuous bargaining and conflict between the state and the private sector, which, as we shall see below, sometimes had to be solved by forceful measures that are difficult to imagine in other countries.[25]

In 1969 the proliferation of inefficient firms after a massive investment boom in the late 1960s (see Table 4.7) prompted the Korean state to set up a task force, accountable only to the Blue House (the presidential office), to deal with the problem. Between 1969 and 1972, the task force forced dozens of inefficient firms (the exact number was never made available to the public) into mergers, sales and liquidation – sometimes sweetened by debt roll-overs by the Korea Development Bank. The programme eventually ended with the notorious 8-3 Decree (named after the date of its announcement, 3 August 1972), involving a total freeze on all curb market loans which were eating into the profits of many firms suffering financial distress, with a subsequent reduction in their interest rates and/or in a debt–equity swap (for details, see S. H. Lee, 1985).

After the investment boom of the late 1970s (see Table 4.7), which led to temporary excess capacity in some major industries, the Korean state stepped in again with the Reorganisation of Heavy and Chemical Industries Programme in 1980. Four existing companies in the power-generating-equipment industry were merged into Korea Heavy Industries and Construction Co. (KHIC), which was subsequently nationalised on the ground that the state support needed to make KHIC profitable was too great to be given to a single private firm.[26] In the passenger-car industry, one of the three existing producers (Kia) was forced to exit and specialise in trucks and buses with a promise that it would be allowed back in again when the demand condition improved – this actually occurred (a conditional entry; see Chapter 3.2.2).[27] One of the three companies in the naval diesel engine industry (Daewoo) was forced to exit, and the other two were forced to split the market into two segments and to specialise (Hyundai in over-6000 hp and Ssangyong in under-6000 hp engines). In the heavy-electrical-machinery industry, where there were eight companies, three (Hyosung, Ssangyong and Kolon) were merged into one (Hyosung) and allowed to produce only highly specialised and expensive products. A subsidiary of Hyundai was asked to produce only for its sister companies. Four other minor companies were forced to produce less sophisticated and cheaper products. Each of the four companies in the electronic-switching-system industry (Samsung, Gold Star, OPC and Daewoo) was forced to specialise in a different product. The two companies in the copper-smelting industry were merged by forcing one to buy the other's equity, which was supported by equity participation of KDB and a moratorium on bank-loan repayment.

Another round of state-led mergers and liquidations of inefficient firms occurred between 1984 and 1988 (for details, see S. H. Lee *et al.*, 1989, pp. 60–2; Leipziger, 1988). This time, the shipping, overseas construction and fertiliser industries, which were identified as declining industries, formed the focus of the programme. In 1984 three fertiliser producers were liquidated and 63 shipping companies were merged into

17. In 1986 a major reorganisation of the overseas construction industry was implemented, again involving mergers and liquidations. And between 1986 and 1988, 82 inefficient firms (23 of them in shipping and overseas construction) were forced into liquidation or merger.

What is notable in the conducting of industrial reorganisation programmes in Korea is that even the economically and politically powerful conglomerates, the *chaebols*, were not immune to state discipline *as individual agents*, although *as a group* they were certainly privileged in their access to various state-created rents. To Korean policymakers it matters little who runs a business so long as it is run efficiently. If a particular *chaebol* runs a plant well, fine; otherwise the ownership has to be transferred to another *chaebol* or even to the public sector (for example the nationalisation of KHIC). The fact that the *chaebols* as conglomerates are potentially able to move into any line of business (on the basis of their activities in related lines) makes it difficult for a *chaebol* to keep a particular industry as its fiefdom. Unless it remains reasonably efficient, other *chaebols* can easily persuade the state that they can do a better job and get the state support in the next round of capacity expansion in that industry.

Therefore the *chaebols* have had a powerful incentive to remain efficient, especially when the loss of state support can mean a sharp downturn in business in a few years' time, given the state control of credit and the high leverage of Korean firms. Many of the *chaebols* that lost state favour (for political and/or efficiency reasons) have either gone into oblivion or been disbanded and their remnants distributed to other *chaebols*, as exemplified by the fact that only two of the 10 biggest *chaebols* in 1966 were among the top 10 in 1974; only five of the 1974 top 10 were in the 1980 top 10; and only six of the 1980 top 10 were in the 1985 top 10 (Paik *et al.*, 1988, p. 352, table 35).

4.5 THE POLITICS OF INDUSTRIAL POLICY IN KOREA

The Korean state has played a central role in the country's economic development through its cunning use of state-created rents as an instrument for industrial development. Of course such a result has been possible only because the Korean state has been a strong state, able to discipline firms whenever necessary. The power of the Korean state has frequently been underrated, especially by some neoclassical economists, on the ground that the 'size' of the Korean state (defined in terms of public-sector expenditure) is relatively small (for example Balassa, 1988, but see Sachs, 1987, for some evidence to the contrary). However, what matters for the effectiveness or ineffectiveness of state intervention is not where the boundary of the state as a legal entity lies, but how far it can exercise its influence. Public-sector expenditure as it is usually defined is a very poor measure of this. What, then, was the basis of the power of the Korean state?

It has often been suggested that the Korean state is strong because the country's historical development left a social structure with no powerful social classes to contest state power (Hamilton, 1983; Lim, 1985; Cumings, 1987; Evans, 1987; Amsden, 1989, ch. 2). The landed class was eliminated through land reforms around about the Korean War, and the incipient (largely socialist) political organisations of the working class and farmers were also crushed during the war and the subsequent era of Cold War politics. Moreover it is argued that the country's history of Confucian tradition produced a society where the state commands the moral high ground and draws in the best talent (for example Luedde-Neurath, 1988).[28] The long tradition of centralisation in Korean history seems to have been another factor serving to legitimatise the power of the central bureaucracy.[29]

We think these historical factors are extremely important, and perhaps are what differentiates the Korean developmental experience most from that of, say, India or Latin America.[30] The weakness of the social classes was certainly important in deciding the balance of power between the state and society in Korea. The Confucian belief in the state as a legitimate social institution (if not necessarily in particular governments and individual political leaders), often lacking in other developing countries, also seems to have been an important factor in making state intervention effective in Korea. Moreover there are reasons to believe that the relatively high cultural and ideological homogeneity of Korean society − although it is not as absolute as is often argued (there have been rather intense regional conflicts) − has also helped in the effective implementation of government policies, as we have discussed earlier.

However we think that such historical factors are, in themselves, not enough to bring about a strong state and effective state intervention. If such conditions have been present since the end of the Korean War, why was the Korean state so weak and incompetent in the 1950s? And, if Confucianism is conducive to a strong and competent state, why was the Kuomintang government before their defeat to the Chinese Communist Party so weak and incompetent? Although a full discussion of the subject is beyond the scope of this chapter, we suggest that the emergence of a strong state in Korea should be understood in relation to the political agenda of the military régime of General Park Chung Hee, which fundamentally shaped the political economy of the country for decades to come. The strong state was as much, if not more, an outcome of calculated political moves and institutional innovations as that of historical conditions and culture.

The political ideas of the top political decision-makers of General Park's military régime were fundamentally shaped under the shadow of the Japanese variety of corporatism.[31] In terms of their economics, the early top Korean political decision-makers were no fans of the free market, although they had to pay constant lip service to free-enterprise economics, given the critical importance of US support for the political survival of the régime.[32] In addition, whatever little economic knowledge the early Korean economic bureaucrats – who were mainly lawyers by training – had was not of neoclassical economics but of the economic theories of Friedrich List, Joseph Schumpeter and, especially, Karl Marx, which dominated Japanese academia and policy-making circles in the first half of the twentieth century (see Morris-Suzuki, 1989). The major themes of Korean economic policy-making, for example, the concern with social waste from excessive competition (a distinctly Marxian notion), the emphasis on scale economies, the obsession with capital accumulation and the desire to develop heavy and chemical industries, make more sense when we understand the intellectual background of the Korean economic bureaucracy. Given such a background, it is more than natural that the political–economic agenda of the Park régime was summarised in the First FYP document as 'guided capitalism' (*Gyodo Jabon-Jui*), where the state plays a guardian role.

As soon as it came to power the Park régime moved swiftly to prepare some institutional grounds for its political–economic agenda. One of the first moves was to nationalise all the banks and thereby gain control over the financial flows in the economy. Subsequently new state-owned banks (for example the Korean Exchange Bank, the Bank for Medium and Small Firms, the Ex-Im Bank) were set up over a period of time, resulting in full state control over investment loans.[33] At the same time, the Park régime imprisoned many prominent businessmen on the charge of having accumulated wealth through illicit means (for example by using political connections), but they were later released in return for their promise to 'serve the nation through enterprise', which basically meant building new plants in state-designated industries (on the so-called 'Illicit Wealth Accumulation' episode; see Jones and Sakong, 1980, pp. 69–70, 281–2). With these two major political blows, the business community suddenly became, morally, a criminal on parole and subject to 'serving the nation through enterprise', and, economically, a paper tiger with little power to make investment decisions – the ultimate capitalist prerogative.

Another important institutional innovation made by the Park régime was the centralisation of economic policy-making power in the hands of a super-ministry, the Economic Planning Board (EPB), headed by the deputy prime minister (see Whang, 1991, pp. 86–7). The integration of *both planning and budgeting authorities* within the EPB eliminated the conflict of interests between the planning and industrial ministries (which are usually more interested in long-term investments) and the finance ministry (which is usually more interested in short-term stability), if at the cost of concentrating power within the government (which may be objected to on other grounds). Elimination of such conflict made the implementation of industrial policy in Korea more effective than in other industrial policy-states such as Japan and France, where such conflict has been a problem.[34]

Even the much-vaunted cultural and ideological homogeneity of Korean society was not purely historical bounty that the nation accidentally stumbled on. The Park régime mobilised the nation with the ideology of 'Renaissance of the Nation' through the building of *Jarip Gyongjé* (independent economy).[35] Workers were described by the state-controlled media and state-issued school textbooks as 'industrial soldiers' fighting a patriotic war against poverty (although the labour movement was brutally suppressed) and businessmen were given medals for achieving export targets as if they were generals who had won major battles. Farmers were mobilised into semi-compulsory (unpaid) labour for rural infrastructural development *à la* Mao Tse Tung, through the *Sémaul* (new village) movement (Michell, 1982, pp. 205–8). Although not all such ideological mobilisations were successful (for example, the *Sémaul* movement was much resented) and some rightly criticised them as 'militarising' the society (for example Halliday, 1980), it is undeniable that they were important in promoting ideological homogeneity.

The Korean state has continued to dominate economic and moral issues throughout the country's developmental period. State control over credit, which has been the most effective means of controlling private firms, given their high leverage, has continued throughout.[36] Although some of the state-owned banks (the so-called 'city banks') were partially privatised in 1982, the independence of these banks is almost nil because of their lending to high-borrowing firms and their consequent dependence on the central bank, which is under the full control of the state.[37] In fact, following their privatisation, the share of policy loans – loans with subsidised interest rates and/or priorities in credit rationing – actually *increased*, from 56.0 per cent (1962–81) to 67.6 per cent (1982–5), making it very difficult to argue that state control over the banking sector has loosened (also see Cole and Park, 1983, p. 173). In addition to their freedom to make loan decisions, the banks' freedom to set interest rates has also been severely limited. Despite the legal deregulation of interest rates on loans and long-term deposits in December 1988, it was reported in 1991 that '[i]nterest rates are still strictly controlled by guidance from the Bank of Korea and the Ministry of Finance, despite the legal deregulation' (*FEER*, 30 May, 1991, p. 52).

In addition to its control over bank loans, the Korean state has maintained tight foreign-exchange controls. The buying and selling of foreign exchange has been tightly regulated, and up until a few years ago it was illegal (subject to prison sentence) to possess foreign exchange except for state-approved business purposes. The state's control over foreign loans and foreign direct investment has been near-absolute. Although foreign borrowing and, to a lesser degree, foreign direct investment have not been discouraged, the state has had the final say in deciding whether a certain loan or foreign direct investment is permitted, and on what terms.

Although far less important than its control over financial resources, the state's control over material resources through public enterprises should not be ignored. The Korean state has owned various strategic industries, including oil, coal (partly), gas, fertiliser, steel and electricity. The fact that such crucial intermediate inputs as oil, coal, gas, electricity, steel and fertiliser are supplied by public enterprises is another important factor contributing to the power of the state in Korea.

Of course the regular threat by the Korean state that it is going to use its power to discipline those firms which do not comply with its policies does not always materialise, partly because large business firms have a strong influence on policy formation and implementation. Nevertheless the threat is not an idle one and it is often realised, as exemplified by the freezing of bank credit (on 8 May 1991) to 14 subsidiaries of eight conglomerates that had not complied with state pressure to sell non-business land (EIU, 1991, p. 20). A still more dramatic example of how far the Korean state can go, if it chooses, was the Kukje-group incident in 1985, when the state deliberately bankrupted the inefficiently-run Kukje group, the then seventh largest conglomerate in the country, by ordering its major lending bank not to honour its cheques, although it is believed that the decision to let Kukje go under was in part motivated by its lukewarm attitude to meeting the ruling party's financial demands (for details, see *FEER*, 21 April 1988, pp. 58–60).

CONCLUSION

The Korean experience shows what an intelligent industrial policy can achieve. To its credit, the Korean state has recognised the limited ability of the market to coordinate interdependent decisions. As expressed in the policymakers' continued concern for excessive competition and the resulting social waste, the possibility of coordination failure and its costs have been taken most seriously when conducting industrial policy in Korea. Again to its credit, the Korean state has not been bound by its own free-enterprise rhetoric and it has been more than willing to intervene in the market to prevent and remedy coordination failures.

That the Korean state has put a restraint on the operations of the market does not mean that it did not believe in the power of the market. If anything, it has taken the market more seriously than anyone else has done as, for example, can be seen in its all-out attempt to help local firms to break into the world market. What differentiates the Korean state's attitude toward the market from that of many other states is that it has taken a dynamic view of the market whereby problems of technical change and learning, rather than allocative efficiency, have taken centre stage. It has fully recognised the inadequacy of the market mechanism to bring about non-marginal change in a late-developing context and it has deliberately created rents in areas where, given the present state of local technological capability, the prospect of technological development was the greatest.

Of course such intervention by the Korean state would not have been as successful as it has been were it not for the historical, political and institutional conditions we have examined – for example the cultural and ideological homogeneity of society, the Confucian tradition, an élite bureaucracy and the state's control over the financial flows in the economy. However, as we have demonstrated, these conditions are not entirely God-sent gifts which other countries cannot aspire to possess. They have been brought to their present forms through an intense process of political struggle, ideological campaigning, and institutional innovation. Only when we recognise this fact will we be able to avoid both the ahistoricism of some orthodox economists who recommend a simplified and biased version of the Korean model as a panacea and the scepticism of some heterodox economists who believe that other countries can never learn from such a 'special' case as Korea.

Conclusion: The Market, the State and Institutions

What is the best way to coordinate the activities of independent, but interdependent, agents with divergent interests and dispersed knowledge? This has been one of the major concerns of economists since the birth of the discipline. Some early economists, notably Adam Smith and Karl Marx, explored this question in relation to two problems. One was the problem of coordination within economic enterprises – that is, the study of the conscious management of the relationships between individuals cooperating within the same enterprise. The other was the problem of coordination between such enterprises – this was seen as the study of spontaneous order of the market mechanism that regulates the behaviour of and the relationships between enterprises without the need for conscious design.

With the rise of modern economics, economists became almost exclusively concerned with the second type of coordination problem – spontaneous regulation through the market – and the first type of coordination problem – conscious coordination within economic organisations – was almost entirely dropped from the research agenda of economics (Pagano, 1985). And the inquiry into the functioning of the market continued to be made in a manner which largely ignored the social nature of the problem. By implicitly assuming a complete and costlessly enforced set of property and other rights underlying the market, the study of the struggle between social groups over the definition of the rights system was ignored (North, 1990b). Furthermore, by supposing the hypothetical system of instantaneous and costless recontracting administered by the Walrasian auctioneer, even the coordination problem within the given system of rights was assumed to be solved at no real cost (Richardson, 1971).

Recently, however, economists have become more critical of the conventional approach. As we mentioned earlier, the learning literature and the labour-process literature are returning to the question of coordination and the division of labour within the enterprise. New institutional economics looks at not only market coordination but also non-market coordination within and between enterprises, and also at the determinants of the scope of individual enterprises. The government-failure literature discusses the problems of the centralised form of coordination between enterprises through state intervention. What is becoming increasingly clear from these writings is that effective coordination both within economic units and between such units can only be achieved at a cost, and that different forms of coordination have different costs under different conditions.

By introducing the costs of *achieving* coordination, or transaction costs in more popular terms, into the picture, we effectively break away from the neoclassical tradition in which perfect coordination is achieved without any cost, either by the Walrasian auctioneer (as in the general-equilibrium version) or by the benevolent, omniscient and omnipotent state (as in the welfare-economics version). In this new framework, the market is but one of many possible economic institutions, or coordination mechanisms, each of which incurs certain transaction costs of different types and magnitudes in resolving the coordination problem (Pagano, 1985, ch. 8). By adopting a theoretical framework that recognises that all institutions are costly to run, we implicitly reject the common view which assigns theoretical primacy to the market and views other institutions as merely surrogates, which are simply 'means of achieving the benefits of collective action in situations in which the price system fails' (Arrow, 1974, p. 33).

By regarding the market as just one of many alternative economic institutions, we also come to realise that the efficient operation of the market depends on many more institutional arrangements than those which are usually recognised in the conventional literature.[1] To begin with, we need at least a minimum degree of morality to have any exchange which is intertemporal, as otherwise the costs of policing and contract-enforcement will be prohibitive (McPherson, 1984). Also, existing exchange relationships are definable only in relation to the existing system of property and other rights (for example social-security entitlements, working conditions, rights for clean air), and the enforcement of such rights necessarily requires certain institutions – the police, the courts, and the prison system. And in this process the state not only plays the role of the ultimate guarantor of property rights and other legal forms but also extensively intervenes in order to establish the market itself as an institution (Polanyi, 1957; Coase, 1988; see also Chapter 1.2.3). Thus seen, the seemingly 'institution-free' market mechanism is sustainable only as a part of the intricate fabric of various institutions. As Simon (1983) succinctly puts it, '[m]arket structures are no substitute for the whole web of social interactions' (p. 78).[2]

Introducing transaction costs – or the costs of coordination – and thereby emphasising that all economic institutions are costly to run allowed us to develop a theory of state intervention which overcomes the limitations of some dominant theories of state intervention. By recognising that state intervention carries certain costs, we were able to avoid the naive view of state intervention as the ultimate solution to the coordination problem that is held by welfare economists and the proponents of central planning. At the same time, by recognising that allocating resources through the market is also costly, we were able to reject the biased view of the government-failure school that the costs of state intervention almost invariably exceed the costs of market transactions.

Our theory of state intervention also suggests that there are many possible types of state intervention other than those implied in the conventional analyses. In addition to the manipulation of the price signals in the manner prescribed by welfare economics, the state can take measures that are intended to reduce the costs of coordination, or transaction costs, in the private sector. For this purpose, it may reduce uncertainty in the economy through aggregate demand management, institute and administer a well-defined property rights system, supersede certain private transactions, change the institutions and values of society, or even simply draw attention to a focal point for coordination.

One interesting point that emerges from our discussion of the diverse forms of state intervention is that state intervention need not be expensive, as is implied by the conventional discussion which equates a state that has a larger expenditure (as a proportion of national income) with a more interventionist state. For example, it is often argued that the Japanese state is not very interventionist on the ground that it has a low ratio of government expenditure to GDP (for example, World Bank, 1991, p. 40, box 2.2). However, as the discussions in Chapters 2 and 3 of this book show, the Japanese state has actively intervened in industrial matters. This apparent puzzle that a 'small' state can also be very interventionist is resolved when we realise that some types of state intervention (for example providing the focal point) can improve greatly the efficiency of the economy at little cost because they have only very modest requirements for information processing and bargaining. The point is that fostering credible commitments to the coordinated outcome among the parties involved need not involve financial transfers, although they may help the process.

Combining our theory of state intervention with some recent developments in the literature on industrial organisation, technical change and evolutionary economics, we set out to provide an analytical discussion of industrial policy. In our discussion of industrial policy we argued, first of all, that in many modern industries where interdependence and asset specificity are important, coordination failures are real possibilities and can be costly, especially when combined with unforeseen demand shocks. Our argument was that the state can coordinate individual decisions *ex ante* to prevent coordination failures in such contexts – an argument analogous to the role of the firm as a device of coordination discussed by Coase (1937) and Williamson (1975). Then we discussed how, given the limited codifiability of human (especially technological) knowledge, the state can intervene in industries in such a way that would encourage experimentation and learning, especially in industries at the earlier phase of the product cycle. Together with coordination of investments in complimentary projects, such intervention would serve to amplify the dynamism of the capitalist economy rather than diminish it, as it is often argued – an argument similar to the Keynesian argument about the socialisation of risk but with a new twist.

Obviously industrial policy is not a panacea. As many sceptics point out, there are some serious difficulties involved in its effective operation. Informational constraints mean that industrial policy may not be effectively designed and implemented, resulting in inefficiencies. It may also create perverse incentives for rent-seeking or turn itself into a vehicle for the advancement of the interests of redistributive coalitions or the preservation of conservative interests. Many also rightly point out that industrial policy poses some serious political questions regarding legitimacy and democratic control. We also recognised that the lack of certain supporting institutions may make industrial policy inapplicable to certain countries which lack such institutions. While recognising all these problems, we pointed out that some of these arguments are based on biased assumptions, and we suggested some ways to alleviate these problems.

The conducting of industrial policy in Korea provided some good examples that clearly brought out the theoretical points made in the earlier chapters. On the one hand the Korean state has used various means of *ex ante* coordination (for example entry restrictions) to minimise the *static* inefficiency from possible coordination failures of the market. On the other hand it avoided the *dynamic* inefficiency that may result from the use of those means intended to reduce static inefficiency of the market – the possibility that productivity growth may slow down because there is not enough competitive pressure – by imposing harsh discipline on the firms through its control over the financial flows in the economy. Thus seen, Korea provides a good example of how active intervention by a strong developmental state in industrial development can, under certain conditions, minimise static inefficiency while maximising the dynamic efficiency of the economy.

The conclusion that emerges from our discussion is that neither the market, nor the state, nor any other economic institution is perfect as a coordination mechanism. Each institution has its costs and benefits, and is therefore better than others under certain conditions and worse under other conditions. This means that different countries facing different conditions can, and should, have different mixes of the market, the state and other institutions. And in fact, as we observed in the Introduction, even economies that are usually lumped together as 'capitalist' or 'market' economies have been based on substantially different institutional mixes. In other words, there are many feasible ways of managing a capitalist economy.

This point, which may seem obvious to the reader by now, however does not seem to be widely recognised by policy-makers in many reforming economies of the ex-socialist world and the developing world. The reform packages applied in these countries are modeled on Anglo-Saxon capitalism, and they are often a crude caricature of it at that. The possibility that this may not be the only, or the most efficient, way of managing a capitalist economy seems to be largely ignored. This is a disturbing state of affairs, especially when within the Anglo-Saxon economies themselves there is growing disillusionment with their own models of economic management. Now their policy-makers are thinking seriously about policy changes which recognise the positive role that the state and other non-market institutions can play in the economy, as exemplified in the renewed interest in industrial policy in these countries.

Of course this does not mean that the reforming countries would necessarily succeed if they were to follow some other model, say that of Scandinavia or East Asia. If there are many different ways of combining different economic institutions, this means that each country has to decide on the exact mix between the market, the state and other institutions on the basis of a careful consideration of its economic, political and social conditions, rather than blindly follow one model or another. Needless to say, finding an appropriate mix of the market, the state and other non-market institutions is not easy. Such a task, especially in a world of ever-changing technology, is formidable, as the sceptics point out. However, as we have repeatedly pointed out with reference to countries such Japan, Korea and France, it can in principle be met through a process of institutional learning and innovation.

Notes and References

Introduction

1. For more detailed discussions on the influence of Keynesian ideas on postwar economic policy-making, see essays in Hall (ed.), 1989.
2. See King, 1987, and Gamble, 1988, for analyses of new-right ideas.
3. For an evaluation of new-right economic policies in the UK, see essays in Green (ed.), 1989.
4. Goldthorpe (ed.), 1984, Schott, 1984, Bruno and Sachs, 1985 and Katzenstein, 1985, are earlier works in the literature. For more recent theoretical developments, see Rowthorn and Glyn, 1990; Rowthorn, 1990; Pekkarinen *et al.* (eds), 1992. For left-wing critiques of the neo-corporatist experience, see Panitch, 1981; Pontusson, 1987. Also see Maier, 1987, for a discussion of the historical origins of corporatist ideas in Western Europe.
5. LO (1963) provides theoretical backings for such policies from the trade unions' point of view.
6. See Jacquemin (ed.), 1984; Johnson (ed.), 1984; Norton, 1986; Thompson (ed.), 1989.
7. Deyo (ed.), 1987, provides an overview of the political economy of Japan and the East Asian NICs. White (ed.), 1988, has useful essays on the role of the state in the East Asian NICs. Magaziner and Hout, 1980, Johnson, 1982; Dore, 1986; and Okimoto, 1989, provide detailed accounts of the role of the state in postwar Japan. Amsden, 1985, and Wade, 1990, do the same for Taiwan. For Korea, see Jones and Sakong, 1980; Amsden, 1989; and Chapter 4 of this book.
8. Coase, 1937, Coase, 1960, Richardson, 1960, and Simon, 1983, are seminal works in the tradition. Williamson, 1975, has established itself as a modern classic. For more recent theoretical developments, see Pagano, 1985; Williamson, 1985; Matthews, 1986; Langlois (ed.), 1986; Putterman (ed.), 1986; Aoki *et al.* (eds), 1990.
9. Schumpeter, 1987, is a classic work in this tradition. For some important contemporary works, see Rosenberg, 1976; Nelson and Winter, 1982; Fransman, 1986; Dosi *et al.* (eds), 1988; Johnson and Lundvall, 1989.
10. See Mueller, 1979; Schott, 1984; and Cullis and Jones, 1987, for a literature survey. Also see Chapters 1 and 2 of this book.

1 Theories of State Intervention

1. Baumol, 1965, is a classic exposition of the literature. For textbook expositions, see Musgrave and Musgrave, 1984, and Stiglitz, 1988. For more recent theoretical developments, see Schotter, 1985; Cullis and Jones, 1987.

2. It has become customary to define a public good, following Samuelson (1954), as a good with 'jointness in supply' or 'non-rivalness in consumption' (that is, one person's consumption not reducing anothers' consumption). Non-excludability is regarded as an additional, but not necessary, feature of a public good (see for example Oakland, 1987, pp. 485–6; Laffont, 1988, pp. 33–5), or at best as one of the two (together with non-rivalness) defining characteristics (see for example Stiglitz, 1988, pp. 119–22). However, along with Olson (1965), we think that non-excludability should be the primary defining characteristic of a public good, because a good with non-rivalness in consumption can be a private good if there are means to exclude other individuals (that is, the so-called club goods). This means that the public-good problem is fundamentally a property-rights problem. Good historical examples in this regard are English public parks, which used to be private goods (or, more exactly, club goods for the upper classes) but later became public goods (for every citizen). Such a change in the nature of the goods occurred not because the parks suddenly acquired non-rivalness in consumption but because the rising political power of the commoners made it impossible to exclude them from access to the parks (a change in the property rights structure). I thank Bob Rowthorn for suggesting this example.

3. Here it is interesting to note some parallel between this argument and some Marxist theories of the state that regard the provision of public goods as one of the major functions of the state (Mandel, 1975; Hirsch, 1978; Fine and Harris, 1979). For example, Hirsch (1978) argues that the capitalist state should and does intervene in areas 'where the "principles of exclusion" cannot be guaranteed' (p. 92). According to Mandel (1975), the capitalist state should provide the general technical preconditions of production (for example means of transport and communication) and the provision of the general social preconditions of production (for example law and order, a currency system) (p. 476) – in other words, public goods.

4. Mishan (1982, p. 154) suggests that, when naming the public good, the term 'public' should be avoided because of the misleading connotation of the term that any good supplied by the state may be called 'public', and that it should be substituted by the term 'collective'.

5. Moreover, given that cooperation is more likely to emerge when the relationship is of a long-term nature (Axelrod, 1984), the state can promote cooperation for the provision of public goods by encouraging the formation of long-term relationships among private-sector agents – for example, the provision of legal backing for industry associations or forum for labour–capital dialogue.

6. The logic behind this is as follows. Regardless of the competitiveness of the market, firms will equate their marginal costs with their marginal revenues in order to maximise their profits. In competitive markets, each firm faces a horizontal demand curve, and therefore marginal revenue coincides with average revenue (that is, price). In a non-competitive market where firms face negatively-sloped demand curves, marginal

revenue – which should still be equated with marginal cost to maximise profit – will be less than average revenue (that is, price). Consequently firms in a non-competitive market will produce less at a higher price than they would if the market were competitive.

7. Moreover, there are non-efficiency reasons to regulate monopoly. For example it is argued that monopoly has to be regulated because it leads to the concentration of economic and political power in private hands, which are not easily subject to democratic control (Cullis and Jones, 1987, p. 182).

8. Anti-interventionists argue that, even when scale economy dictates a non-competitive market structure, the state should regulate private firms rather than set up a public enterprise, because private monopoly is better than public monopoly. According to this argument, private monopoly is subject to some form of market discipline (for example takeover, bankruptcy) and is therefore more responsive to the changing needs of the consumers, whereas public monopoly is unlikely to be subject to such discipline. Although we do not have enough space to discuss the merits and demerits of public monopoly vis-à-vis private monopoly, it has to be pointed out there are ways and means to discipline public enterprises (for a detailed discussion of this issue, see Chang and Singh, 1993).

9. Nelson and Winter (1982) generate some computer-simulation results where, under certain plausible assumptions concerning firm behaviour, a reasonably competitive market transforms itself into an oligopolistic one through a stochastic process.

10. The concept of freedom employed by Friedman is that of negative freedom ('freedom from'), but it is not the only acceptable concept of freedom. There is another widely-accepted concept of positive freedom ('freedom to'). On different notions of freedom, see Berlin, 1969.

11. The 'liberalism' of Peacock and Rowley is what is usually called 'libertarianism'. They argue, quite correctly, that this position should be differentiated from Paretian arguments (for example market-failure arguments), because the latter are ends-oriented whereas the former is process-oriented (also see Rowley, 1983).

12. Hayek (1972) contends that non-market coordination of the economy ('planning' in his terminology) is doomed to technical failure due to insurmountable information costs. This important point need not detain us here since our main concern is the politico–philosophical side of the argument. For a discussion of the informational problem in central planning, see Lavoie, 1985. For an exposition of the information problem in general, see Arrow, 1974. See also Chapters 1.4.1, 2.1.1 and 3.4.1 of this book.

13. Although Brennan and Buchanan (1985) reject the 'state-of-nature-as-a-fiction' type of criticism as irrelevant, they are correct only when one makes such criticism and at the same time endorses contractarianism (as Brennan and Buchanan themselves admit; see p. 22), a position that is not held in this chapter.

14. For example Bobbio (1987) justifies the state's concern for social inequality on contractarian grounds (p. 136).

15. For Marxist theories of the state, see Miliband, 1969, and Jessop, 1982.
16. According to neoclassical political economy, what differentiates the market from the polity is not the different behavioural principle of the participants (always self-interested) but the different constraints that they face (the individual bearing or otherwise of the whole effects of one's decision) (McCormick and Tollison, 1981, p. 5). Still emergent, this school has many different names, such as economics of politics (Buchanan *et al.*, 1978), neoclassical political economy (Colander [ed.], 1984), public-choice school (Mueller, 1979), new political economy (Findlay, 1990), or positive political economy (Alt and Shepsle [eds], 1990).
17. In some models of interest-group theory, interest groups – acting as maximisers of utility (or wealth) – make demands to claim the largest possible amount of state largesse, which the politicians who make up the state distribute with a view to maximising their votes, and not to maximising social welfare. The result often is the generation of policies that are 'irrational' from the social point of view, for example 'political business cycles'.
18. From the viewpoint of extreme methodological individualism this argument is a *non sequitur*, because if these norms restrict the formation of a certain interest group, the individuals who belong to that potential interest group can organise themselves first to remove such restrictions. However, in the real world, as Eggertsson (1990) argues, 'various factors work against special interest groups and limit their effectiveness, including laws against bribery, rules regulating the behaviour of lobbyists, and public-spiritedness of civil servants and legislators' (pp. 66–7). Moreover norms may have arisen due to the utility-maximising behaviour of individuals but they acquire an autonomous life once they come into being, because individuals who join the society by birth or immigration after these norms have been established will internalise them through the socialisation processes.
19. Moreover, even when assuming that there are no unnecessary activities initiated by the budget-maximising attempts of the bureaucrats, the state activities may not be fully cost-efficient. The fact that the state bureaucracy is in a monopolistic position may mean that there is x-inefficiency in their activities (see Peacock, 1979b, pp. 123–4). x-inefficiency, as defined by Leibenstein (1966), is generated when production units use inputs in the right proportion, but on an unnecessarily large scale. Thus, even when strict marginal pricing is conducted within the state bureaucracy, it may operate with considerable slack due to the lack of competitive pressures.
20. Marxists emphasise this problem when they discuss the need for the state in a class society to ensure the legitimacy of the system (see Gramsci, 1988; O'Connor, 1973; Gough, 1979).
21. Even from a purely selfish point of view, there is far more scope for cooperation in a stable organisation like the bureaucracy than in a strictly atomised world. Firstly, since an organisation by definition implies a long-lasting relationship between a given set of people, there is

much more possibility of evolutionary cooperation, that is, development of cooperative behaviour through continued reciprocity (see Axelrod, 1984). Secondly, the environment to which a self-seeker has to adapt himself/herself is not just the material world, but also the human actors around him/her (Simon, 1991). Then adaptation will inevitably mean collaboration with those other actors (this is an analogy to Dawkins' genetic argument; see Dawkins, 1986, pp. 170–1). In an organisation, its members will be treated more as a part of the environment than those who people encounter on a more precarious basis in the atomised world.

22. The informational problem also has a politico-philosophical dimension, especially from the point of view of the individualism–contractarianism. As Rowley (1983) argues, the belief 'that reason is paramount and that appropriate rule of social choice can be devised to encompass public sector decision-making in a manner fully compatible with the Paretian emphasis upon the primacy of individual preferences' is misguided because the pervasive uncertainties in human life make it inevitable that such as approach ends up with the imposition of the social decision-makers' individual preference 'to fill the void that otherwise would destroy the smooth calculus of social choice' (pp. 35–6).

23. In this sense, the self-seeking bureaucrats approach (see Chapter 1.3.3) is also partly an informational argument. However we included it in the political-economy literature because it emphasises the difference between the objectives of the public, or the top politicians, and the bureaucrats. An asymmetric information problem would exist even if the bureaucrats genuinely want to serve the public interest, because of the limited scope for knowledge transmission (Hayek, 1949a, 1978).

24. It is interesting to note that this explanation of the dynamic rent-seeking process in a competitive setting is similar to the Marxian argument on surplus profit (Marx, 1981) and the Schumpeterian argument on entrepreneurial profit (Schumpeter, 1961, 1987). More on this in later chapters of the book.

25. Buchanan argues that, unless no single set of winners can secure benefits on each and every occasion, a 'constitutional revolution' will become more feasible with the *increase* in opportunities for rent-seeking behaviour, since each group gains more than it loses in net from the revolution. In the case of a single set of groups constantly securing benefits, a 'nonconstitutional revolution' – or violent revolution – becomes a possibility (Buchanan, 1980b, p. 366).

26. Of course this point does not hold if the bribed had to spend extra time to change the state's decision in the briber's favour. In this case, the bribery should be regarded, at least from the analytical point of view, as an implicit wage to the bribed rather than as pure bribery (a pure transfer).

27. That bribery does not have *direct* efficiency consequences – that it is a pure transfer – does not mean that it has no efficiency consequences. It may have *negative indirect* efficiency consequences when it enables less efficient producers to get monopoly rights (see below). Moreover widespread bribing can lead to loss in legitimacy of the political–economic system of the country (Krueger, 1974). The loss of legitimacy may create

uncooperative attitudes among the underprivileged and therefore more monitoring and enforcement costs will have to be incurred. Bribery, however, may have *positive indirect* efficiency consequences when it is used as a 'signal' for one's superior ability as a producer (as heavy advertising may be used as a signal for superior quality).

28. I thank John Toye for reminding me of this important point.
29. The proposal for constitutional revolution is reminiscent of the 'rigidities' argument put forward by the new right, whose favourite recipe for a restoration of dynamism in advanced capitalist economies is to undo oligopolistic arrangements, enforce the principles of fair trade, break union monopolies, break institutional constraints that prevent wages from 'finding their real level' and make labour mobile and market-responsive again. See some essays in Balassa and Giersch (eds), 1986. For a critique of such views, see Johnson and Lundvall, 1989.
30. Market failure does not necessarily mean that state intervention is the solution. As new institutional economics argues, the history of capitalism is full of institutional innovations to deal with the failure of the market to coordinate individual activities. The rise of the factory system, joint-stock companies, multidivisional firms, and vertical integration and conglomeration are but a few such innovations (see for example essays in Langlois [ed.], 1986).

2 A New Institutionalist Theory of State Intervention

1. This view of rationality and decision-making has been employed not only by the orthodox economists but also by the proponents of central planning. On this point, see Lavoie, 1985.
2. On the role of expertise in decision-making, see Simon, 1983. On the problem of knowledge transfer, see Hayek, 1949a, 1949b, 1978, and Chapter 3.3.1 of this book.
3. In 1957 the Polish Economic Council suggested that '[p]lanning is improved not by introducing a multiplicity of indices, by making extremely detailed projects, and by formal balancing, but by securing a more profound economic analysis and well-founded estimates of economic development *in those areas where precise economic calculation is impossible*' [emphasis added] (quoted from Brus, 1972, p. 154).
4. Public enterprises in an industry with public *and* private firms may also play a valuable role in reducing the informational asymmetry between the state and the firms in that industry, by providing the state with first-hand knowledge about the workings of the industry.
5. These conditions are assumed to be satisfied in empirical studies that estimate the magnitude of resources involved in rent-seeking in some developing countries. These studies assume that an amount of resources equivalent to the rent is dissipated through the competitive process, yielding estimates that put the magnitude of resources involved at 7–45 per cent of GNP in countries like Turkey and India (for example Krueger, 1974; Mohammad & Whalley, 1984). However, as we discuss below, these conditions are frequently not met, and therefore the quantitative

estimates of these studies should be accepted with great caution.

6. Farrell (1987) raises the same point from the perspective of information economics when he says that 'if a central authority fails to succeed in *committing himself to ignore information*, it can lead to excessive incentives for subjects to try to influence his decisions; this is the idea of "rent-seeking" behaviour, which often has important social costs' [emphasis added] (p. 121).

7. Some qualifications, which emerged from a discussion with Terence Moll, may be needed here. First of all, it may be necessary to invest resources to qualify for the queue (you do not get a license to run a petrochemical plant just because you applied earlier). In this case, people will 'waste' some resources in order to qualify, although it is possible that in the process they will create socially beneficial by-products (see below), for example in the form of enhanced managerial skills (to prove that you are able to run a modern plant well). Secondly, it may be possible to jump the queue by paying the administrator of the queue, although the payment to the administrator should not be counted as a rent-seeking cost if it does not make the administrator do any more work (see Chapter 1.4.2).

8. For example, all firms in a protected industry may benefit from tariff protection whether or not they contributed to lobbying efforts of the industry association.

9. Strategic uncertainty (uncertainty due to interdependence) is a crucial element in a game-like situation. After all, the use of randomised (or mixed) strategies is a way to prevent other players from capitalising on the certainty of one's future action by deliberately creating uncertainty about one's future course of action. The existence of parametric uncertainty (uncertainty due to nature) also affects the magnitude of rent-seeking 'waste'. If there is uncertainty about the size of the rent (for example the case of a monopoly right to an infant industry whose growth prospect is uncertain), the outcome of rent-seeking is not clear (Fisher, 1985), although we may suppose a strong bias *against* the standard conclusion of total rent dissipation (Rogerson, 1982).

10. Moreover, monopolistic or oligopolistic incumbency in a rent market helps one to build up the ability to enter into other such markets. However, as we discuss later in the Korean context, rather than multiplying rent-seeking costs, such 'interlocked' rent-seeking may, under certain conditions, work to decrease such costs (see Chapter 4.4.2).

11. However, education may generate some positive externalities, thus partially offsetting the social loss from rent-seeking (a case of the beneficial by-stander effect). I thank Jay Min Lee for raising this point.

12. Although it may sound objectionable to say that rent-seeking may create some values because the rent-seekers derive utility from the very act of rent-seeking, this is only because we are already assuming that the rent-seekers are sinister people. If we imagine that the rent-seekers are those poor fish farmers who want to acquire the right to restrict entry into their stretch of river by a chemical factory or workers fighting for better working conditions, the difficulty of accepting this argument may be reduced.

13. For example, a society may encourage competition in education while restricting competition in politics, while another does the opposite.
14. On the question of 'learning', see Rosenberg, 1976, 1982; Amsden and Hikino (forthcoming); and Chapter 3 of this book.
15. See Braverman, 1974; Marglin, 1974; Bowles, 1985; and Pagano, 1985, on the Marxian labour-process literature. See essays in Akerlof and Yellen (eds), 1986, for the efficiency-wage argument. See Alchian and Demsetz, 1972, for the theory of team production.
16. There exists no agreed or exact definition of 'new institutional economics', which still is emergent as a school. Transaction-cost economics *à la* Oliver Williamson (for example Williamson, 1975, 1988) and property-rights economics *à la* Ronald Coase (for example Coase, 1960; Alchian and Demsetz, 1972; North, 1990b) are probably the two most important strands within new institutional economics (Putterman, 1986, p. 20, n. 27). However there also exist strong influences from the Schumpeterian, Austrian and behaviouralist (*a là* Herbert Simon) traditions (Langlois, 1986a, pp. 1–2). Eggertsson (1990, pp. 7–10) argues that transaction-cost economics – what he calls new institutional economics – is different from property-rights economics – what he calls neoinstitutionalist economics – in that it rejects the 'hard-core' assumption of neoclassical economics about full rationality and adopts the heterodox concept of bounded rationality. Although Eggertsson's point is valid, the demarcation between the above two groups is not as clear as he suggests, and the two groups share enough commonalities to be put under the single heading of 'new institutional economics'.
17. Needless to say, whether or not it can better allocate resources than the market is another matter.
18. To date, there is no agreed definition of transaction costs, but we are in general agreement with Matthews (1986), who defines transaction costs as 'the costs of arranging a contract *ex ante* and monitoring and enforcing it *ex post*, as opposed to production costs, which are the costs of executing the contract' (p. 906). At this point it should also be noted that it is not easy to differentiate the production-cost elements and the transaction cost elements in practice, even of a single activity, not to mention the activities of the firms and of other organisations which partially perform economic functions (for example the state, the family). For example it is difficult to tell how much of a foreman's labour belongs to the domain of production cost (for example his technical advice to the supervisee) and how much to the domain of transaction cost (for example his monitoring activities). I thank Bob Rowthorn for reminding me of this important point.
19. Matthews (1986) is opposed to defining transaction costs as the costs of interaction between people on the ground that there are production costs that involve relations between people, particularly the costs of providing personal services (p. 906). However the object of transaction in the provision of personal service is the service and not the human being who is providing the service. Imagine a future society where all personal services are conducted by robots. Even in this society, there will still be

transaction costs due to the interaction between the recipient of the services and the owner of the robots. If this is the case, it may be useful to define transaction costs as 'the costs of interaction between people'.

20. One intriguing point that emerges by reinterpreting rent-seeking costs as variants of transaction costs is that someone who thinks rent-seeking is wasteful is compelled to take the controversial position that other activities that incur transaction costs – informational, bargaining and enforcement costs (for example stockbrokers, lawyers, judges, policemen) – are also wasteful or unproductive (for discussions of unproductive activities, see Wolff, 1987, ch. 2, and Boss, 1990). There may be two possible responses to this point, neither of which are convincing. (1) It may be argued that rent-seeking costs are artificially created by state intervention, whereas other transaction costs are natural. However influencing the state is only one of many ways of changing the existing property rights structure and is not more or less natural than other methods of changing it. (2) It may be argued that other transaction costs are necessary evils whereas rent-seeking costs are unnecessary evils because the former are more than offset by gains in efficiency – which is achieved through the transfer of resources to the best (or at least better) users – but the latter are not. However such difference exists only because any efficiency gain from the state intervention which starts off the rent-seeking process is assumed away (for an example, see Buchanan, 1980b, p. 359)

21. Expanding on the above example of the pure coordination problem, this will be the case when a society, in which people have been driving on any side of the road they like, tries belatedly to decide on one side. Given the higher possibility of accidents when people drive on both sides, everyone will prefer there to be a designated side. However different people will prefer different sides because say, they have cars with steering wheels on different sides and/or may be reluctant to change their driving habits.

22. This may be somewhat counterintuitive for those who are familiar with the neoclassical model of perfect competition, where the the existence of many agents does not lead to a coordination failure. However such a result obtains only because some stringent assumptions are made in this model to eliminate the interdependence between individual decisions and therefore any need for coordination. For a more detailed discussion of this point, see Chapter 3.2.1.

23. In addition to the reduction of transaction costs involved in people's attempts to overcome the strategic uncertainty inherent in the coordination problem, the state also has an important role to play in reducing what Koopmans (1957) calls 'primary uncertainty', which arises from random acts of nature and unpredictable changes in consumers' preferences (p. 163). First of all, the state can provide information whose provision is subject to scale economy, for example information regarding the condition of the world market. It is well known that the information on export markets collected by the Japanese and Korean government trading agencies (JETRO and KOTRA) and diplomatic services played

an important role in the exporting successes of these countries. Secondly, the state can provide information with externalities, for example technical knowledge. Basic technical knowledge generated by non-profit-making institutions (for example universities) will generate externalities in the sense that those who utilise that information can improve their productivity without paying the full cost for it. If such a piece of information is not readily available to the firms because of a lack of communication between them and the knowledge-generating institutions, the state can act as a sort of information-clearinghouse, as is actually practiced in many countries.

24. Organising society will not only reduce transaction costs in the private sector but also the transaction costs involved in state intervention, by delegating the responsibility of monitoring and enforcement to organisations such as industry associations and labour unions. Indeed the early Marxist belief in the increasing feasibility of central planning was also partly based on the belief that the continued process of 'concentration and centralisation of capital' would reduce the (transaction) costs involved in state intervention (for a critical discussion of this view, see Tomlinson, 1982).

25. Here the term 'ideology' is used as a shorthand for a set of social norms and values and not as meaning 'false belief' or 'pseudo-science', as in some studies of ideology. See McLellan (1986) for different concepts of ideology.

26. Many ideologies frame the decision-making process so as to encourage people to identify themselves with people who are outside the usual boundaries of an individual's limited personal and other channels of identification (professional, ethnic and so on). For example, the American ideology of industrial productivity and the German and Italian fascist ideologies, which dismissed the liberal concept of trade-off between growth and equity and emphasised the non-zero-sum nature of distributive struggle, were accepted by different classes with conflicting interests (Maier, 1987, chs 1–3).

27. Of course, as Hall (1987, p. 155) argues, this type of planning exercise cannot be *purely* indicative and would probably have to involve a degree of coercion in order to be effective, not least because most coordination problems involve some conflicts of interest, as in our example of the generalised coordination problem.

28. Commissioning pilot research projects, organising cooperative (among firms) research projects, and providing 'signalling' subsidies for sunrise industries are other examples of the state providing of a focal point (for examples from various countries, see Porter, 1990, especially pp. 635–6, 639–40).

29. Our theory is also able to accommodate insights from the political economy literature by explicitly introducing the role of institutions and ideas (or values) in the political process, although we did not fully pursue this line of inquiry. For some works trying to incorporate the role of institutions and ideas in explaining the economic policy process, see Tomlinson, 1980; Evans *et al.* (eds) 1985; and Hall (ed.), 1989.

3 The Political Economy of Industrial Policy

1. See NEDO, 1978; Stout, 1979; Cairncross *et al.*, 1983.
2. See Singh, 1977; Blackaby (ed.), 1979; Rowthorn and Wells, 1987.
3. See Pinder (ed.), 1982; Jacquemin (ed.), 1984; Cox (ed.), 1986; Duchêne and Shepherd (eds), 1987.
4. For some interesting reviews of the debate, see Norton, 1986; Thompson, 1989.
5. See essays in Kirzkowski (ed.), 1984, and Krugman (ed.), 1988.
6. For example Dornbusch *et al.*, 1988, take a pro-manufacturing position but recommend better macroeconomic management rather than industrial policy as the major solution to the current industrial decline in the USA.
7. Of course this is not to argue that a change in the employment structure has no impact on our socioeconomic life. The growing importance of service activities may have a significant impact on people's life-styles, on their relationship with others, on their perception of the world, and so on, especially by providing people with different work experiences from those in the manufacturing sector (on the 'constitutive' nature of labour processes, see Bowles and Gintis, 1990). I thank Michael Landesmann for raising this important point.
8. Lawrence (1984) argues against using industrial policy as a surrogate regional or group-oriented policy on the grounds that 'particular objectives – such as meeting national defense needs, redistributing incomes, and promoting regional development – can all be achieved by more precise policies' (p. 115).
9. Our definition of industrial policy is based on a stylised version of industrial policy conducted in 'industrial-policy states' such as Japan, France and Korea. On Japanese industrial policy, see Magaziner and Hout, 1980; Johnson, 1982; Dore, 1986; Okimoto, 1989; Best, 1990, ch. 6. On Korean industrial policy, see Jones and Sakong, 1980; Luedde-Neurath, 1986; Amsden, 1989; and Chapter 4 of this book. On French industrial policy, see Cohen, 1977; Hayward, 1986; Hall, 1987.
10. For example, in their study of Japanese industrial policy, Magaziner and Hout (1980) document that MITI will often 'suggest that a company participate in an unappealing foreign investment project or delay a capacity addition *to accomplish a broader end*' [emphasis added] (p. 34).
11. This part of the definition helps us deal with those who downgrade the importance of industrial policy, say in Japan, by saying that Japan would have grown quickly and become rich anyway given factors like the 'catching-up effect' and high savings ratios (for example Krugman, 1984). From our perspective, however, the important point is not whether Japan would have become rich or not without industrial policy but whether *the structure* of the present Japanese economy is in line with what the Japanese state intended when it implemented industrial policy measures (by choosing what technology to deploy, where to channel the savings and so on). And in this respect, there is no doubt that Japanese industrial policy has played a crucial role.

12. Moreover, as Williamson (1988) states, 'it does not suffice to demonstrate that a condition of large numbers competition obtains at the outset. It is also necessary to examine whether this continues or if, by reason of transaction specific investments and incomplete contracting, a condition of bilateral trading *evolves* thereafter' (p. 71).
13. What Hayek calls the 'competition as a state of affairs' view is still dominant in the field of industrial economics (on different notions of competition, see Hayek, 1949b, 1978; McNulty, 1968; O'Driscoll, 1986). For example, even a most updated industrial economics textbook, Tirole (1988), argues that replacement of one monopolist by another through a patent race 'does not mean competition, as one monopolist replaces another' (p. 396, n. 12). However Hayek would have argued that the replacement was a result of 'the activity called competition'.
14. Dobb (1925, ch. 23) expresses a similar concern. He describes the capitalist economy as an 'economic anarchy' that gives fluidity to the economy but at the cost of instability due to coordination failure. In particular, he points out that miscalculations by competing firms might not cancel out because expectations tend to move in the same direction.
15. It should, however, be noted that Marx had another vision of socialist society organised on the basis of a more democratic and less specialised division of labour, which Pagano (1985) aptly calls 'anti-firm communism' (p. 60).
16. Amadeo and Banuri (1991) argue that there is a correlation between the liquidity of the assets owned by different groups (for example financiers, industrialists, workers) and their degrees of support for unregulated competition in the market.
17. Some recent developments in mainstream theory attempt to incorporate these observations through modelling 'wasteful R&D' and the like. However this type of model is not generally extended to the theory of competition in general.
18. The very diversity of coordination devices in a capitalist economy is a testimony to the diversity of coordination problems to be solved. And this is one reason why we emphasise the particularistic nature of industrial policy, since, to be successful, it has to be custom-designed to fit the nature of the coordination problem involved in a particular instance.
19. Marx's concept of 'constant capital' (which was absent in the Ricardian system) and the Austrian concept of 'roundabout methods of production' are two important ways of theorising such a characteristic.
20. Of course there are other options open to firms. One is to find a hitherto unexploited market, say, through exporting. Another is to diversify into other related industries, as shown in the examples of some Japanese firms in declining industries like textiles, brewing and food-processing that have successfully diversified into biotechnology (see Okimoto, 1989, p. 128).
21. However, devising a side-payments scheme is not easy because the estimate of future costs and benefits from exit may differ among the agents concerned. For example, in the branches of the Japanese textile industry that are dominated by many small-scale firms, who were hard-pressed by imports from the NICs in the early 1980s, the government

took the view that exit compensation should be financed by the remaining firms who would benefit from such exit, while the remaining firms argued that the exiters' share of the total market was minute (and hence benefit negligible) and that any room left in the market by the exit of home producers was likely to be taken up by imports (see Dore, 1986, p. 236).

22. In this case, side-payments will mainly involve compensation for workers who are laid off. For example, in the case of the Japanese shipbuilding industry, additional unemployment benefits and special placement services for workers, provided by the state, were important in arranging a speedy capacity-scrapping arrangement (see Renshaw, 1986, p. 145; Dore, 1986, p. 143).

23. In the case of the Japanese textile industry, some equipment was mothballed in 1978, but it was eventually scrapped in 1981 as the demand downturn proved to be permanent (Dore, 1986, pp. 235–6).

24. More generally, given the limited human capacity to process information, the introduction of rigidity in behaviour through such long-term binding contracts may well be essential to achieve rational decisions (Simon, 1983; Heiner, 1983).

25. In this particular case, no exit was negotiated, and the cut was graduated to the size of the firm, ranging from 40 per cent for the seven biggest firms to 15 per cent for the 21 smallest (Dore, 1986, p. 145).

26. And this is why '[c]onsumers do not wish to contract for their future purchases because they cannot foretell what their future needs and opportunities will be; and producers do not generally wish to commit themselves to forward purchases of inputs because they cannot predict the productive possibilities that will be open to them' (Richardson, 1971, p. 437).

27. In the case of the Japanese aluminium-smelting industry, one reason put forward for not cutting capacity to the level dictated by current relative prices (mainly due to the oil price hike and the consequent rise in electricity prices) was the need to maintain a sizeable industry to support an R&D capacity, which is an important precondition for regaining international competitiveness if the cost situation improves in the future (Dore, 1986, p. 143).

28. While arguing that the coordination failures of the market entails enormous waste and therefore needs to be replaced by less wasteful *ex ante* coordination through central planning, Marx was also a precursor of the Schumpeterian, and to some extent the Austrian, 'process' view of competition, which emphasises the role of market competition in developing the 'forces of production' (see, for example, Marx, 1981, pp. 373–4).

29. In contrast, in the neoclassical framework every piece of information (or knowledge) is seen as obtainable, albeit at a cost (for example search cost) (for similar views, see Heiner, 1988, p. 148, and Pelikan, 1988, p. 385).

30. The importance, in the nineteenth century, of the migration of skilled technicians in transmitting technical knowledge from one to another part of the then industrialised world (that is, Europe and the USA) documented by Rosenberg (1976, pp. 154–5) shows the difficulty of codifying technical knowledge.

31. For evolutionary arguments in economics, see Alchian, 1950, and Nelson and Winter, 1982.
32. The same view of economic evolution lies in the French state's claim that it was involved in rescue operations of declining sectors not 'to save endangered spieces but to provide funds for their *mutation*' [emphasis added] (*Fortune*, 9 April 1978; quoted in Hall, 1987, p. 190).
33. On the notion of cumulative causation, see Young, 1928; Kaldor, 1985; Stigler, 1951.
34. Of course computer firms may decide on in-house production of semiconductors, but there is no guarantee that scale economies in computer production and semiconductor production will be of the same magnitude. If the semiconductor industry is subject to a larger scale economy (as is the case), the in-house production option will be costly compared with the option of production by independent semiconductor producers.
35. Porter (1990) reports that '[i]n the United States and often in Europe, the process of reaching technical standards is frequently protracted as firms jockey for their individual positions. In Japan, MITI has frequently applied significant pressure on firms to set basic standards, pushing them to move on to the next stage in the innovation cycle' (p. 653). See also the examples of the Japanese computer and machine tools industries in Dore, 1986, pp. 134–6.
36. It may not matter, for example, whether a country goes for superconductivity or biotechnology, but it matters whether enough complementary investments are made in either of these industries.
37. For a classic discussion of the problem of coordinating complementary investments, see Richardson, 1960. Also related are concepts like Hirschman's 'linkages' (Hirschman, 1958) and Dahmén's 'development blocks' (Dahmén, 1988).
38. Magaziner and Hout (1980) argue that 'MITI's greatest strength appears to be its understanding of the competitive stages through which an industry moves and its ability to fashion appropriate policy' (p. 38). They document that '[f]or businesses in the early, rapid growth phases of development ... policy calls for protection from foreign competition, concentration among producers, government support of the industry's cash flow, and stimulation of new technology .... For businesses which are already internationally competitive ... government assistance recedes [with the significant exception of occasional officially sanctioned recession and export cartels co-ordinated by the industry associations] as it is no longer necessary. Finally, for businesses in competitive decline, MITI becomes active again, this time trying to bring about capacity reduction and rationalisation' (pp. 38–9).
39. Of course we should not forget the possibility of *rejuvenation*, whereby a new series of exogenous technical changes turn a mature industry into a young one again, although we may not go as far as Pierre Dreyfus, a former French minister of industry, who argued that '[t]here are no condemned sectors; there are only outmoded technologies' (quoted in Hall, 1987, p. 210). I thank Nathan Rosenberg for reminding me of this important point.

40. A good example of the shift in policy emphasis according to product cycle is the production cartel among six Japanese computer peripheral equipment producers organised by MITI in the late 1970s. 'The products handled through the cartel included [mainly] standard peripherals whose design had stabilised and where further innovation was remote' (Magaziner and Hout, 1980, pp. 83–4).

41. On the role of diversity in the economic system, see Johnson and Lundvall, 1989, pp. 103–4. On the role of genetic diversity in the biological world, see Axelrod, 1984, p. 170.

42. See the 'long purse story' (pp. 337–9) and the case of high fixed-R&D costs (p. 414) in Tirole (1988) for the implications of an imperfect capital market for R&D activities.

43. Needless to say, due to the limited human ability to process information, the greater availability of information does not guarantee a better decision (see Chapter 2.1.2).

44. Of course it has to be recognised that there exists 'second-mover disadvantage', because the first-movers would reap more rents from innovation. I owe this point to Sandeep Kapur. See also Landes, 1990; and Amsden and Hikino, forthcoming.

45. Interestingly some Marxist denunciation of the 'revisionist' strategies of 'co-opted' trade-union leaderships in favour of rank-and-file militancy (for example Panitch, 1981) is based on the same view of information. As Tomlinson (1982) argues, this position ultimately depends on 'a belief that the experience of the ordinary employee, his/her experience of the oppressive and exploitative relations of capitalist wage labour will guarantee the appropriate socialist direction in the struggle. The experience gives a privileged access to the appropriate means to change the capitalist enterprise whereas the experience of the trade union official may lead him or her to a different *and wrong assessment*' [emphasis original] (pp. 44–5).

46. For discussions of the different relationships between the state and finance in different OECD countries and their implications for industrial adjustment, see Zysman, 1983, and Cox (ed.), 1986. On the same issue in the French context, see Hall, 1987. For the Korean case, see Chapter 4.

47. For a discussion of this problem in the French context, see Hall, 1987, pp. 176–80.

48. And he continues: as a consequence, 'harmony can only be obtained by coercion or by a series of compromises ... and purely strategic considerations may tend more and more to override any considerations of maximum welfare and efficiency'. It 'may also produce class struggle', and, '[i]n conflicts of this kind, *a considerable part of the economic resources of a community may be consumed, either in their conduct or in their prevention* [emphasis added]' (p. 158).

49. It has to be pointed out, however, that parliamentary representation (the representation of individuals as individuals) is not the only legitimate form of representation. Representation along class lines (as in Scandinavian social corporatism) or even issues (as in some American lobbying organisations) are too pervasive to be dismissed as illegitimate (see Maier, 1987, on different forms of representation).

50. Interestingly, American authors such as Badaracco and Yoffie (1983), Schultze (1983, pp. 9–10), and Lawrence (1984, pp. 112–15) usually emphasise the absence of an élite bureaucracy and British authors such as Hare (1985, pp. 112–13) emphasise the hostility between the state and the capitalists as the major obstacles to an effective industrial policy, reflecting the institutional characteristics in their respective countries.

4 Industrial Policy in Action – The Case of Korea

1. The earlier view of Korea as a free-market and free-trade economy is represented by Ranis and Fei, 1975, and Balassa, 1982. Jones and Sakong, 1980, is a seminal work in the alternative explanation, emphasising the role of the state. Luedde-Neurath, 1986, provides a detailed empirical study criticising the free-trade view of Korea. Amsden, 1989, is, to date, the most comprehensive study in this alternative tradition.
2. It is interesting to note that recently one of the authors just quoted, by emphasising the role of 'institutional/organisational changes orchestrated by the governments' of Korea and Taiwan, in effect contradicted his earlier position (see Ranis, 1989).
3. Although there has been more trade liberalisation since Luedde-Neurath's study, all of the following 'invisible' import restrictions are still being imposed, if less widely and less rigorously.
4. For instance, the domestic price of imported scotch whisky, whose tariff was 100 per cent, was over nine times that of the c.i.f. price after the imposition of various inland taxes, for example liquor tax, luxury consumption tax and value added tax (Luedde-Neurath, 1986, p. 130).
5. In other words, '[b]y paying depositors low real interest rates and by controlling capital outflows, the government implicitly taxed depositors, then channelled the proceeds to favoured sectors for investment' (Dornbusch and Park, 1987, p. 418).
6. In 1980 Korea experienced negative growth for the first time since the industrialisation drive began in the early 1960s. For a different interpretation of the early 1980s crisis, see Chang, 1987.
7. This is reminiscent of the situation in Japan during the 1950s and 1960s, when 'only machinery which could not be made in [the country] was allowed to be imported' (Magaziner and Hout, 1980, p. 75).
8. The Korean shipbuilding industry raised its share of world shipbuilding output from nil in 1973 (when the first modern shipyard started production) to 4 per cent in 1980 and then to 21.6 per cent in 1986. This made Korea the second largest shipbuilding nation in the world (next to Japan), producing more ships (in gross tonnes) than Western Europe as a whole, whose world-production share was 12.2 per cent in 1986 (NRI, 1988, pp. 162–4).
9. In Korean newspapers one always reads that 'the government has allowed', and not that 'firm A has decided on', a certain percentage price rise of a product.
10. The most important policy documents include various Five-Year-Plan (FYP) documents and the White Paper on the Economy (WP), produced

annually by the Economic Planning Board (EPB), the planning ministry. The First FYP (1962–6) was issued in 1961 and revised in 1964. Some of the later FYPs, for example, the Fourth and the Sixth, were also revised during the plan period, but the changes were mainly ones of macroeconomic forecasting rather than of policy.

11. For a critique of the dependency view on Korea, see Chang, 1990.
12. WP (1968) states that 'it is needless to say that the attainment or otherwise of efficient scale of production is the most fundamental determinant of productivity' (p. 174).
13. On the same practice in France, see Hall, 1987, p. 167.
14. On the issue of technology assimilation, see Rosenberg, 1982; Abramovitz, 1986; Dore, 1989.
15. Of course this does not necessarily mean that it is impossible to develop a national technological capability by inviting multinationals in. For example Singapore has developed a sophisticated technological capability with a large multinational presence (see Evans, 1987, pp. 208–9). Likewise there has been a substantial technological diffusion through subcontracting by multinationals in the Malaysian electronics industry in Penang (see Rasiah, 1990). The important question then becomes: what kind of policies are necessary to promote technological transfer by multinationals?
16. In the country's earlier period of development, the Japanese state also legislated that no repatriation of earnings or capital would be guaranteed from foreign investment in sectors that were deemed to generate few externalities (for example marketing), and that, even in other industries, repatriation would be guaranteed only when the investment 'contributes to the development of the domestic industry' (Magaziner and Hout, 1980, p. 56).
17. The most important tool of industrial policy in Korea has been policy loans – loans with subsidised interest rates and/or priorities in the (ubiquitous) credit rationing. Policy loans accounted for 57.9 per cent of total bank loans made between 1962 and 1985 (Y. S. Lee et al., 1987, p. 53, table III-1). See 4.5 below for a more detailed discussion of the use of policy loans.
18. The concept of 'basic' industry is also employed in other industrial-policy states such as France and Japan. In early French planning, coal, steel, cement, agricultural machinery, electricity and transportation were identified as 'basic' sectors (Cohen, 1977, p. 86). In Japan the office of MITI that deals with the steel, chemicals and fertiliser industries is called the 'Basic Industries Bureau' (Magaziner and Hout, 1980, p. 34).
19. This is in contrast with the Japanese practice whereby industries become eligible for assistance according to the Structurally Depressed Industries Law only if more than two-thirds of the producers petition MITI (Magaziner and Hout, 1980, p. 40).
20. For details, see Kim, 1989, pp. 36–62; Paik et al., 1988, pp. 46–7; S. H. Lee et al., 1989, pp. 64–73.
21. After the three abovementioned unsuccessful attempts to raise money for the steel mill, the Korean state finally secured funds through war repatriation from the Japanese government and loans from the Japanese

Ex-Im Bank (EPB, 1982, pp. 92–4). Ten years after it started operation, the state-owned steel mill (POSCO) became the fourth largest and one of the most cost-efficient steelmakers in the world (Amsden, 1989, pp. 298–9). The success of the Japanese automobile industry is too obvious to discuss further.

22. On the problem of 'learning', see Rosenberg, 1982; Abramovitz, 1986; Dore, 1989; Amsden and Hikino (forthcoming).

23. On the basis of his theory of prescriptive state intervention, Bhagwati (1988) suggests that 'prescriptive governments provide fewer inducements for such unproductive activities, because the prescriptions leave large areas open for initiatives' (p. 100). Nevertheless prescriptive policy is no less prone to rent-seeking, because the logic of rent-seeking is precisely that even if there are many areas open for private initiatives, individuals will *not* engage in activities in such areas if their rates of return are lower than in unproductive areas. For example it is well known in Korea that obtaining subsidised credits (for example by being a producer in a priority sector) is a very profitable business in itself, because one can divert that money into the curb market where real interest rates are much higher (see Table 4.6).

24. The introduction of limited lifetimes for rationalisation programmes due to the implementation of IDL may be understood as an attempt to make the state-created rents more 'transitory'.

25. For a discussion of the role of bargaining and conflicts in the process of imposition of state discipline on the private sector, see Khan, 1989.

26. In addition to rolling over KHIC's debt (details not released), the state tried to boost its activities by giving it monopoly rights to produce certain power-generation components and certain heavy-construction equipment (*FEER*, 2 June 1983, pp. 67–8).

27. The history of the passenger-car industry characterises how the Korean state shapes up a targeted industry (the following account is based on KDB, 1981, pp. 501–6). The Korean passenger car industry started in 1962 by assembling imported semi-knock-down (SKD) kits. In 1965 there was a state-led merger between the two existing passenger-car makers (Sénara and Shinjin) into one (Shinjin). In 1968 there were two more entries (Hyundai and Asia), and thereafter new entries were banned until 1972, when a lorry producer, Kia, was allowed to enter. In 1974 the government announced the Long-term Plan for Promotion of the Automobile Industry to develop local passenger-car models – at this point producers were still assembling complete-knock-down (CKD) kits from Toyota, Ford, GM and Fiat – and forced Asia, which had failed to submit a plan for the development of its own models, to exit and sell its capacities to Kia. From 1974 local models were developed (Kia's 'Brisa' in 1974, Hyundai's 'Pony' in 1975, GMK's 'Gemini' in 1977). In the meantime Shinjin withdrew from GMK (its joint venture with GM since 1972) due to a sales crisis of the newly introduced Chevrolet models. Shinjin's stake was bought by the state-owned Korea Development Bank (KDB) (hence a KDB–GM joint venture), which

ultimately sold it to Daewoo in 1978 (it has been a GM–Daewoo joint venture since then until 1992). In the 1980 reorganisation of the sector the original plan had been to force Kia to exit and to merge Hyundai and Daewoo, but the plan was dropped because Korean policymakers would not accept Daewoo's wish to abandon its local models in favour of the 'world car' models of GM. The market was maintained as a duopoly between Hyundai and Daewoo until 1987, when Kia was allowed to re-enter.

28. It has to be pointed out that Confucianism in itself is *not* necessarily beneficial to economic development. Its contempt for commercial and industrial pursuits – the merchant and the craftsman occupied the two lowest castes in the traditional Confucian social hierarchy – could have acted as an obstacle to industrialisation. Actually, Confucian contempt for commercial and industrial pursuits was often blamed for the relatively poor Korean economic performance in the 1950s.

29. Korea has traditionally been even more centralised than other Confucian countries. The Japanese feudal system was fairly decentralised until the Meiji Restoration, and the Chinese system, because of the sheer size of the country, had a strong tendency to dissolve into a decentralised one except in the heights of a dynasty.

30. For a comparison of Korea with India, see Datta-Chaudhuri, 1990. For comparisons of Korea with Latin America, see Fishlow, 1990; Shapiro and Taylor, 1990; Hughes and Singh, 1991.

31. Park Chung Hee was a fierce nationalist strongly influenced by corporatist ideas: his education in the Japanese military academy in Manchuria, which he joined after a brief career as a school teacher, left him deeply influenced by the Japanese version of corporatism. Such influence is illustrated well by his naming his 1972 mid-career political coup (to guarantee himself a lifetime presidency) the 'October Restoration', after the Meiji Restoration. Park was also strongly influenced by communism, which played an important role in the Korean nationalist movement during Japanese colonial rule. His brother was an influential local communist leader, and he himself was sentenced to death (but earned an amnesty by publicly denouncing communism) as one of the leaders of a communist mutiny within the Korean army in 1949. His close political aides shared similar ideas. On the debate concerning the fascist nature of Japanese corporatism, see Halliday, 1975, pp. 133–40. On the influence of fascist ideology on the Japanese élite during the interwar period, see Johnson, 1982, ch. 4.

32. With the growing sophistication of the economy, which puts more informational demand on the state, there is a growing recognition among Korean policymakers of the need for decentralisation in economic policy-making. Hence, talk of the government's commitment to the 'private-led economy' in later policy documents (especially the Fifth and Sixth-FYP documents). However such an emphasis, paradoxically, testifies to the persisting dominance of the state – if the economy had already been privately led, no comments of this sort would have been necessary.

33. Short-term working capital, given credit rationing, was mainly provided either by small non-bank financial institutions or by the curb market.
34. For example, in the French case the Planning Commission had to engage in interdepartmental competition with the Ministry of Finance which had 'control over macroeconomic management, the flow of funds and all forms of public spending' (Hall, 1987, p. 172). See Johnson, 1982, p. 256, for the conflict between MITI and the Ministry of Finance in Japan.
35. On the issue of ideological mobilisation in the Korean developmental process, see You and Chang (1993).
36. The average equity participation ratio (as a proportion of total assets) for Korean manufacturing firms was 22.7 per cent during 1971–9 (Cha, 1983, table V-30). For 1986 it was 22.2 per cent, which is even lower than for Japanese firms (28.3 per cent), which are known for their high leverages. Compare this with the 47 per cent for US firms (1986) and the 46.8 per cent for Taiwanese firms (1985) (see Paik *et al.*, 1988, p. 43, table 1–6).
37. 'The government [still] appoints senior bank officials and major credit allocation decisions have traditionally been cleared with government authorities' (*FEER*, 21 April 1988, p. 58).

Conclusion: The Market, the State and Institutions

1. I benefited greatly from discussions with Bob Rowthorn and Richard Wright in clarifying this point.
2. In this respect the following passage by Coase is also illuminating: '[T]he [neoclassical] analysis proceeds in terms of a comparison between a state of laissez faire and some kind of ideal world. This approach inevitably leads to a looseness of thought since the nature of the alternatives being compared is never clear. In a state of laissez faire, is there a monetary, a legal or a political system and if so, what are they? In an ideal world, would there be a monetary, a legal or a political system and if so, what would they be? The answers to all questions are shrouded in mystery and every man is free to draw whatever conclusion he likes. Actually very little analysis is required to show that an ideal world is better than a state of laissez faire, unless the definitions of a state of laissez faire and an ideal world happens to be the same. But the whole discussion is largely irrelevant for questions of economic policy. Since whatever we may have in mind as our ideal world, it is clear that we have not yet discovered how to get to it from where we are. *A better approach would seem to be to start our analysis with a situation approximating that which actually exists, to examine the effects of a proposed policy change and to attempt to decide whether the new institution would be, in total, better or worse than the original one.* In this way, conclusions for policy would have some relevance to the actual situation' [emphasis added] (Coase, 1960, p. 43).

Bibliography

Abramovitz, M. (1986) 'Catching Up, Forging Ahead, and Falling Behind', *Journal of Economic History*, vol. 46, no. 2.
Akerlof, G. and J. Yellen (eds) (1986) *Efficiency Wage Models of the Labour Market* (Cambridge University Press).
Alavi, H. (1972) 'The State in Post-Colonial Societies: Pakistan and Bangladesh', *New Left Review*, no. 74.
Alchian, A. (1950) 'Uncertainty, Evolution and Economic Theory', *Journal of Political Economy*, vol. 58, no. 3.
Alchian, A. and H. Demsetz (1972) 'Production, Information Costs, and Economic Organisation', *American Economic Review*, vol. 62, no. 5.
Alt, J. and K. Shepsle (eds) (1990) *Perspectives on Positive Political Economy*, (Cambridge University Press).
Amadeo, E. and T. Banuri (1991) 'Policy, Governance, and the Management of Conflict', in T. Banuri (ed.), *Economic Liberalisation: No Panacea*, (Oxford: Clarendon Press).
Amsden, A. (1985) 'The State and Taiwan's Economic Development', in P. Evans, D. Rueschemeyer and T. Skocpol (eds), *Bringing the State Back In*, (Cambridge University Press).
Amsden, A. (1989) *Asia's Next Giant* (New York: Oxford University Press).
Amsden, A. and T. Hikino (forthcoming) 'Borrowing Technology or Innovating: An Exploration of Paths of Industrial Development', in R. Thomson (ed.), *Learning and Technological Change* (London and Basingstoke: Macmillan).
Aoki, M., B. Gustafsson and O. Williamson (eds) (1990) *The Firm as a Nexus of Treaties* (London: Sage Publications).
Armstrong, P., A. Glyn and J. Harrison (1991) *Capitalism since 1945* (Oxford: Basil Blackwell).
Arrow, K. (1974) *The Limits of Organisation* (New York and London: W. W. Norton).
Axelrod, R. (1984) *The Evolution of Co-operation* (New York: Basic Books).
Badaracco, J. and D. Yoffie (1983) '"Industrial Policy": It Can't Happen Here', *Harvard Business Review*, Nov./Dec..
Balassa, B. (1982) 'Development Strategies and Economic Performance', in B. Balassa et al., *Development Strategies in Semi-Industrial Economies* (Baltimore: Johns Hopkins University Press).
Balassa, B. (1985) 'French Industrial Policy under the Socialist Government', *American Economic Review*, vol. 75, no. 2.
Balassa, B. (1988) 'The Lessons of East Asian Development: An Overview', *Economic Development and Cultural Changes*, vol. 36, no. 3 (Apr.), Supplement.
Balassa, B. and H. Giersch (eds) (1986) *Economic Incentives* (London and Basingstoke: Macmillan).

Bardhan, P. (1984) *The Political Economy of Development in India* (Oxford: Basil Blackwell).
Baumol, W. (1965) *Welfare Economics and the Theory of the State*, 2nd edition (London: London School of Economics).
Baumol, W. (1990) 'Entrepreneurship: Productive, Unproductive, and Destructive' *Journal of Political Economy*, vol. 98, no. 5.
Baumol, W., S. Blackman and E. Wolff (1989) *Productivity and American Leadership* (Cambridge, Mass: MIT Press).
Bell, M., B. Ross-Larson and L. Westphal (1984) 'Assessing the Performance of Infant Industries', *Journal of Development Economics*, nos 1/2.
Berlin, I. (1969) 'Two Concepts of Liberty', in *Four Essays on Liberty* (Oxford University Press).
Best, M. (1990) *The New Competition* (Cambridge: Polity Press).
Bhagwati, J. (1985) 'Foreign Trade Regimes', in J. Bhagwati, *Dependence and Interdependence* (Oxford: Basil Blackwell).
Bhagwati, J. (1987) 'Outward Orientation: Trade Issues' in V. Corbo, M. Khan and M. Goldstein (eds), *Growth-Oriented Structural Adjustment* (Washington DC: IMF and World Bank).
Bhagwati, J. (1988) *Protectionism* (Cambridge, Mass: MIT Press).
Bhagwati, J. (1989) 'U.S. Trade Policy at Crossroads', *The World Economy*, vol. 12, no. 4.
Blackaby, F. (ed.) (1979) *De-Industrialisation* (London: Gower).
Bobbio, N. (1987) *The Future of Democracy*, translated by R. Griffin (Cambridge: Polity Press).
BOK (Bank of Korea) (1987) *National Accounts* (Seoul: BOK).
BOK (Bank of Korea) (1988) *Economic Statistics Yearbook 1988* (Seoul: BOK).
Boltho, A. (1985) 'Was Japan's Industrial Policy Successful?', *Cambridge Journal of Economics*, vol. 9. no. 2.
Boss, H. (1990) *Theories of Surplus and Transfer* (Boston: Unwin Hyman).
Bowles, S. (1985) 'The Production Process in a Competitive Equilibrium: Walrasian, Neo-Hobbesian, and Marxian Models', *American Economic Review*, vol. 75, no.1.
Bowles, S. and H. Gintis (1990) 'Contested Exchange: New Microfoundations for the Political Economy of Capitalism', *Politics and Society*, vol. 18, no. 2.
Braverman, H. (1974) *Labour and Monopoly Capital* (New York: Monthly Review Books).
Brennan, G. and J. Buchanan (1985) *Reason of Rules* (Cambridge University Press).
Bruno, M. and J. Sachs (1985) *Economics of Worldwide Stagflation* (Cambridge, Mass: Harvard University Press).
Brus, W. (1972) *The Market in a Socialist Economy* (London: Routledge & Kegan Paul).
Brus, W. and K. Laski (1989) *From Marx to the Market* (Oxford: Clarendon Press).
Buchanan, J. (1980a) 'Rent Seeking and Profit Seeking', in J. Buchanan, R. Tollison and G. Tullock (eds), *Towards a Theory of the Rent-Seeking Society* (College Station: Texas A&M University Press).

Buchanan, J. (1980b) 'Reform in the Rent-Seeking Society in J. Buchanan, R. Tollison and G. Tullock (eds), *Towards a Theory of the Rent-Seeking Society* (College Station: Texas A&M University Press).

Buchanan, J. (1986) 'Contractarianism and Democracy', in J. Buchanan, *Liberty, Market and State* (Brighton: Wheatsheaf Books).

Buchanan, J. et al. (1978) *The Economics of Politics* (London: The Institute of Economic Affairs).

Buchanan, J., R. Tollison and G. Tullock (eds) (1980) *Toward a Theory of the Rent-Seeking Society* (College Station: Texas A&M University Press).

Burton, J. (1983) *Picking Losers ... ? The Political Economy of Industrial Policy* (London: Institute of Economic Affairs).

Cairncross, A., J. Kay and Z. Silberston (1983) 'Problems of Industrial Recovery', in R. Matthews and J. Sargent (eds), *Contemporary Problems of Economic Policy* (London: Methuen).

Cha, D. S. (1983) Öja Do-ip ui Hyokkwa Boonsok (The Effects of Foreign Capital Inflow) (Seoul: Korea Institute for Economics and Technology [KIET]).

Chandler, A. (1962) *Strategy and Structure* (Cambridge, Mass: MIT Press).

Chang, H-J. (1987) 'Crisis of Capital Accumulation in South Korea, 1979-82 — An Analysis of Policy Solutions', unpublished M. Phil. dissertation, Faculty of Economics and Politics, University of Cambridge.

Chang, H-J. (1990) 'Interpreting the Korean Experience - Heaven or Hell?', research paper series, no. 42, Faculty of Economics and Politics, University of Cambridge.

Chang, H-J. and A. Singh (1993) 'Public Enterprise in Developing Countries and Economic Efficiency', *UNCTAD Review*, no. 4.

Coase, R. (1937) 'The Nature of the Firm', *Economica*, Nov.

Coase, R. (1960) 'The Problem of Social Cost', *Journal of Law and Economics*.

Coase, R. (1988) 'The Firm, the Market, and the Law', in *The Firm, the Market, and the Law* (University of Chicago Press).

Cohen, S. (1977) *Modern Capitalist Planning: The French Model*, 2nd edition, (Berkeley: University of California Press).

Cohen, S. and J. Zysman (1987) *Manufacturing Matters* (New York: Basic Books).

Colander, D. (ed.) (1984) *Neoclassical Political Economy* (Cambridge, Mass: Ballinger Publishing).

Cole, D. and Y. Park (1983) *Financial Development in Korea, 1945-78* (Cambridge, Mass: Harvard University Press).

Congleton, R. (1980) 'Competitive Process, Competitive Waste, and Institutions', in J. Buchanan, R. Tollison and G. Tullock (eds), *Towards a Theory of the Rent-Seeking Society* (College Station: Texas A&M University Press).

Corden, W. (1980) 'Relationships between Macro-economic and Industrial Policies', *The World Economy*, vol. 3, no. 2.

Cox, A. (ed.) (1986) *State, Finance, and Industry in Comparative Perspective* (Brighton: Wheatsheaf Books).

Cullis, J. and P. Jones (1987) *Microeconomics and the Public Economy: A Defence of Leviathan* (Oxford: Basil Blackwell).

Cumings, B. (1987) 'The Origins and Development of the Northeast Asian Political Economy: Industrial Sectors, Product Cycles, and Political Consequences', in F. Deyo (ed.), *The Political Economy of the New Asian Industrialism* (Ithaca: Cornell University Press).

Dahlman, C. (1979) 'The Problem of Externality', *Journal of Law and Economics*, vol. 22, no. 1.

Dahmén, E. (1988) '"Development Blocks" in Industrial Economics', *Scandinavian Economic History Review*, vol. 36, no. 1.

Datta-Chaudhuri, M. (1990) 'Market Failure and Government Failure', *Journal of Economic Perspectives*, vol. 4, no. 3.

David, P. (1985) 'Clio and the Economics of QWERTY', *American Economic Review* vol. 75, no. 2.

Dawkins, R. (1986) *The Blind Watchmaker* (Harmondsworth: Penguin Books).

Deane, P. (1989) *The State and the Economic System* (Oxford University Press).

Demsetz, H. (1964) 'The Exchange and Enforcement of Property Rights', *Journal of Law and Economics*, vol.7.

Demsetz, H. (1982) *Economic, Legal, and Political Dimensions of Competition* (Amsterdam: North-Holland).

Deyo, F. (ed.) (1987) *The Political Economy of the New Asian Industrialism* (Ithaca and London: Cornell University Press).

Dobb, M. (1925) *Capitalist Enterprise and Social Progress* (London: George Routledge & Sons).

Dobb, M. (1970) *Socialist Planning: Some Problems* (London: Lawrence & Wishart).

Dobb, M. (1974) 'Some Reflections on Market and Planning in Historical Perspective', in C. Abramsky (ed.), *Essays in Honour of E. H. Carr* (London and Basingstoke: Macmillan).

Donges, J. (1980) 'Industrial Policies in West Germany's Not So Market-oriented Economy', *The World Economy*, vol. 3, no. 2.

Dore, R. (1986) *Flexible Rigidities: Industrial Policy and Structural Adjustment in the Japanese Economy 1970–80* (London: The Athlone Press).

Dore, R. (1987) *Taking Japan Seriously* (London: The Athlone Press).

Dore, R. (1989) 'Latecomers' Problems', *European Journal of Development Research*, vol. 1, no. 1.

Dornbusch, R. and Y. Park (1987) 'Korean Growth Policy', *Brookings Papers on Economic Activity*, no. 2.

Dornbusch, R., Poterba, J. and Summers, L. (1988) 'Macroeconomic Policy Should Make Manufacturing More Competitive', *Harvard Business Review*, Nov./Dec.

Dosi, G., C. Freeman, R. Nelson, G. Silverberg and L. Soete (eds) (1988) *Technical Change and Economic Theory* (London: Pinter Publishers).

Duchêne, F. and G. Shepherd (eds) (1987) *Managing Industrial Change in Western Europe* (London: Frances Pinter).

Eatwell, J. (1982) 'Competition', in I. Bradley and M. Howard (eds), *Classical and Marxian Political Economy* (London: Macmillan).

Eggertsson, T. (1990) *Economic Behaviour and Institutions* (Cambridge University Press).

EIU (Economist Intelligence Unit) (1991) *South Korea – Country Report*, no. 2.

Ellman, M. (1989) *Socialist Planning*, 2nd edition (Cambridge University Press).
Elster, J. (1983) *Sour Grapes* (Cambridge University Press).
Elster, J. (1984) *Making Sense of Marx* (Cambridge University Press).
Elster, J. (1989) *The Cement of Society* (Cambridge University Press).
EPB (Economic Planning Board) (1982) *Gaebal Nyondae ui Gyong-jé Jonngchek* (Economic Policy in the Developmental Period) (Seoul: EPB).
EPB (Economic Planning Board) (1989) *Major Statistics of Korean Economy 1989* (Seoul: EPB).
Evans, P. (1987) 'Class, State, and Dependence in East Asia: Lessons for Latin Americanists' in F. Deyo (ed.), *The Political Economy of the New Asian Industrialism* (Ithaca: Cornell University Press).
Evans, P., Rueschemeyer, D. and Skocpol, T. (eds), 1985, *Bringing the State Back In* (Cambridge University Press).
Farrell, J. (1987) 'Information and the Coase Theorem', *Journal of Economic Perspectives*, vol. 1, no. 4.
FEER (Far Eastern Economic Review), various issues.
Findlay, R. (1988) 'Trade, State, and Development', in G. Ranis and T. Schultz (eds), *The State of Development Economics* (Oxford: Basil Blackwell).
Findlay, R. (1990) 'New Political Economy', *Economics and Politics*, vol. 2, no. 2.
Fine, B. and L. Harris (1979) *Rereading Capital* (London and Basingstoke: Macmillan).
Fisher, F. (1985) 'The Social Costs of Monopoly and Regulation: Posner Reconsidered', *Journal of Political Economy*, vol. 93, no. 2.
Fishlow, A. (1990) 'The Latin American State', *Journal of Economic Perspectives*, vol. 4, no. 3.
Fransman, M. (1986) *Technology and Economic Development* (Brighton: Wheatsheaf).
Freeden, M. (1991) *Rights* (Milton Keynes: Open University Press).
Freeman, C. (1989) 'New Technology and Catching Up', *European Journal of Development Research*, vol. 1, no. 1.
Friedman, M. (1962) *Capitalism and Freedom* (Chicago and London: University of Chicago Press).
Fudenberg, D. and J. Tirole (1986) 'A Theory of Exit in Duopoly', *Econometrica*, vol. 54, no. 4.
FYP (Five Year Plan), various years (Seoul: Republic of Korea Government).
Gamble, A. (1988) *The Free Economy and the Strong State: The Politics of Thatcherism* (London and Basingstoke: Macmillan).
Gerschenkron, A. (1966) *Economic Backwardness in Historical Perspective* (Cambridge, Mass: Belknap Press).
Ghemawat, P. and B. Nalebuff (1985). 'Exit', *The Rand Journal of Economics*, vol. 16, no. 2.
Goldthorpe, J. (ed.) (1984) *Order and Conflict in Contemporary Capitalism* (Oxford University Press).
Goodin, R. (1986) 'Laundering Preferences', in J. Elster and A. Hylland (eds), *Foundations of Social Choice Theory* (Cambridge University Press).

Gough, I. (1979) *The Political Economy of the Welfare State* (London and Basingstoke: Macmillan).

Gould, S. (1983) *The Panda's Thumb*, (Harmondsworth: Penguin Books).

Gramsci, A. (1988) *A Gramsci Reader*, edited by D. Forgacs (London: Lawrence & Wishart).

Green, F. (ed.) (1990) *Restructuring the British Economy* (London: Routledge).

Grossman, G. (1988) 'Strategic Export Promotion: A Critique', in P. Krugman (ed.), *Strategic Trade Policy and the New International Economics* (Cambridge, Mass: MIT Press).

Hadley, E. (1989) 'The Diffusion of Keynesian Ideas in Japan', in P. Hall (ed.), *The Political Power of Economic Ideas: Keynesianism Across Nations* (Princeton University Press).

Hall, P. (1987) *Governing the Economy* (Cambridge: Polity Press).

Hall, P. (ed.) (1989) *The Political Power of Economic Ideas: Keynesianism across Nations*, (Princeton University Press).

Halliday, J. (1975) *A Political History of Japanese Capitalism* (New York: Monthly Review Books).

Halliday, J. (1980) 'Capitalism and Socialism in East Asia', *New Left Review*, no. 124.

Hamilton, C. (1983) 'Capitalist Industrialisation in East Asia's Four Little Tigers', *Journal of Contemporary Asia*, vol. 13, no.1.

Hardin, R. (1982) *Collective Action* (Baltimore: Johns Hopkins University Press).

Hare, P. (1985) *Planning the British Economy* (London and Basingstoke: Macmillan).

Hargreaves Heap, S. (1989) *Rationality in Economics* (Oxford: Basil Blackwell).

Harris, L. (1987) 'Financial Reform and Economic Growth: A New Interpretation of South Korea's Experience', in L. Harris (ed.), *New Perspectives on the Financial System* (London: Croom Helm).

Hayek, F. (1949a) 'Economics and Knowledge', in F. Hayek, *Individualism and Economic Order* (London: Routledge & Kegan Paul).

Hayek, F. (1949b) 'The Meaning of Competition', in F. Hayek, *Individualism and Economic Order* (London: Routledge & Kegan Paul).

Hayek, F. (1949c) 'The Use of Knowledge in Society', in F. Hayek, *Individualism and Economic Order* (London: Routledge & Kegan Paul).

Hayek, F. (1972) *The Road to Serfdom* (London: Routledge & Kegan Paul).

Hayek, F. (1978) 'Competition as a Discovery Procedure', in F. Hayek, *New Studies in Philosophy, Politics, Economics and the History of Ideas* (London: Routledge & Kegan Paul).

Hayek, F. (1988) *The Fatal Conceit – The Errors of Socialism* (London: Routledge & Kegan Paul).

Hayward, J. (1986) *The State and the Market Economy* (Brighton: Wheatsheaf Books).

Heiner, R. (1983) 'The Origin of Predictable Behaviour', *American Economic Review*, vol. 73, no. 4.

Heiner, R. (1988) 'Imperfect Decisions and Routinised Production: Implications for Evolutionary Modeling and Inertial Technical Change' in G. Dosi, C. Freeman, R. Nelson, G. Silverberg and L. Soete (eds), *Technical Change and Economic Theory* (London: Pinter Publishers).

Hindess, B. (1987) *Politics and Class Analysis* (Oxford: Basil Blackwell).
Hirsch, F. (1978) 'The State Apparatus and Social Reproduction: Elements of A Theory of the Bourgeois State', in J. Holloway and S. Picciotto (eds), *State and Capital* (London: Edward Arnold).
Hirschman, A. (1958) *The Strategy of Economic Development* (New Haven and London: Yale University Press).
Hirschman, A. (1970) *Exit, Voice, and Loyalty* (Cambridge, Mass: Harvard University Press).
Hirschman, A. (1982) *Shifting Involvements* (Princeton University Press).
Hodgson, G. (1988) *Economics and Institutions* (Cambridge: Polity Press).
Hughes, A. and A. Singh (1991) 'The World Economic Slowdown and the Asian and Latin American Economies: A Comparative Analysis of Economic Structure, Policy, and Performance', in T. Banuri (ed.), *Economic Liberalisation: No Panacea* (Oxford: Clarendon Press).
Ito, K. (1984) 'Development Finance and Commercial Banks in Korea', *The Developing Economies*, vol. 22, no. 4.
Jacquemin, A. (ed.) (1984) *European Industry: Public Policy and Corporate Strategy* (Oxford: Clarendon Press).
Jessop, B. (1982) *The Capitalist State* (Oxford: Basil Blackwell).
Johnson, B. and B. Lundvall (1989) 'Limits of the Pure Market Economy', in *Samhällsventenskap, Ekonomi och Historia – Festskrift till Lars Harlitz* (Göteborg: Daidalos).
Johnson, C. (1982) *MITI and the Japanese Miracle* (Stanford University Press).
Johnson, C. (1984) 'Introduction: The Idea of Industrial Policy', in C. Johnson (ed.), *The Industrial Policy Debate* (San Francisco: Institute for Contemporary Studies).
Johnson, C. (ed.) (1984) *The Industrial Policy Debate* (San Francisco: Institute for Contemporary Studies).
Jones, L. and E. S. Mason (1982) 'Role of Economic Factors in Determining the Size and Structure of the Public-enterprise Sector in Less-developed Countries with Mixed Economies' in L. Jones (ed.), *Public Enterprise in Less-developed Countries* (Cambridge University Press).
Jones, L. and I. Sakong (1980) *Government, Business and Entrepreneurship in Economic Development: The Korean Case* (Cambridge, Mass: Harvard University Press).
Jorde, T. and D. Teece (1990) 'Innovation and Cooperation: Implications for Competition and Antitrust', *Journal of Economic Perspectives*, vol. 4, no. 3.
Kaldor, N. (1985) *Economics without Equilibrium* (Cardiff: University College of Cardiff Press).
Katzenstein, P. (1985) *Small States in World Markets* (Ithaca: Cornell University Press).
KDB (Korea Development Bank) (1981) *Palship Nyondae ui Jonryak Sanup* (Strategic Industries of the 1980s) (Seoul: KDB).
Khan, M. A. (1987) 'Perfect Competition', in *The Palgrave Dictionary of Economics*, vol. 3 (London: Macmillan).
Khan, M. H. (1989) 'Clientelism, Corruption, and Capitalist Development: An Analysis of State Intervention with special reference to Bangladesh', unpublished Ph. D. thesis, Faculty of Economics and Politics, University of Cambridge.

Kim, J. H. (1989) 'Korean Industrial Policies for Declining Industries', Korea Development Institute (KDI) working paper no. 8910 (Seoul: KDI).

King, D. (1987) *The New Right: Politics, Markets and Citizenship* (London and Basingstoke: Macmillan).

Kirzkowski, H. (ed.) (1984) *Monopolistic Competition and International Trade* (Oxford University Press).

Kirzner, I. (1973) *Competition and Entrepreneurship* (University of Chicago Press).

Kitching, G. (1983) *Rethinking Socialism: A Theory for a Better Practice* (London: Methuen).

Knight, F. (1921) *Risk, Uncertainty, and Profit* (University of Chicago Press).

Koopmans, T. (1957) 'The Construction of Economic Knowledge', in *Three Essays on the State of Economic Science* (New York: McGraw-Hill Books).

Korpi, W. (1983) *The Democratic Class Struggle* (London: Routledge & Kegan Paul).

Krueger, A. (1974) 'The Political Economy of the Rent-Seeking Society', *American Economic Review*, vol. 64, no. 3.

Krueger, A. (1980) 'Trade Policy as an Input to Development', *American Economic Review*, vol. 70, Papers and proceedings.

Krueger, A. (1990) 'Government Failure in Economic Development', *Journal of Economic Perspective*, vol. 4, no. 3.

Krugman, P. (1984) 'The U.S. Response to Foreign Industrial Targeting', *Brookings Papers on Economic Activity*, no. 1.

Krugman, P. (ed.) (1988) *Strategic Trade Policy and the New International Economics* (Cambridge, Mass: MIT Press).

Kuisel, R. (1981) *Capitalism and the State in Modern France: Renovation and Economic Management in the Twentieth Century*, (Cambridge University Press).

Laffont, J-J. (1988) *Fundamentals of Public Economics*, translated by J. Bonin and H. Bonin (Cambridge, Mass: MIT Press).

Laffont, J-J. and J. Tirole (1988) 'The Politics of Government Decision-making: A Theory of Regulatory Capture', working paper, no. 506, Department of Economics, MIT.

Lal, D. (1983) *The Poverty of Development Economics* (London: Institute of Economic Affairs).

Landes, D. (1990) 'Why are we so rich and they so poor?', *American Economic Review*, vol. 80, no. 2.

Landesmann, M. (1992) 'Industrial Policies and Social Corporatism', in J. Pekkarinen, M. Pohjola and B. Rowthorn (eds), *Social Corporatism* (Oxford: Clarendon Press).

Langlois, R. (1986a) 'The New Institutional Economics: An Introductory Essay', in R. Langlois (ed.), *Economics as a Process* (Cambridge University Press).

Langlois, R. (1986b) 'Rationality, Institutions, and Explanation', in R. Langlois (ed.), *Economics as a Process* (Cambridge University Press).

Langlois, R. (ed.) (1986) *Economics as a Process* (Cambridge University Press).

Lavoie, D. (1985) *Rivalry and Central Planning* (Cambridge University Press).

Lawrence, R. (1984) *Can America Compete?* (Washington DC: Brookings Institution).

Lee, S. H. (1985) '*Gookka, kyegup mit jabon chookjok*' (The state, classes and capital accumulation), in J. J. Choi (ed.), *Hangook jabonjui wa gookka* (Korean Capitalism and the State) (Seoul: Hanwool).

Lee, S. H., S. D. Kim and S. H. Hahn (1989) *Hangook ui Sanup Jongchek – Sanup Goojo Jongchek Gwanryon Jaryojip* (Korean Industrial Policy – Policies concerning Industrial Structure) (Seoul: Korea Institute for Economics and Technology).

Lee, Y. S., J. H. Lee and D. H. Kim (1987) *Sanup Goomyoong Jongchek ui Hyoyool-hwa Bang-ahn* (A Proposal for Improving the Efficiency of Industrial Financial Policy) (Seoul: Korea Institute for Economics and Technology).

Leibenstein, H. (1966) 'Allocative Efficiency vs X-Efficiency', *American Economic Review*, vol. 56, no. 3.

Leipziger, D. (1988) 'Industrial Restructuring in Korea', *World Development*, vol. 16, no. 1.

Leijonhufvud, A. (1981) 'The Wicksell Connection: Variations on A Theme', in *Information and Coordination* (New York: Oxford University Press).

Lim, H-C. (1985) *Dependent Development in Korea*, (Seoul National University Press).

Lindbeck, A. (1981) 'Industrial Policy as an Issue in the Economic Environment', *The World Economy*, vol. 4, no. 4.

Lippincott, B. (ed.) (1938) *On the Economic Theory of Socialism* (Minneapolis: University of Minnesota Press).

Lipsey, R. and K. Lancaster (1956) 'General Theory of the Second Best', *Review of Economic Studies*, vol. 24, no. 63.

Little, I. (1982) *Economic Development* (New York: Basic Books).

Littlechild, S. (1981) 'Misleading Calculations of the Social Costs of Monopoly Power', *Economic Journal*, vol. 91, no. 2.

LO (Landsorganisationen i Sverige) (1963) *Economic Expansion and Structural Change*, edited and translated by T. Johnston (London: George Allen and Unwin).

Luedde-Neurath, R. (1986) *Import Controls and Export-Oriented Development; A Reassessment of the South Korean Case* (Boulder and London: Westview Press).

Luedde-Neurath, R. (1988) 'State Intervention and Exported-Oriented Development in South Korea', in G. White (ed.), *Development States in East Asia* (London: Macmillan).

Maddison, A. (1989) *The World Economy in the 20th Century* (Paris: OECD).

Magaziner, I. and T. Hout (1980) *Japanese Industrial Policy* (London: Policy Studies Institute).

Maier, C. (1987) *In Search of Stability* (Cambridge University Press).

Mandel, E. (1975) *Late Capitalism* (London: New Left Books).

March, J. and H. Simon (1958) *Organisations* (New York: John Wiley & Sons).

Marglin, S. (1974) 'What do Bosses do?', *Review of Radical Political Economy*, vol. 6, no. 2.

Marglin, S. and J. Schor (eds), (1990) *The Golden Age of Capitalism* (Oxford: Clarendon Press).

Marx, K. (1934) *The Eighteenth Brumaire of Louis Bonaparte* (Moscow: Progress Publishers).

Marx, K. (1976) *Capital*, vol. 1 (Harmondsworth: Penguin Books).

Marx, K. (1981) *Capital*, vol. 3 (Harmondsworth: Penguin Books).

Matthews, R. (1986) 'The Economics of Institutions and the Source of Growth', *Economic Journal*, vol. 96, no. 4.

Maynard Smith, J. (1982) *Evolution and the Theory of Games* (Cambridge University Press).

McCormick, R. and R. Tollison (1981) *Politicians, Legislation, and the Economy* (Boston: Martinus Nijhoff Publishing).

McLellan, D. (1986) *Ideology* (Milton Keynes: Open University Press).

McNulty, P. (1968) 'Economic Theory and the Meaning of Competition', *Quarterly Journal of Economics*, vol. 82, no. 4.

McPherson, M. (1984) 'Limits of Self-Seeking: The Role of Morality in Economic Life', in D. Colander (ed.), *Neoclassical Political Economy* (Cambridge, Mass: Ballinger Publishing).

Michell, T. (1982) 'South Korea: Vision of the Future for Labour Surplus Economies?', in M. Bienefeld and M. Godfrey (eds), *The Struggle for Development: National Strategies in International Context* (New York: John Wiley & Sons).

Milgrom, P. and Roberts, J. (1990) 'Bargaining Costs, Influence Costs, and the Organisation of Economic Activity', in J. Alt and K. Shepsle (eds), *Perspectives on Positive Political Economy* (Cambridge University Press).

Miliband, R. (1969) *The State in Capitalist Society* (London: Quartet Books).

Mises, L. (1929) 'Interventionism' in L. Mises, *A Critique of Interventionism*, translated by H. Sennholz (1977) (New Rochelle, NY: Arlington House).

Mises, L. (1979) *Economic Policy* (Chicago: Regnery Gateway).

Mishan, E. (1982) *Introduction to Political Economy* (London: Hutchinson).

Mohammad, S. and J. Whalley (1984) 'Rent Seeking in India: Its Costs and Policy Significance', *Kyklos*, vol. 37, no. 3.

Morris-Suzuki, T. (1989) *A History of Japanese Economic Thought* (London and New York: Routledge).

Mueller, D. (1979) *Public Choice* (Cambridge University Press).

Musgrave, R. and P. Musgrave (1984) *Public Finance in Theory and Practice*, 4th edition (New York: McGraw Hill).

Nath, S. K. (1973) *A Perspective on Welfare Economics* (London and Basingstoke: Macmillan).

NEDO (National Economic Development Office) (1978) *Competition Policy* (London: HMSO).

Nelson, R. (1981) 'Assessing Private Enterprise: An Exegesis of Tangled Doctrine', *The Bell Journal of Economics*, vol. 12, no. 1.

Nelson, R. (1986) 'Incentives for Entrepreneurship and Supporting Institutions', in B. Balassa and H. Giersch (eds), *Economic Incentives* (London and Basingstoke: Macmillan).

Nelson, R. (1991) 'Diffusion of Development: Post-World War II Convergence Among Advanced Industrial Nations', *American Economic Review*, vol. 81, no. 2.

Nelson, R. and L. Soete (1988) 'Policy Conclusions', in G. Dosi, C. Freeman, R. Nelson, G. Silverberg and L. Soete (eds), *Technical Change and Economic Theory* (London: Pinter Publishers).

Nelson, R. and S. Winter (1982) *An Evolutionary Theory of Economic Change* (Cambridge, Mass: Belknap Press).

Niskanen, W. (1973) *Bureaucracy: Servant or Master?* (London: Institute of Economic Affairs).

North, D. (1981) *Structure and Change in Economic History* (New York: W. W. Norton).

North, D. (1990a) 'Institutions, Transaction Costs, and Exchange', in J. Alt and K. Shepsle (eds), *Perspectives on Positive Political Economy* (Cambridge University Press).

North, D. (1990b) *Institutions, Institutional Change and Economic Performance* (Cambridge University Press).

Norton, R. (1986) 'Industrial Policy and American Renewal', *Journal of Economic Literature*, vol. 24, no. 1.

Nozick, R. (1974) *Anarchy, Utopia and the State* (Oxford: Basil Blackwell).

NRI (Nomura Research Institute) (1988) *Sekai ni Hiyakusuru Kankoku Sangyo* (Korean Industries are Joining the World Class) (Tokyo: NRI) (Korean language edition: Seoul, Panmun Book Company).

Oakland, W. (1987) 'Theory of Public Goods', in A. Auerbach and M. Feldstein (eds), *Handbook of Public Economics*, vol. II, (Amsterdam: Elsevier).

O'Connor, J. (1973) *The Fiscal Crisis of the State* (New York: St. Martin's Press).

O'Driscoll, G. (1986) 'Competition as a Process: a Law and Economics Perspective in R. Langlois (ed.), *Economics as a Process* (Cambridge University Press).

OECD (Organisation for Economic Cooperation and Development) (1989) *Industrial Policy in OECD Countries; Annual Review 1989* (Paris: OECD).

Okimoto, D. (1989) *Between MITI and the Market: Japanese Industrial Policy for High Technology* (Stanford University Press).

Olson, M. (1965) *The Logic of Collective Action* (Cambridge, Mass: Harvard University Press).

Pagano, U. (1985) *Work and Welfare in Economic Theory* (Oxford: Basil Blackwell).

Paik, N. K., S. I. Chang and D. H. Lee (1988) *Hangook ui Sanup Jongcheck – Sanup Jojick Jongchek Gwanryon Jaryojip* (Industrial Organisation Policies of Korea) (Seoul: Korea Institute for Economics and Technology).

Panitch, L. (1981) 'Trade Union and the Capitalist State', *New Left Review*, no. 125.

Parker, G. and J. Maynard Smith (1990) 'Optimality Theory in Evolutionary Biology', *Nature*, vol. 348, 1 Nov.

Peacock, A. (1979a) 'The Limitations of Public Goods Theory: The Lighthouse Revisited', in A. Peacock, *The Economic Analysis of Government* (Oxford: Martin Robertson).

Peacock, A. (1979b) 'Appraising Government Expenditure: A Simple Economic Analysis', in A. Peacock, *The Economic Analysis of Government* (Oxford: Martin Robertson).

Peacock, A. and C. Rowley (1979a) 'Welfare Economics and the Public Regulation of Natural Monopoly', in A. Peacock, *The Economic Analysis of Government* (Oxford: Martin Robertson).

Peacock, A. and C. Rowley (1979b) 'Pareto Optimality and the Political Economy of Liberalism', in A. Peacock, *The Economic Analysis of Government* (Oxford: Martin Robertson).

Pekkarinen, J., M. Pohjola and B. Rowthorn (eds) (1992) *Social Corporatism* (Oxford: Clarendon Press).

Pelikan, P. (1988) 'Can the Innovative System of Capitalism be Outperformed?' in G. Dosi, C. Freeman, R. Nelson, G. Silverberg and L. Soete (eds), *Technical Change and Economic Theory* (London: Pinter Publishers).

Peltzman, S. (1976) 'Toward a More General Theory of Regulation', *Journal of Law and Economics*, vol. 19.

Pinder, J. (1982) 'Causes and Kinds of Industrial Policy', in J. Pinder (ed.), *National Industrial Strategies and the World Economy* (London: Croom Helm).

Poggi, G. (1990) *The State: Its Nature, Development and Prospect* (Cambridge: Polity Press).

Polanyi, K. (1957) *The Great Transformation* (Boston: Beacon Press).

Pontusson, J. (1987) 'Radicalisation and Retreat in Swedish Social Democracy', *New Left Review*, no. 165.

Popkin, S. (1979) *The Rational Peasant* (Los Angeles and Berkeley: University of California Press).

Porter, M. (1990) *Competitive Advantage of the Nations* (London and Basingstoke: Macmillan).

Posner, R. (1975) 'The Social Costs of Monopoly and Regulation', *Journal of Political Economy*, vol. 83, no.4.

Price, V. (1980) 'Alternatives to Delayed Structural Adjustment in "Workshop Europe"', *The World Economy*, vol. 3, no. 2.

Putterman, L. (1986) 'The Economic Nature of the Firm: An Overview', in L. Putterman (ed.), *The Economic Nature of the Firm* (Cambridge University Press).

Putterman, L. (ed.) (1986) *The Economic Nature of the Firm* (Cambridge University Press).

Putterman, L. (1990) *Division of Labour and Welfare* (Oxford University Press).

Ranis, G. (1989) 'The Role of Institutions in Transition Growth: The East Asian Newly Industrialising Countries', *World Development*, vol. 17, no. 9.

Ranis, G. and J. Fei (1975) 'A Model of Growth and Employment in the Open Dualistic Economy: The Cases of Korea and Taiwan', in F. Stewart (ed.), *Employment, Income Distribution and Development* (London: Frank Cass)

Rasiah, R. (1990) 'Electronics Industry in Penang', mimeo., Faculty of Economics and Politics, University of Cambridge.

Rasmusen, E. (1989) *Games and Information* (Oxford: Basil Blackwell).

Reich, R. (1982) 'Why the U.S. Needs an Industrial Policy', *Harvard Business Review*, Jan./Feb.

Renshaw, J. (1986) *Adjustment and Economic Performance in Industrialised Countries* (Geneva: ILO).

Richardson, G. B. (1960) *Information and Investment* (Oxford University Press).

Bibliography

Richardson, G. B. (1971) 'Planning versus Competition', *Soviet Studies*, vol. 22, no. 3.

Richardson, G. B. (1972) 'The Organisation of Industry', *Economic Journal*, vol. 82, no. 3.

Robbins, L. (1932) *An Essay on the Nature and Significance of Economic Science* (London: Macmillan).

Rogerson, W. (1982) 'The Social Costs of Monopoly and Regulation: A Game-theoretic Approach', *The Bell Journal of Economics*, vol. 13, no. 2.

Rosenberg, N. (1976) *Perspectives on Technology* (Cambridge University Press).

Rosenberg, N. (1982) 'The International Transfer of Technology: Implications for the Industrialised Countries', in *Inside the Black Box: Technology and Economics* (Cambridge University Press).

Rosenberg, N. and L. Birdzell (1986) *How the West Grew Rich* (London: I. B. Tauris).

Rowley, C. (1983) 'The Political Economy of the Public Sector', in B. Jones (ed.), *Perspectives on Political Economy* (London: Frances Pinter).

Rowthorn, B. (1990) 'Wage Dispersion and Employment: Theories and Evidence', Department of Applied Economics working paper, no. 9001, Department of Applied Economics, University of Cambridge.

Rowthorn, B. and A. Glyn (1990) 'The Diversity of Unemployment Experience since 1973', in S. Marglin and J. Schor (eds), *The Golden Age of Capitalism* (Oxford: Clarendon Press).

Rowthorn, B. and J. Wells (1987) *Foreign Trade and De-Industrialisation* (Cambridge University Press).

Sachs, J. (1987) 'Trade and Exchange Rate Policies in Growth-Oriented Adjustment Programs', in V. Corbo, M. Khan and M. Goldstein (eds), *Growth-Oriented Structural Adjustment* (Washington DC: IMF and World Bank).

Salter, W. (1960) *Productivity and Technical Change* (Cambridge University Press).

Samuels, W. and N. Mercuro 1984. 'A Critique of Rent-Seeking Theory', in D. Colander (ed.), *Neoclassical Political Economy* (Cambridge, Mass: Ballinger).

Samuelson, P. (1954) 'The Pure Theory of Public Expenditure', *Review of Economics and Statistics*, vol. 36, no.4.

Schelling, T. (1960) *The Strategy of Conflict* (Cambridge, Mass: Harvard University Press).

Schelling, T. (1984) 'Command and Control', in *Choice and Consequence* (Cambridge, Mass: Harvard University Press).

Schott, K. (1984) *Policy, Power and Order* (New Haven and London: Yale University Press).

Schotter, A. (1981) *The Economic Theory of Social Institutions* (Cambridge University Press).

Schotter, A. (1985) *Free Market Economics– A Critical Appraisal* (New York: St Martin's Press).

Schultze, C. (1983) 'Industrial Policy: A Dissent', *The Brookings Review*, Fall.

Schumpeter, J. (1961) *The Theory of Economic Development* (London: Oxford University Press).

Schumpeter, J. (1987) *Capitalism, Socialism and Democracy*, 6th edition (London: Unwin).

Scitovsky, T. (1954) 'Two Concepts of External Economies', *Journal of Political Economy*, vol. 62, no. 2.

Sen, A., (1982) 'Rational Fools: A Critique of the Behavioural Foundations of Economic Theory', in *Choice, Welfare and Measurement* (Oxford: Basil Blackwell).

Shapiro, H. and L. Taylor (1990) 'The State and Industrial Strategy', *World Development*, vol. 18, no. 6.

Simon, H. (1975) *Administrative Behaviour*, 3rd edition (New York: The Free Press).

Simon, H. (1979) 'Rational Decision Making in Business Organisation', *American Economic Review*, vol. 69, no. 4.

Simon, H. (1982) *Models of Bounded Rationality – Behavioural Economics and Business Organisation*, vol. 2 (Cambridge, Mass: MIT Press).

Simon, H. (1983) *Reason in Human Affairs* (Oxford: Basil Blackwell).

Simon, H. (1991) 'Organisations and Markets', *Journal of Economic Perspectives*, vol. 5, no. 2.

Simon, H. *et al.* (1955) 'Organising for Controllership: Centralisation and Decentralisation', *The Controller*, no. 33, reprinted in Simon (1982).

Singh, A. (1977) 'UK Industrialisation and the World Economy: A Case of De-Industrialisation', *Cambridge Journal of Economics*, vol. 1, no. 2.

Skocpol, T. (1985) 'Bringing the State Back In', in P. Evans, D. Rueschemeyer and T. Skocpol (eds), *Bringing the State Back In* (Cambridge University Press).

Stigler, G. (1951) 'The Division of Labour is Limited by the Extent of the Market', *Journal of Political Economy*, vol. 59, no. 3.

Stigler, G. (1975) *The Citizen and the State* (University of Chicago Press).

Stiglitz, J. (1987) 'Principal-Agent Problem', in *The Palgrave Dictionary of Economics*, vol. 3 (London and Basingstoke: Macmillan).

Stiglitz, J. (1988) *Economics of the Public Sector*, 2nd edition (New York: W. W. Norton).

Stinchcombe, A. (1990) *Information and Organisation* (Berkeley and Los Angeles: University of California Press).

Stout, D. (1979) 'De-industrialisation and Industrial Policy', in F. Blackaby (ed.), *De-industrialisation* (London: Gower).

Taylor, M. (1987) *The Possibility of Cooperation* (Cambridge University Press).

Telser, L. (1987) *A Theory of Efficient Cooperation and Competition* (Cambridge University Press).

Thompson, G. (1989) 'The American Industrial Policy Debate: Any Lessons for the UK?' in G. Thompson (ed.), *Industrial Policy: USA and UK Debates* (London: Routledge).

Thompson, G. (ed.) (1989) *Industrial Policy: USA and UK Debates* (London: Routledge).

Tirole, J. (1988) *The Theory of Industrial Organisation* (Cambridge, Mass: MIT Press).

Tollison, R. (1982) 'Rent-seeking: A Survey', *Kyklos*, vol. 35, fasc. 4.

Tomlinson, J. (1980) *Problems of British Economic Policy 1870–1945* (London, Methuen).

Tomlinson, J. (1982) *The Unequal Struggle?: British Socialism and the Capitalist Enterprise* (London: Methuen).

Trezise, P. (1983) 'Industrial Policy is not the Major Reason for Japan's Success', *The Brookings Review*, vol. 1, Spring.

Tullock, G. (1984) 'The Backward Society: Static Inefficiency, Rent Seeking and the Rule of Law', in J. Buchanan and R. Tollison (eds), *The Theory of Public Choice II* (Ann Arbor: Michigan University Press).

Tversky, A. and D. Kahneman (1986) 'The Framing of Decisions and the Psychology of Choice', *Science*, no. 211 (1981); reprinted in J. Elster (ed.), *Rational Choice* (Oxford: Basil Blackwell).

UN (United Nations), *The Growth of World Industry*, various years (New York: United Nations).

UN (United Nations), *Industrial Statistics Yearbook*, various years (New York: United Nations).

UN (United Nations), *Trade Statistics Yearbook*, various years (New York: United Nations).

Varian, H. (1984) *Microeconomic Analysis* (New York: W. W. Norton).

Varian, H. (1989) 'Measuring the Deadweight Costs of DUP and Rent Seeking Activities', *Economics and Politics*, vol. 1, no. 1.

Vernon, R. (1987) 'Product Cycle', in *The Palgrave Dictionary of Economics*, vol. 3 (London: Macmillan).

Wade, R. (1990) *Governing the Market* (Princeton University Press).

Watanabe, T. (1987) *Venture Capitalism* (translated from Japanese) (Seoul: The Korea Economic Daily).

Whang, I. J. (1991) 'Government Direction of the Korean Economy', in G. Caiden and B. W. Kim (eds), *A Dragon's Progress – Development Administration in Korea*, (West Hartford, Conn: Kumarian Press)

White, G. (ed.) (1988) *Developmental States in East Asia* (London and Basingstoke: Macmillan).

Williamson, O. (1975) *Markets and Hierarchies; Analysis and Antitrust Implications* (New York: The Free Press).

Williamson, O. (1985) *The Economic Institutions of Capitalism* (New York: The Free Press).

Williamson, O. (1988) 'The Logic of Economic Organisation', *Journal of Law, Economics and Organisation*, vol. 4, no. 1.

Winter, S. (1988) 'On Coase, Competence, and the Corporation', *Journal of Law, Economics and Organisation*, vol. 4, no. 1.

Wolff, E. (1987) *Growth, Accumulation, and Unproductive Activity – An Analysis of the Postwar U.S. Economy* (Cambridge University Press).

World Bank, *World Development Report*, various years (New York: Oxford University Press).

WP (the White Paper on the Economy), various years (Seoul: Economic Planning Board [EPB]).

Yamamura, K. (1988) 'Caveat Emptor: The Industrial Policy of Japan', in P. Krugman (ed.), *Strategic Trade Policy and the New International Economics* (Cambridge, Mass: MIT Press).

You, J. and H-J. Chang (1993) 'The Myth of Free Labour Market in Korea', *Contributions to Political Economy*, vol. 12.

Young, A. (1928) 'Increasing Returns and Economic Progress', *Economic Journal*, vol. 38, no. 4.

Yusuf, S. and R. Peters (1985) 'Capital Accumulation and Economic Growth: The Korean Paradigm', World Bank staff working paper no. 712.

Zysman, J. (1983) *Governments, Markets and Growth: Financial Systems and the Politics of Industrial Change* (Oxford: Martin Robertson).

Index

Abdication: of power by the state, 39
Abramovitz, M., 74, 75, 77, 118, 153n14, 154n22
Accelerated depreciation, 113
Administrative guidance, 58
Agency costs, 37
Agency problem, see Principal–agent problem
Agenda formation, 21–2; see also State
Aggregate demand management, 49, 110
Agriculture, 58; in Korea, 94
Akerlof, G., 144n15
Alavi, H., 18
Alchian, A., 144n15, 150n31
Allocative efficiency, 48, 53, 99, 101, 131
Alt, J., 140n16
Altruism, 23, 39; see also Self-interest
Amadeo, E., 22, 148n16
Amsden, A., 97, 112, 118, 121, 124, 137n7, 144n14, 147n9, 151n44, 152n1, 154n21
Animal spirits, 81
Antitrust, 9–10, 55, 66
Aoki, M., 137n8
Argentina, 92, 93, 94
Armstrong, P., 1
Arrow, K., 132
Asset specificity, 65, 68, 75, 89, 112, 134
Asymmetric information, see Information: asymmetric
Austria, 52, 92, 93
Austrian economics, 26; see also Hayek, F.; Mises, L.
Autonomous state, 18, 19, 31; see also State
Axelrod, R., 138n5, 140–1n21, 151n41

Badaracco, J., 89, 152n50
Balance of payments, 58; see also Trade balance
Balassa, B., 82, 118, 119, 124, 142n29, 152n1
Banuri, T., 22, 148n16
Bardhan, P., 22, 119
Bargaining costs, 43, 47, 51, 52, 68, 89, 120, 145n20

Basic industries, 113, 153n18
Baumol, W., 11, 57, 137
Bell, M., 26, 121
Benevolence, of the state, 22, 39; see also State
Berlin, I., 139n10
Best M., 147n9
Bhagwati, J., 56, 57, 101, 107, 108, 120; see also Rent-seeking; State intervention, prescriptive vs. proscriptive
Biology, 73, 78, 151n41
Birdzell, L., 72, 79
Blackaby, F., 147n2
Bobbio, N., 139n14
Boltho, A., 58
Boss, H., 145
Bounded rationality, 27, 46, 49, 78, 144n16; see also Rationality
Bowles, S., 144n15, 147n7
Braverman, H., 144n15
Brazil, 92, 93, 94, 102, 103–4, 113
Brennan, G., 139n13
Bribery, 43, 119, 140n18, 141n26, 141–2n27
Britain, see UK
Bruno, M., 137n4
Brus, W., 26, 142n3
Buchanan, J.
 on contractarianism, 13, 14, 15, 17, 27, 29, 31, 139n13, 140n16, 141n25, 142n29
 on rent-seeking, 27, 28, 30, 31, 44, 145n20
Budget maximisation, 22, 24, 140n19, 141n23; see also Self-seeking bureaucrats
Bureaucracy, 19, 21, 23, 25, 26, 28, 32, 43, 86–9, 152n50
Burton J., 57, 72, 79, 80
Business groups, see Conglomerates; Korea, chaebols

Cairncross, A., 80, 147n1
Capacity scrapping, 68–9, 71, 77
Capacity utilisation, 111
Capital accumulation, 2, 22, 56, 125

173

Capital-intensive industries, *see* Korea, Heavy and chemical industries
Capitalism: different types of, 2–4, 142n30, 156n2; origins of, 16–7
Capitalists, 20
Cartels, *see* Investment cartels; Recession cartels
Catching-up, 81, 84, 147n11; *see also* Late development
Central planning, 26, 52, 55, 64–5, 72, 89, 133, 139n12, 141n1, 146n24, 149n28; *see also* Planning; Planning debate
Centralisation (and decentralisation), 35–6, 53, 124
Cha, D., 156n36
Chaebols, see Korea, *chaebols*
Chandler, A., 82
Chang, H-J., 96, 111, 139n8, 152n6, 153n11, 156n35
Chemical industries, *see* Korea, heavy and chemical industries
Chicago school, 18, 20
Chile, 92, 93, 94, 103–4
China, 53, 92, 93, 94
Class interests, 20, 146n26
Clientelism, 22, 154n25
Coase, R, 11, 49, 52, 132, 134, 137n8, 144n16, 156n2
Cohen, S., 39, 53, 56, 88, 147n9, 153n18
Colander, D., 27, 140n16
Cole, D., 127
Collective action problem, 8–9, 14–5, 20–1, 31
  and public goods, 8–9
  in rent-seeking, 38, 40–1
  selective incentives to overcome, 21
  see also Public goods; Olson
Collusion, 9, 42, 43, 112; *see also* Cooperation; Cartels
Colonialism, 155n31
Communism, 148n15
Comparative advantage, 98, 101
Competition, 38, 59, 73, 76, 141n24, 144n13, 145n22, 148n12, 148nn16–7
  as a process vs. as a state of affairs, 62–3, 148n13, 149n28
  in R&D, 77
  in rent-seeking, 41–2, 43, 44–5, 53, 62–3
  socially wasteful, 64–5, 111–12, 114, 125, 128

Competitive markets, 138–9n6; the self-perpetuation of, 8, 30, 31
Competitive politics, 44, 45; *see also* Rent-seeking
Competitiveness, 149n27
Conditional entry, 67, 71, 122; *see also* Industrial policy; Investment coordination
Conflict, during the process of structural change, 5, 14, 19, 121, 126
Confucianism, *see* Japan, Confucian tradition in; Korea, Confucian tradition in
Congleton, R., 38, 39
Conglomerates, 142n30; *see also* Korea, *chaebols*
Constant returns to scale, *see* Returns to scale
Constitutional revolution, *see* Buchanan, on constitutional revolution
Contractarianism, 5, 7, 12–18, 31, 139nn13–14
Contracts, 5, 11, 12–4, 15, 47, 68–9, 75, 82, 132
  binding, 42–3, 82, 149n24
  enforcement of, 11
  plan contracts, *see* Plan contracts
  social contracts, *see* Contractarianism
  writing of, 47–8
Cooperation, 138n5, 140–1n21
Coordination, 41, 70, 72, 83, 89, 146n27, 148n14, 149n28
  ex ante vs. *ex post*, 49, 53, 54, 62, 63, 132, 133, 135
  failure of, 49, 50, 63, 145n22
  generalised, 51–2
  and information, 73, 74
  pure, 50, 145n21
Corden, M., 59, 82
Corporatism
  social corporatism, *see* Social corporatism
  Japanese, *see* Japan, corporatism in
Corruption, 85, 86
Costs and benefits: private vs. social, 7, 9, 10, 29
Costs: production vs. transaction, *see* Production costs; Transaction costs
Cox, A., 147n3, 151n46
Creative destruction, 82; *see also* Schumpeter
Credibility, 70–1
Credible commitments, 43, 70–1, 134

Index

Credit rationing, *see* Korea, credit policy in
Cullis, J., 137, 139, 156
Culture, and economic development, *see* Japan, Confucian tradition in; Korea, Confucian tradition in
Cumings, B., 124
Cumulative causation, 74, 150n33

Dahlman, C., 11
Dahmén., E, 150n37
Datta-Chauduri, M., 155n30
David, P., 51, 75
Dawkins, R., 73, 141n21
De-industrialisation, 56–60
Deadweight loss, 9, 27, 66, 67, 82
Deane, P., 7
Decentralisation, *see* Centralisation
Decision-making, 35–7, 85
Declining industries, 68–9, 112, 114, 153n19
Decreasing returns to scale, *see* Returns to scale
Demand downturn, *see* Recession cartels; Capacity scrapping
Democracy, 88
Democratic control, 86–7, 134, 139n7
Demsetz, H., 10, 46, 47, 62, 144n15
Denmark, 3
Dependency, 153n11
Development, 82, 123, 155n28, 156n35, 142n3
Deyo, F., 137n7
Dictatorship, 22
Directly unproductive profit-seeking (DUP), *see* Rent-seeking
Disciplining, of business, 135
Distortion, 10, 97, 101; *see also* Allocative efficiency; Korea, virtual free trade
Diversity, 151n41
  of innovatory sources, i 77–8.
  of institutional mix, 2–4, 135
Division of labour, 64, 131
Dobb, M., 26, 83, 85, 148n14
Donges, J., 59
Dore, R., 67, 68, 69, 70, 71, 81, 87–8, 137n7, 147n9, 148–9n21, 149nn22–24, 149n25, 149n27, 150n35, 153n14
Dornbusch, R., 99, 147n6, 152n5
Dosi, G., 137n9
Duchêne, F., 147n3

Dynamic efficiency, 44, 72, 79, 121, 135, 141n24; *see also* Schumpeter
Eatwell, J., 70
Economic change, 5, 72, 73, 74–5, 78; and interdependence, 75–6, 79
Economic costs, 46–8; *see also* Costs
Economic development, *see* Development
Economic growth, 44, 72; *see also* Korea, economic growth of
Economic management, 1–3; *see also* Social corporatism; Industrial policy
Economic restructuring, 2
Economies of scale, 41, 65, 66, 84, 111, 112, 145n23; *see also* Returns to scale
Education, 11, 29, 52, 143n11
Efficiency, 23, 30, 33, 86, 101, 120, 133, 139n7, 141n27, 144n15, 145n20, 151n49
  dynamic, *see* Dynamic efficiency
  static, *see* Static efficiency
Eggertsson, T., 18, 23, 140n18, 144n16
Ellman, M., 26
Elster, J., 8, 11, 39
Enclosure, 16
Enforcement, 15, 47, 52; *see also* Contracts, enforcement of
Entrepreneurship, 82–4; productive and unproductive, 82–4; *see also* Schumpeter
Entry barriers, 10, 20, 28–31, 38, 45, 76; to rent-seeking markets, 41–3, 45
Equilibrium, 50, 51; *see also* General equilibrium
Evans, P., 113, 124, 146n29, 153n15
Evolution, 72, 150n31
  biological vs. social, 72–4
  as a Darwinian vs. Lamarckian process, 73–4
Evolutionarily stable strategy (ESS), 63; *see also* Game theory
Excess capacity, 30, 122; *see also* Capacity scrapping; Exit
Exchange rates, 97, 98, 108
Exit, 60, 65, 67, 69–71, 73, 116, 122
Export targets, *see* Korea, export targeting in
External shocks, 66
Externalities, 10–2, 49, 74, 77, 145n23, 153n16
  definition of, 10
  network, *see* Network externalities
  pecuniary, *see* Pecuniary externalities

Externalities *cont.*
    positive and negative, 143n11

Fairness, 40, 69–71
Farrell J., 143n6
Fei., 98, 152n1
Findlay, R., 18, 140n16
Fine, B., 138n3
Fisher, F., 143n9
Fishlow, A., 22, 155n30
Five-year plans, *see* Korea, Five-Year Plans; Planning; Central planning
Flexibility, 6, 70–1
Focal point, 53, 71, 76, 131–2
Foreign debt, of Korea, *see* Korea, foreign borrowing by
Foreign direct investments (FDI), in Korea, *see* Korea, foreign direct investment in
France
    basic industries in, 153n18
    bureaucracy of, 38, 86, 151n47
    financial sector in, 151n46
    indicative planning in, 39, 53, 76, 153n18, 156n34
    industrial policy in, 82–4, 91, 113, 147n9, 150n32, 150n39
    plan contracts in 37, 82
Franchise bidding, 28, 30, 43
Fransman, M., 137n9
Free rider problem, 9, 21; *see also* Collective action problem
Free trade, 97, 101, 102; *see also* Korea, trade policy; Virtual free trade
Free trade zone (FTZ), *see* Korea, free trade zones
Freeden, M., 16
Freedom, 107, 139n10
Friedman, M., 10, 12, 13, 15, 139n10
Fudenberg, D., 68
Full employment, 1, 29

Gamble, A., 137n2
Game theory
    mixed strategy in, 63, 143n9
    evolutionarily stable strategy (ESS) in, 63
    war of attrition in, 68, 77
    side payments and, 120, 148–9nn21–2
    strategic uncertainty in, 42, 66, 70, 83, 143n9, 145n23
General equilibrium, 132

General industrial policy, *see* Industrial policy, general vs. selective
Germany, West, 87, 117, 118, 146n26
Gerschenkron, A., 81
Ghemawat, P., 68
Giersch, H., 142n29
Gintis, H., 147n7
Glyn, A., 137n4
Golden Age, of capitalism, 1, 93
Goldthorpe, J, 137n4
Goodin, R., 16, 21, 24
Gough, I., 20, 140n20
Gould, S., 73
Government, *see* State
Government failure, 4, 5, 25–31, 33, 34–45, 48, 53, 54, 132; *see also* Information problem; Market failure; Rent-seeking
Government intervention, *see* State intervention
Government–business relationship, 37, 87, 121
Gramsci, A., 140n20
Greece, 94, 103–4
Green, F., 137n3
Grossman, G., 79, 80
Growth, *see* Economic growth
Guided capitalism, *see* Korea, *Gyodo Jabon Jui*

Hadley, E., 35
Hall, P., 37, 69, 82, 84, 137n1, 146n27, 147n9, 150n32, 150n39, 151n46, 151n47, 153n13, 156n34
Halliday, J., 127, 155n31
Hamilton, C., 124
Hard state, *see* State
Hardin, R., 8, 20
Hare, P., 152n50
Hargreaves Heap, S., 34
Harris, L., 99, 138n3
Hayek, F., 5, 13, 14, 61, 62, 63, 72, 73, 76, 77, 139n12, 141n23, 142n2, 148n13
Hayward, J., 37, 147n9
Heavy and chemical industrialisation (HCI), *see* Korea, heavy and chemical industries
Heavy industries, *see* Korea, heavy and chemical industries
Heiner, R., 149n24
Hierarchy, 25, 36, 64, 88
Hikino, T., 144n14, 151n44 154n22

Index

Hindess, B., 20
Hirsch, F., 138n3
Hirschman, A., 11, 23, 37, 45, 150n37
Hobbes, T., 13
Hodgson, G., 13, 74
Hong Kong, 1
Hout, T., 37, 67, 68, 76, 87, 118, 137n7, 147nn9–10, 150n38, 151n40, 152n7, 153n16, 153nn18–9
Hughes, A., 155n30

Ideology
    as a device to overcome collective action problem, 21
    as a device to reduce transaction costs, 52, 54
    as a set of social norms and values vs. as false belief, 52–3, 146n25
Import restrictions, *see* Korea, trade policy
Import substitution industrialisation (ISI), 98–9, 102, 116
    chaotic, 97
    easy, 97
Incentive neutrality, *see* Korea, incentive neutrality in; Virtual free trade
Increasing returns to scale, *see* Returns to scale
Independent economy, *see* Korea, *Jarip Gyongjé*
India, 52, 92, 93, 94, 142n5, 155n30
Indicative planning, 39, 53, 76, 153n18, 156n34; *see also* France, indicative planning in; Japan, indicative planning in; Korea, Five-Year Plan in
Individualism, 13, 14, 15, 155n30
Industrial policy, 3–4, 54, 55–90, 119, 121, 147n6, 147n9, 148n18, 152n50
    conditional entry, 67, 71, 122
    and coordination failure, 61–72, 73, 75–7
    debates on, 56–61
    definitions of, 58–61
    and élite bureaucracy, 84–6
    and evolution, 71–89
    general vs. selective, 60–1, 80, 82
    and information problem, 79–82
    logic of, 61–79
    optimal entry, 66–7
    and picking the winner, 39, 73, 80, 81
    and political economy, 55–90
    problems of, 79–89
    and the product cycle, 76–9
    and rent-seeking, 82–4
    and technological change, 66–70, 74–9
    transparency of, 86
    see also France; Japan; Korea; UK; USA
Industrial reorganisation, *see* Korea, industrial reorganisation in
Industrial restructuring, 1, 3
Industrial targeting, *see* Targeting
Industrial upgrading, *see* Upgrading; Japan, industrial policy; Korea, industrial policy
Industrialisation, 53
Industry associations, 40, 116
Infant industry protection, 26, 30, 45, 76, 121
Inflation, 22
Information, 72, 134, 139n12, 141n23
    asymmetric, 26, 27, 36–7, 81–2, 141n23, 142n4
    costs of gathering and processing, 11, 27, 35–6, 47, 53
    insufficient 26–7, 35–6, 80–1
    localised vs. global, 36
    and state intervention, 26–7
    with externalities, 79–82
Infrastructure, 118, 126
Innovation, 27–8, 44; *see also* Schumpeter; Institutions, institutional innovation
Institutional design, 27, 37
Institutional innovation, *see* Institutions, institutional innovation
Institutions, 56, 77, 87, 88, 91, 132, 133, 139, 152n2
    institutional innovation, 27, 87, 142n30; *see also* Korea, institutional innovation in
Insufficient information, *see* Information, insufficient
Interdependence, 65–6
    and economic changes, 75–6, 79
    and externalities, 10–1
    see also Externalities
Interest-group politics, 18, 19–22, 31, 43, 86, 140n17
Interest groups, *see* Interest-group politics
Intervention, state, *see* State intervention
Investment cartels, *see* Investment coordination
Investment coordination, 66–7, 70–83; *see also* Industrial policy

Investment management, 110
Italy, 92, 117, 146n26
Ito, K., 111

Jacquemin. A., 137n6, 147n3
Japan
  administrative guidance, 53
  aluminium industry in, 69, 149n27
  automobile industry, 118, 153n21
  Bank of Japan, 118
  bureaucracy, 38
  Confucian tradition in, 88, 155n29
  corporatism in, 155n31
  industrial policy in, 69, 81, 86, 87, 88, 89, 91, 113, 147n9, 147nn10–11, 152n7, 153n18
  indicative planning in, 39, 53
  Japan Export–Import Bank, 153–4n21
  Japan External Trade Organisation (JETRO), 145n23
  Meiji Restoration in, 155n31
  Ministry of International Trade and Industry (MITI), 35, 53, 81, 87, 92, 93, 118, 137n7, 145n23, 148n20, 153n16, 153n18
  shipbuilding industry in, 69, 152n8
  Structurally Depressed Industries Law, 153n11
  vision for the future economy, 53, 81
Jessop, B., 140n15
Johnson, B., 137n9, 142n29, 151n41
Johnson, C., 35, 39, 53, 56, 59, 87, 137nn6–7, 147n9, 156n34
Jones, L., 8, 23, 108, 114, 126, 137n7, 147n9, 152n1
Jones, P., 8, 23, 137n1, 139n7
Jorde, T., 78

Kahneman, D., 24
Kaldor, N., 150n23
Kapur, S., 151n44
Katzenstein, P., 137n4
Kenya, 94
Keynes, J. M., 65
Khan, M. A., 62
Khan, M. H., 22, 121, 154n25
Kim, J. H., 116, 153n20
King, D., 137n2
Kirzkowski, H., 147n5
Kirzner, I., 72, 83
Kitching, G., 21, 86
Knight, F., 63
Knowledge

  codifiability of, 72, 74–6, 134, 149n29, 149n30
  dispersed, 73, 131
  tacit, 46
  utilisation of, 73
  see also Hayak
Koopmans, T., 50, 145n23
Korea (South)
  antitrust policy in, 111–12
  automobile industry in, 114, 122, 154n27
  balance of payments in, 109
  Bank of Korea, 127
  bank nationalisation in, 125–6
  bank privatisation in, 127
  basic industries in, 113
  Blue House, 121
  bureaucracy in, 98, 117, 124, 129
  catching up by, 93, 97
  chaebols, 120, 123–4
  comparative industrial performance of, 103–4, 155n30, 156n36
  competition policy in, 112, 117
  Confucian tradition in, 124–5, 129, 155nn28–29
  credit policy in, 102, 128, 153n19, 154n23, 156n37
  Daewoo group 122, 154n27
  economic development of, 135
  economic growth of, 92
  Economic Planning Board, 109, 111, 126, 152n10, 154n21
  export targeting in, 114, 126
  financial reform in, 99, 107
  fiscal policy in, 109–10, 152n4
  Five-Year Plan in, 109–10, 113, 114, 125, 152n10, 155n32
  foreign borrowing by, 127
  foreign direct investment in, 112, 127
  Free Trade Zones in, 113
  free-market view of, 97, 152n1
  government–business relationship in, 121
  Gyodo Jabon Jui (Guided Capitalism), 125–6
  heavy and chemical industries in, 93, 96, 102, 104, 107, 109, 111, 113, 122, 125
  Hyundai group, 108, 120, 122
  'Illicit Wealth' episode in, 126
  import substitution industrialisation in, 97–9, 102, 116
  incentive neutrality in, 101–2

Industrial Development Law in, 114, 117, 154n24
industrial policy in, 91, 97, 108–113, 128–9, 147n9
industrial policy, the economics of, 113–23
industrial policy, the politics of, 123–8
industrial reorganisation in, 111, 122–3
institutional innovation in, 126–7, 129
investments in, 100
Jarip Gyongjé (Independent Economy), 109, 126
Kia group, 122
Korea Development Bank, 108, 111, 122
Korea Heavy Industries and Construction Company, 122, 123, 154n26
Korea International Steel Associates, 117
Korea Trade Organisation (KOTRA), 145n23
Kukje group, 128
learning in, 118
liberalisation in, 98–9
macroeconomic policy in, 110–11
manufacturing growth in, 93, 96
nature of the state in, 124
politics of, 91, 125–7
price controls in, 108, 116–17
production structure of, 93–7
public enterprises in, 108, 127
push and pull factors in the structural change of, 97
rent-seeking in, 117–23
research and development in, 116–7
scale economies in, 111, 125
Sémaul movement in, 126
shipbuilding industry in, 108, 111, 114, 118, 122, 152n8
Special Laws, 113, 122
social structure of, 124
state intervention in, 91, 97, 101, 108–13, 121, 155n32
state intervention, porous, 107
state intervention, proscriptive vs. prescriptive, 107–8, 154n23
state intervention, self-cancelling, 101–6
state intervention in, efficiency of, 124
steel industry in, 118, 127, 153n21
structural change in, 92, 94, 96, 97

technology policy in, 113, 118, 128
trade policy in, 97–8, 105–6, 116–17
virtual free trade in, 101–6
Korpi, W., 88
Krueger, A., 28, 29, 85, 101, 119, 141n27, 142n5
Krugman, P., 147n5, 147n11
Kuisel, R. 88
Labour market, 1, 2, 60, 87–8
Labour process, 46, 131, 144n15, 147n7, 151n45
Labour-intensive industries, 59, 98
Laffont, J.-J., 20, 138n2
Laissez-faire, 17, 53, 78, 88
Lal, D., 101, 102
Lancaster, K., 9, 99
Land reform, 124
Landes, D., 151n44
Lange, O., 26, 72
Landesmann, M., 60, 147n7
Landsorganisationen i Sverige (LO), 137n5; *see also* Sweden
Langlois, R., 34, 137n8, 142n30, 144n16
Laski, K., 26
Late development, 81, 118; *see also* Catching-up
Latin America, 118, 124, 155n30
Lavoie, D., 26, 72, 139n12, 142n1
Lawrence, R., 82, 147n8
Learning, 46, 73, 76, 89, 118, 131, 134, 144n14, 154n22
Learning by doing, 30
Lee, J. M., 143n11
Lee, S. H. (1985), 122
Lee, S. H. (1989), 116, 117
Lee, Y. S., 153n11
Legitimacy, 85–6, 134, 140n20, 141n27
Leibenstein, H., 140n19
Leijonhufvud, A., 50
Leipziger, D., 111, 122
Li, Kwan Yew, 19
Liberalism, 14, 139n11
Libertarianism, 139n11
Liberty, *see* Freedom
Licensing, 40–1, 67, 84
Lim, H. C., 124
Lindbeck, A., 60, 80
Linkages, 11, 150n37
Lippincott, B., 72
Lipsey, R., 9, 99
Liquidity, of assets, *see* Asset specificity
List, F., 125

Little, I., 101
Littlechild, S., 29-30
Lobbying, 20, 47, 140n18, 143n8
Loyalty, *see* Organisation, loyalty to
Luedde-Neurath, R., 98, 102, 124, 147n9, 152n1
Lundvall, B., 137n9, 142n29, 151n41
Luxury goods
  controls on the imports of, 98, 152n4
  the psychology of consuming, 11

Macroeconomic (in)stability, 49, 54, 55, 83
Maddison, A., 92, 94
Magaziner, I., 37, 67, 68, 76, 87, 118, 137n7, 147nn9-10, 150n38, 151n40, 152n7, 153n16, 153nn18-9
Maier, C., 137n4, 146n26, 151n49
Malaysia, 153n16
Mandel, E., 138n3
Manufacturing, the importance of, 109, 147n7
Mao, T. S., 126
March, J., 35, 37
Marglin, S., 1, 144n15
Market
  critique on the institutional primacy of, 132
  failure, 5, 7-12, 18, 33, 46, 53-4, 139nn11-2, 142n30; *see also* Government failure
  forces, 89
  as an institution, 4, 7, 16, 132
  share 69, 70
  sharing, 70, 71, 120, 122
Marshall, A., 4, 5
Marshallian triangle, *see* Deadweight loss
Marx, K., 4, 5, 18, 64, 65, 83, 121, 125, 131, 141n24, 148n14, 148n19, 149n28
Marxism, 20, 21, 140n20
Marxist theories of the state, 18, 138n3, 139n15
Mason, E., 108
Matthews, R., 49, 137n8, 144nn13-19
Maynard Smith, J., 63, 64
McCormick, R., 140n16
McLellan, D., 146n25
McNulty, P., 148n13
McPherson, M., 15, 23, 132
Measurement costs, 47-8
Meiji Restoration, *see* Japan, Meiji Restoration in

Mercuro, N., 29
Merger, 69
Merit goods, 12
Mexico, 92, 93, 94, 103-4, 113
Michell, T., 109, 126
Milgrom, P., 40, 47, 48
Miliband, R., 20, 140n15
Mises, L. 10, 13, 14
Mishan, E., 138n4
Minimal state, 17, 21; *see also* Contractarianism; *Laissez-faire*
Mixed economy, 1
Mixed strategy, 63, 143n9; *see also* Game theory
Mohammad, S., 119, 142n5
Moll, T., 143n7
Monetarism, 1, 2
Monitoring, 26, 46-7, 49, 51-2, 68, 141n27, 144n18, 146n24
Monopoly, 9-10, 139nn7-8, 141n27, 142n29, 143n9
  public vs. private, 10
  in rent-seeking, 41-2
Monopoly profit, 27-8, 67
Morality, 12-8, 23, 132
Morris-Suzuki, T., 125
Moth-balling, 69, 71; *see also* Capacity scrapping; Exit
Mueller, D., 23, 137n10, 140n16
Multinational corporations (MNCs), *see* Korea, foreign direct investment in
Musgrave, P., 12, 137n1
Musgrave, R., 12, 137n1
Mutation: biological vs. industrial, 73, 81; *see also* Evolution; Natural selection

Nalebuff, B., 68
Nath, K., 11
National Economic Development Office (NEDO), 147n1
Nationalisation, *see* Public enterprises; Korea, bank nationalisation in
Natural selection, 57, 64, 73-4; *see also* Evolution; Mutation
Negotiated exit, *see* Exit; Capacity scrapping; Moth-balling; Recession cartel
Neighbourhood effects, 12, 15
Nelson, R., 61, 74, 77, 78, 83, 137n9, 139n9, 150n31
Neoclassical economics, 46, 101, 139n16, 156n2

Neoclassical Political Economy, 18, 139n16
Network externalities, 51, 74; *see also* System scale economies
New Institutional Economics, 4, 5, 6, 13, 15, 53–4, 142n30, 144n16
  and transaction costs, 49–50
New Political Economy, *see* Neoclassical Political Economy
New Right, 2, 137n3
Newly Industrialising Countries (NICs), 1, 3, 93
Nirvana state, 46, 48
Niskanen, W., 22
Non-competitive markets, 9–10, 138n6, 139n8
Non-excludability, 8, 138n2; *see also* Public goods
Non-rivalness in consumption, 8, 138n2; *see also* Public Goods
Norms, 50–1, 140n18
North, D 18, 19, 21, 49, 52, 79, 83, 131, 144n16
Norton, R., 137n6, 147n4
Nozick, R., 13, 16, 17

O'Connor, J., 140n20
O'Driscoll, G., 148n13
Oakland, W., 138n2
Oil shock, 1, 93
Okiomoto, D., 67, 69, 76, 81, 137n7, 147n9, 148n20
Oligarchy, 41
Oligopoly, 65, 139n9, 142n29, 143n9
Olson, M., 8, 9, 20, 138n2
Olympian rationality, *see* Rationality
Order: spontaneous vs. constructed, 131
Organisation for Economic Cooperation and Development (OECD), 5–6
Organisation
  design of, 37
  as a device to deal with complexity and uncertainty, 34, 52
  and the fallacy of composition, 34
  loyalty to, 23–4, 27, 37
  decision-making structure of, 35–7
Over-investment, *see* Investment coordination

Pagano, U., 62, 64, 65, 131, 132, 137n8, 144n15, 148n15
Paik, N. K., 112, 153n20, 156n36
Panitch, L., 137n4, 151n45

Pareto efficiency, 7
Park Chung Hee, 108, 125, 155n31; *see also* Korea, politics of
Park, Y., 99. 127, 152n5
Parker, G., 64
Patents, 30, 40, 47, 76, 84
Paternalism, 12–14; *see also* Contractarianism
Peacock, A., 8, 10, 14, 139n11, 140n19
Pecuniary externalities, 11; *see also* Externalities
Pekkarinen, J., 137n4
Pelikan, P., 149n29
Peltzman, S., 20
Perfect competition
  Hayek's critique of the notion of, 62–3
  Demsetz's nirvana state and, 47
  perfect decentralisation and, 82
Peters, R., 102
Philosopher King, 18
Picking the winner, 39, 73, 80, 81; *see also* Industrial policy
Pinder, J., 58, 147n3
Plan contracts, 37, 82; *see also* France, industrial policy in
Planning, *see* Central planning; Indicative planning
Planning debate, 26, 72, 139n12, 142n1
Poggi, G., 16, 19, 23
Polanyi, K., 16, 49, 132
Policing costs, 47–8
Political economy, 18–32, 43, 45, 146n29
Political entrepreneurs, and collective action, 9; *see also* Collective action problem
Political market, 20–2, 29
Politics, 21, 44–5, 85–9
Pontusson, J., 137n4
Poor Law, 16–17
Popkin, S., 9
Porous state intervention, *see* Korea, state intervention, porous
Porter, M., 52, 76, 146n28, 150n35
Posner, R., 28, 29
Power, 7, 22, 40
Predatory state, 18–9, 25; *see also* State
Preference, 11, 21, 51
  counteradaptive, 11
  endogenous preference formation, 24
  interdependence of preferences, 11
  preference for preferences, 16
Price control, *see* Korea, price controls in

Price wars, 66–8
Price, V., 80
Principal–agent problem, 24, 26–7, 82; *see also* Agency costs; Information, asymmetric
Priority sectors, 110–11, 112–114, 154n23; *see also* Korea, industrial policy in
Private costs and benefits, *see* Costs and benefits
Private goods, 8, 40, 138n2; *see also* Public goods
Private sector, 133
Process-orientation, 139n11
Product cycle, 76–7, 134, 141n40, 150nn38–9
Production costs, 46–8, 66, 144n18
Productive vs. unproductive activities, *see* Rent-seeking; Entrepreneurship, productive and unproductive
Productivity, growth of, 30–1, 45, 56–8, 67–8, 83, 135
Property, 15
Property rights, 5–6, 18, 24, 47–9, 54, 85, 131–3
 and externalities, 11
 instituting, 49
 protection of, 15
 and public goods, 8, 138n2
Protection, *see* Korea, trade policy
Public choice, 140n16
Public enterprises, 142n4; in Korea, 108, 127
Public goods, 8–9
 collective action problem and, 8–9, 15, 40, 138n2, 138n4
 definition of, 8
 see also Private goods
Public sector, *see* Public enterprises
Putterman, L., 137n8, 144n16

QWERTY, 75

Ranis, G., 98, 152n2
Rasiah, R., 153n15
Rasmusen, R., 63
Rationalisation, 114, 115, 117; *see also* Korea, industrial policy in; Japan, industrial policy in
Rationality
 bounded, 27, 34–5, 46, 49, 71, 144n16
 different notions of, 34–5, 142n1
 individual vs. collective, 8, 27–8

Olympian vs. bounded, 34–5
 substantive vs. procedural, 34–5
Rawls, J., 13
Recession cartel, 59, 67–71
Reciprocity, 140–1n21; *see also* Cooperation
Regulation, 20, 61, 114–15, 131
Regulatory capture, 20, 39
Reich, R., 56, 58
Rejuvenation, of industries, 150n39
Relative prices, 102; *see also* Korea, incentive neutrality in *and* trade policy in
Relocation, of industries, 77
Renshaw, J., 55, 149n22
Rent-seeking, 25, 33, 38–45, 82–4, 142nn24–7, 142n5, 143n6, 143nn9–10, 143n12
 bystander effect in, 39
 collective action problem in, 38, 40–1
 competitiveness of, 41–4
 competitive politics vs. competive markets, 30, 44–5
 costs of, 27
 definition of, 27
 monopolistic, 27, 41
 entry barriers to, 41–3, 45
 oligopolistic, 41–3
 productive vs. unproductive, 20, 30–1, 82–4
 second-tier, 43–4, 119
Rents, 44
 state-created, 27–31, 38–45, 83–4, 118–19, 120–1, 123, 145n20
 see also Monopoly profit; Rent-seeking
Research and development (R&D), 30, 44, 47, 59, 78, 84, 148n17, 149n27
Resource allocation, 48
Restrictive practices, 44; *see also* Collusion; Schumpeter
Restructuring: industrial, *see* Industrial restructuring
Retraining, 77
Returns to scale, 62–3
Revolution, 23; constitutional, 29, 31
Richardson, G. B., 62, 65, 66, 70, 75, 80, 84, 121, 131, 137n8, 149n26, 150n37
Rights, 13, 47, 49, 131; *see also* Property rights
Rigidities, 2, 3
Risk, *see* Socialisation of risk
Robbins, L., 46

Roberts, J., 40, 47, 48
Rogerson, W., 143n9
Role of the state, *see* State
Rosenberg, N., 72, 73, 79, 137n9, 144n14, 149n30, 150n39, 153n14, 154n22
Rowley, C., 10, 14, 139n11, 141n22
Rowthorn, B., 3, 57, 137n4, 138n2, 144n18, 147n2, 156n1

Sachs, J., 124, 137n4
Sakong, I., 108, 114, 126, 137n7, 147n9, 152n1
Salter, W., 69
Samuels, W., 29
Samuelson, P., 138n2
Savings, 59, 60, 98, 99, 109
Savings gap, 109, 112
Schelling, T., 34, 39, 43, 53, 120
Schor, J., 1
Schott, K., 24, 137n4, 137n10
Schotter, A., 8, 11, 13, 50–1, 137n1
Schultze, C., 152n50
Schumpeter, J., 70, 73, 79, 82–3, 121, 125, 137n9, 141n24, 149n28
Scitovsky, T., 11
Second best, theory of, 9, 10, 99
Selection, *see* Natural selection
Selective incentives, 9, 21; *see also* Collective action problem
Selective industrial policy, *see* Industrial policy, general vs. selective
Self-interest, 22–4, 140n16, 140–1n16
 and organisational loyalty, 37
 see also Altruism
Self-seeking bureaucrats, 18, 22–4, 31, 142n23; *see also* Budget maximisation
Sémaul (New Village) Movement, *see* Korea, *Sémaul* Movement
Sen, A., 34
Service sector, 56–8
Shapiro, H., 155n30
Shepherd, G., 147n3
Shepsle, K., 140n16
Shortages: in socialist economies, 26
Side payments, 120, 148–9nn21–2; *see also* Game theory
Signalling, 76, 141–2n27, 146n28
Simon, H., 24, 27, 34–7, 49, 133, 137n8, 141n21, 142n2, 149n24
Singapore, 1, 19, 92–3, 153n15
Singh, A., 139n8, 147n2, 155n30

Skilled workforce, 58, 60, 118
Skocpol, T., 19–21
Small firms, 59, 125
Small number competition, 42, 63; *see also* Oligopoly
Smith, A., 4, 5, 131
Social contract, 31; *see also* Contractarianism
Social corporatism, 2–3, 52, 137n4, 151n49
Social costs and benefits, *see* Costs and benefits, private vs. social
Socialisation of risk, 6, 42, 78–9, 89, 134
Socialism, 14
Soete, L., 77
South Africa, 94, 103–4
South Korea, *see* Korea
Soviet Union, 53
Spain, 93, 103–4
Specific assets, *see* Asset specificity
Spontaneous coordination, 61
Spontaneous order, 131; *see also* Order
State
 abdication of power by, 39
 agenda formation and, 20–1
 autonomous, 18, 19, 31
 benevolent, 22, 39
 failures of, *see* Government failure
 hard, 25
 monopolisation of violence by, 49
 predatory, 23, 39
 role of, 33, 52, 54, 55, 78, 132
 self-cancelling, 101–4
 vulnerability of, 38–40, 86
State intervention, 16, 29, 33, 48, 53–4, 55, 70, 81
 New Institutionalist theory of, 45–54
 porous, 107
 prescriptive vs. proscriptive, 107–8, 154n23
 transaction costs and, 48–54
Static efficiency, 46, 72, 77, 101; *see also* Efficiency
Stigler, G., 5, 11, 20, 150n33
Stiglitz, J., 26, 137n1, 138n2
Stinchcombe, A., 80
Stout, D., 147n1
Strategic behaviour, 8
Strategic industry, 110, 127
Structural change, 10, 57; *see also* Korea, structural change in
Structuralism, 21

Sub-goal identification, 35–7; see also
    Information, localised vs. global
Subcontracting, 49
Subsidies, 20, 76, 78, 84, 101
Supply-side economics, 2
Svennilson, I., 73
Sweden, 3, 88
System scale economies, 51; see also
    Network externalities

Tacit knowledge, see Knowledge, tacit
Taiwan, 35, 92–3, 96–7, 125
Targeting, 47; see also Industrial policy
Tariffs, see Korea, trade policy
Taylor, F., 72
Taylor, L., 155n30
Taylor, M., 21
Technical change, 4, 46, 71–2, 80, 81, 89
Technical progress, see Technical change
Technological change, see Technical change
Technological development, see Technical change
Technology, 46, 51, 77, 118, 147n11, 150n38, 153nn14–5
Teece, D., 78
Telser, L., 66
Thompson, G., 137n6, 147n4
Tirole, J., 20, 68, 148n13, 151n42
Tollison, R., 27, 140n16
Tomlinson, J., 146n26, 146n29, 151n45
Toye, J., 142n28
Trade balance, 2, 104–6
Trade liberalisation, 98
Trade unions, 146n29, 151n45:
    centralised, 3, 52
Transaction costs, 11, 29, 82, 145n23
    definitions of, 47, 144n18, 144–5n19
    and state intervention, 5–6, 46, 67–8, 119, 132–3, 144n16, 145n20, 146n24
Trezise, P., 58, 89
Trust, 68, 85
Tullock, G., 40, 41
Turkey, 142n5
Tversky, A., 24

Unanimity rule, 14; see also
    Contractarianism
Uncertainty, 34, 42, 80, 83, 141n22, 145n23
    parametric vs. strategic, 42, 66, 70, 83, 143n9, 145n23
    primary and secondary, 50
    see also Organisation; Rationality; Game theory

Under-investment, see Investment coordination
United Kingdom (UK), 56, 84, 87, 89, 117, 137n3
United States of America (USA), 39, 52, 56, 117, 149n30, 150n35
Untraded interdependence, 11; see also Externalities
Upgrading, 109, 112, 117, 121

Varian, H., 29, 48, 62
Venture capital, 78, 81
Vernon, R., 76
Vested interests, 31; see also Interest-group politics
Virtual free trade, 101–6; see also Korea, incentive neutrality in, State intervention
Vision, for the future economy, 53, 81; see also Japan, vision for the future economy
Voice, 23
Vulnerability, of the state, see State, vulnerability of

Wade, R., 35, 94, 96, 97, 137n7
Walrasian auctioneer, 131–2
War of attrition, 68, 77; see also Game theory
Waste, 28, 30, 43, 64–5, 112, 120, 143n7
Watanabe, T., 118
Welfare economics, 4, 22, 24–5, 30, 46–8, 132–3
Wells, J., 57, 147n2
Whalley, J., 119, 142n5
Whang, I. J., 126
White, G., 137n7
Williamson, O., 64, 65, 80, 134, 137n8, 144n16, 148n12
Winter, S., 65, 137n9, 139n9, 150n31
Wolff, E., 145n20
World Bank, 99, 132
Wright, R., 156n1

x-efficiency, 140n19

Yamamura, K., 66
Yellen, J., 144n15
Yoffie, D., 89, 152n50
You, J., 156n35
Young, A., 150n33
Yusuf, S., 102

Zysman, J., 56, 151n46